Denial and Defense in the Therapeutic Situation

THEODORE L. DORPAT, M.D.

Jason Aronson, Inc.
New York and London

Library of Congress Cataloging in Publication Data

Dorpat, Theodore L.
  Denial and defense in the therapeutic situation.

  Bibliography: p. 271
  Includes index.
    1. Denial (Psychology)   2. Defense mechanism
(Psychology)   3. Psychotherapy.   4. Parent and child.
I. Title.
RC455.4.D45D67   1985   616.89′14   84-24257
ISBN 0-87668-755-9

Manufactured in the United States of America.

Contents

Preface

This book presents an integrated and comprehensive clinical theory of denial and defense. Though there have been notable contributions to the theory of defense since Anna Freud's (1936) classic work, there have been no systematic efforts to integrate these contributions into a comprehensive theory.

Past efforts to construct a theory of defense have worked from the "top down." Concepts derived from clinical and theoretical studies of high level defenses (e.g., repression) have been extended and generalized to all defensive activities. In contrast, this book develops a theory of defense from the "bottom up." That is to say, my emphasis is on the most primitive kinds of defense, and I have tried to show how more developmentally advanced defenses are modifications of the lower level defensive actions.

There have been several competing nominees for the basic or primordial defense, including splitting, primal repression, and denial. In different chapters I review and discuss the Kleinian literature on splitting and the classical literature on primal repression. I present empirical as well as logical evidence for the proposition that denial, and not primal repression or splitting, is the basic defense.

My principal research method has been the clinical method, and the data I provide is taken from my own cases, cases I supervise, or from the literature. Multiple perspectives and methods of approach are used in this book. Chapter 1 presents a microanalysis of denial and defense and formulates the "Cognitive Arrest Theory of Denial." A major hypothesis is that denial brings about an arrest of cognition regarding something disturbing to the subject. In denying something, an individual interrupts the normal process of thought formation, and this prevents the construction of realistic verbal representations of whatever he or she is denying. The cognitive arrest concerning something disturbing stimulates a need to form a "cover story" or screen to conceal the deficit caused by the cognitive arrest. Denial is an aspect of all defensive activity, and it is one of the essential and defining elements of defense.

Freud's contributions to psychoanalytic knowledge of denial are taken up in Chapter 2. Chapter 3 covers the contributions of other, chiefly classical, analysts. Chapter 4 provides a critique and discussion of Kleinian writings on primitive defenses. Chapters 5 through 8 emphasize the developmental approach to integrate the findings from child analysis, child observation, and reconstructions from adult analyses to provide a theory about the precursors of denial and the ontogenesis of denial.

Classic analysis has neglected the interactional approach to the development and maintenance of defensive activity. Chapter 10 provides a critical review and discussion of the literature on the interactional aspects of denial, and Chapters 11 and 12 apply the communicative (or interactional) approach to the study of defensive activity in the analytic situation.

Other chapters cover the relationship between denial and unconscious perception and between denial and memory pathology. One chapter explains how denial brings about psychic defects, dyscontrol, and symptom formation. A clinical case study is used in Chapter 14 to describe the working through of denial in psychoanalytic psychotherapy. The final chapter reviews the psychoanalytic, neurological, and psychiatric literature on denial and brain function.

Acknowledgments

The writing and publication of this book would not have been possible without the help and inspiration of many people. Several people encouraged this project by giving me valuable advice at critical points and by reading all or parts of the manuscript. They include, Jason Aronson, Joan Langs, James Raney, Robert Dickinson, Charles Mangham, Hugo Van Dooren, Damaris Rice, David Rowlett, George Allison, Maxine Anderson, and Marga Rose-Hancock.

My thanks are also due a number of colleagues who allowed me to use material from cases they analyzed in consultation with me. The names of the colleagues who generously provided case material are not mentioned, as a special safeguard lest, despite careful disguise, their patients' identities might be recognized.

Financial help supporting all phases of the investigations I am presenting here came to me from the Edith Buxbaum Foundation. I acknowledge this support with gratitude.

My thanks go also to the editors and publishers of the *International Journal of Psycho-Analysis*, the *International Review of Psychoanalysis*, *Psychoanalytic Inquiry*, and the *Annual of Psychoanalysis* for their permission to reprint material that first appeared in these publications.

Marga Rose-Hancock deserves a special expression of gratitude for the care and patience she showed in preparing and editing the manuscript; Mrs. N. Lewis pitched in ably to help get the job done.

1

The Cognitive Arrest Theory of Denial and Defense

This chapter provides an overview of the cognitive arrest theory of denial and defense and a microanalysis of the psychic actions and processes in defensive denial. Later chapters deal with other aspects of denial from a variety of perspectives, for example, developmental, interactional, object relations, and brain functions.

One of my main hypotheses is that denial causes an arrest of cognition regarding something disturbing to the subject, and this chapter proposes answers to questions concerned with the how, what, when, and why of the cognitive arrest.

Freud (1923) first described the defense of denial, and Chapter 2 will review his writing on the subject. He hypothesized that some young boys, not seeing a penis in girls, reject the evidence of their senses and imagine that they did see the girl's penis after all. This defensive activity Freud termed *denial* (or *disavowal*).

Basic Terms and Definitions

Goldberger's (1983) review of the literature shows that denial is, and always has been, a fuzzy and complex concept that has acquired many meanings and connotations, depending on the context in which it is used.

In addition to the dictionary definition—namely, "denial is the act of saying no"—the term in its strict psychoanalytic application means an *unconscious defense mechanism* against unpleasurable ideas, affects, and perceptions.

Strachey (Freud 1923, p. 143) points out that the English word *denial,* which had previously been used to translate the German word *Verleugnung,* was too ambiguous, and he proposes that *disavowal* be used instead. Despite Strachey's objections, denial rather than disavowal has become the most widely used term for designating the defensive action. In this book I shall use denial and disavowal as synonyms.

In the psychoanalytic and psychiatric literatures, denial has been used in a narrow sense to refer to a *unitary* defense mechanism and in a broad sense to refer to a *unifying concept* of different defensive actions (Weisman 1972). In this book I shall use denial in the broad sense to refer to the unconscious repudiation of some or all of the meanings of an event to allay anxiety or other unpleasurable affects. Denial covers situations in which individuals in words, fantasies, or overt actions attempt to avoid painful reality. Used in this way, denial refers to the reality-repudiating aspect of defensive operations rather than to a discrete defense mechanism. An implicit denial is part of all defensive activities. Defense always contains an aspect of denial, but also more than denial.

As Breznitz (1983) indicates, there are different degrees and kinds of denial, ranging from forms having massive reality distortions to forms having minor and selective reality distortions. Though much of the early psychoanalytic literature emphasized the more pathological kinds of denial, such as the kinds observed in the psychoses, the trend in recent decades (as reviewed in Chapter 3) has been toward a broader, more inclusive definition of denial that includes normal and neurotic as well as psychotic types.

Many writers on defenses have committed the error of misplaced concreteness insofar as they have conceptualized defenses as separable entities. The words we use to denote denial and defensive activities should not be thought of as describing discrete entities; they should rather be used to refer to the defensive *aspect* of an individual's thinking, communicating, or relating.

When persons defend themselves, they may, in addition to denying something, be attempting to carry out other conscious and unconscious aims. Intellectualization, for example, may serve as a defense against sexual and aggressive wishes in puberty, representing an attempt to master those impulses. But this process also has another, reality-oriented aspect, showing that the defense against instinctual impulses may at the same time be regarded as an adaptation process (Hartmann 1939). The description of any activity as a denial or defense does not fully define it: a comprehensive description must also include its reality-oriented and adaptation-facilitating characteristics and regulations.

At the present time, the term *defense* is usually used in both psychoanalysis and psychiatry in the broad sense, to designate unconscious protective responses to any kind of psychic pain or unpleasure. It includes, especially, reactions to anxiety, guilt, sorrow, danger, temptation (instinctual drives), and trauma.

Both S. Freud and A. Freud used the word *defense* in a narrow sense, to "cover all these processes that have the same purpose—namely, *the protection of the ego against instinctual demands* . . ." (Freud 1926; italics mine). The broader usage is justified, I believe, by the many clinical reports indicating that the same kinds of defensive actions are used against non-instinctual dangers and traumas as are used to protect against threatening instinctual drives (sexual and aggressive impulses).

Any psychic function can be used defensively. Affects, ideas, percepts, ego functions, and so on may at times be used for defensive purposes. Lampl-deGroot (1957) noted that neurotic defense mechanisms are pathologically exaggerated or distorted ego regulation and adaptive mechanisms. According to Brenner (1981), there are no special ego functions used for defense and defense alone. The various modes of defense are as diverse as psychic life itself. The terms we use for specific defenses (e.g., repression and reaction formation) are abstractions denoting aspects of psychic actions.

Psychoanalytic writings on repression and defense, including Freud's, abound in vivid and sometimes misleading metaphors. The reader is told that thoughts and feelings are "expelled," "rejected," "split," "cast out," and so on. These terms should always be used and recognized as figures of speech. Otherwise, one will misinterpret the metaphor as being literal. That is, ideas and feelings are not physical things that can literally be expelled, rejected, split, and so forth. Only in fantasy and not in reality is it possible to expel or to split psychical contents such as ideas and emotions.

Freud (1915a) described the mechanism of repression as an "after-expulsion," and he likened the repression process to ordering an undesirable guest out of one's drawing room. Other psychoanalytic writers since Freud have continued the mistake of conceptualizing the mechanism of repression as an after-expulsion. A prominent psychoanalytic glossary misinterprets metaphors in a literal way (Moor and Fine 1967). Repression, they write, "consists of the expelling and withholding from conscious awareness of an idea or feeling" (p. 24).

Freud and others are mistaken in their notions that ideas and percepts are first admitted to consciousness and then expelled. The mind is not a container, like the gastrointestinal tract, that receives and expels physical things. As I shall later demonstrate, the defensive process occurs at a presymbolic or prelinquistic level. The denier aborts his or her cognition process before transforming presymbolic and embryonic forms of thought into verbal thought. In short, denial prevents the formation of verbal ideas; it does not involve the expulsion, rejection, or splitting of ideas.

Still, there is some truth in reifications such as the expulsion or splitting of ideas, because these vivid terms do describe some of the common kinds of unconscious fantasies underlying defensive activity. Analysts, in fact, have confused the content of the unconscious fantasies in defensive actions with the processes and mechanisms of defensive activity.

Psychoanalytic science asks "how" questions as well as "why" questions (Wallerstein 1976). "How" questions are answered in terms of mechanisms, processes, and causes; "why" questions are answered in terms of reasons and motives. The cognitive arrest theory explains how individuals unconsciously defend themselves. In the following section I shall define the basic mechanisms of defense as the arrest of cognition of something threatening and the shifting of the subject's focal attention to something less threatening.

The Microanalysis of Defenses

The microanalytic approach to defenses was used by Freud (1926) in his account of isolation and undoing. For example, he traced the obsessional patient's defensive need to *isolate* to unconscious prohibitions against erotic touching. The following examination of denial will be carried out by means of a microanalysis and a sequential account of the following four phases of denial reactions:

1. preconscious appraisal of danger or trauma
2. painful affect
3. cognitive arrest
4. screen behavior.

Before examining these four phases, I shall first outline where we are heading. The subject's preconscious appraisal of a situation as actually or potentially traumatic or dangerous produces the formation of a painful affect. This affect triggers a reaction in which the subject turns his or her focal attention from what is disturbing to something else. A cognitive arrest is brought about by unconscious fantasies of destroying or rejecting whatever is considered to be the cause of the psychic pain (or what I have termed the *painful object*). Such unconscious fantasies of destroying the painful object arrest the subject's thinking about the painful object at a primary-process level.

The unconscious fantasy attacks on the painful object and the consequent arrest of higher-level cognitive processes are followed by screen behavior. Ideas, fantasies, and/or affects are used by the subject to fill in the gaps formed by the cognitive arrest phase and to support its defensive aims.

The Preconscious Appraisal of Danger or Trauma

Freud (1926) was the first to describe the mental mechanisms wherein the subject's expectation of danger evoked signal anxiety, which in turn elicited defensive reactions. Most often, a dangerous or traumatic situation is appraised preconsciously, although in some situations there may also be conscious appraisals. The concept of a preconscious appraisal phase preceding and preparing for the formation of painful affects is consonant with studies by psychologists of the antecedent conditions for affective responses. According to Lazarus (1968), emotions result from conscious, preconscious, or unconscious acts of appraising the subject's situation. Underlying such actions are the subject's perceptions, expectations, and beliefs, as well as learning and memory.

Painful Affects and Defensive Actions

Following Freud (1926), psychoanalysis and, later, psychiatry made anxiety the central point of defensive operations and symptom formation. This view has been modified by the accumulated clinical evidence of recent decades, which has shown that defensive operations and symptom formation are elicited by the subject's need to avoid awareness of any of several unpleasurable affects, including depressive affect, shame, guilt, anxiety, grief, and helplessness (Brenner 1975, Dorpat 1977). In other words, defensive actions may be initiated not only by anxiety but also by any one or several of many different painful affects. Affects initiating defensive activity may be conscious, preconscious, or unconscious.

Focal Attention and Consciousness

A comprehensive account of denial should include a description of the alterations in consciousness associated with the cognitive arrest and the defensive action. This I aim to do by discussing the role of *focal attention in denial*. Denial is a defensive strategy for the deployment and inhibition of focal attention. Neisser (1967) and Schachtel (1959) distinguish between focal attention and a more diffuse and peripheral sort of sensing. By focal attention, Schachtel (1959) designates a person's capacity to center his or her attention on an object. Acts of focal attention exclude the rest of the field (both environmental and internal) from conscious awareness.

Focal attention is a constructive cognitive process in which the subject seeks to comprehend and represent in words the meaning of whatever within himself or herself or the object world is being attended to. When we read a text, our focal attention is directed toward the meaning of the words and not toward the words as marks on the paper. This is what we mean when we say we *read* a text and why we do not say that we *observe* it (Polanyi 1964, p. 32). Focal attention is a consciously intentional process concerned with the formation of meanings, and it employs higher-level modes of cognition.

The dynamic defensive function of denial is carried out by the active exclusion of information from focal attention, that is, from explicit conscious awareness. Information processed by focal attention achieves full conscious awareness, whereas one is only very briefly and minimally aware of stimuli processed by the more diffuse and peripheral kinds of attention. Stimuli or information processed by the peripheral kind of sensing are available at a preconscious level of awareness. In denial, the subject shifts his or her focal attention from disturbing stimuli emanating from either himself or herself or the environment to less disturbing stimuli, fantasies, or ideas. Denial, then, is both turning away from something painful or potentially painful and focusing on something that is less painful or is pleasurable. The defensive and restitutive functions of turning toward something less painful we shall discuss later, in the section on screen behavior.

Schafer (1976) suggests that self-deception "is an incorrect or faulty way of observing one's own actions" (p. 238). Faulty self-observation means acting inattentively, unheedfully, unobservantly, or inaccurately. Sullivan (1956) describes a defensive maneuver as "selective inattention." In their study of 104 brain-damaged patients who denied their illness or disability, Weinstein and Kahn (1955) observed many patients who showed a marked inattention to their illness. Some stroke patients, for example, held their eyes and heads averted from the side of their paralyzed extremities.

In negative hallucination experiments cited by Neisser (1967), the hypnotized subjects who were told that they would not see a chair nevertheless did not bump into the chair when they were instructed to walk around in the room. Even though they avoided bumping the chair, they did not recognize or represent it as a "chair." For them it was simply a thing to avoid bumping into. A puzzled reader might ask "How can you say that the hypnotized subjects did not recognize the chair when the fact that they avoided bumping into it indicated that they recognized it?" The answer is that the hypnotized subjects did have a purely visual awareness of the object and they did form a registration of it, but they had not represented or perceived the object as a chair. The registration of their visual sensation of the chair accounts for their avoiding bumping into it.

One of the most intractable problems of the perceptual defense hypotheses advanced by psychologists and psychoanalysts was what appears to be a logical paradox. As Bruner and Postman (1949) and later others note, the paradox resides in the idea that the perceiver both perceives and does not perceive something. Or, as Erdelyi (1974) puts it, "If the perceptual defense is really perceptual, how can the perceiver selectively defend himself against a particular stimulus unless he *first perceives* the stimulus against which he should defend himself?" As Erdelyi (1974) points out, the implication of this point of view is that perception is some sort of singular event that either happens or fails to happen. The supposed contradiction in the perceptual defense hypothesis dissolves in the face of evidence that perception is a multistage process and that it can be aborted at any of the several sequential stages.

Both psychological and neurological studies agree that certain stimulus inputs reach unconscious levels of registration and sensory identification but are blocked from conscious perception (Brown 1972, Erdelyi 1974, G. Klein 1959, Werner 1948, 1956). Registration and perception are distinct processes, and registration of a stimulus object can occur without perception of the object that has been registered (G. Klein 1959). Fisher's (1954, 1956) experiments offer convincing evidence that subliminal stimuli are registered. What is excluded from focal attention by denial or other means may be recovered by techniques such as hypnosis, free association, or dream analysis.

The Role of Unconscious Fantasy in Denial

Thus far we have seen that the defensive function of denial is caused by excluding information from focal attention. The emotionally charged contents in denial reactions are not excluded merely by passive attention. Rather, the process of exclusion is an active one, which is explained by the denier's unconscious fantasies of destroying whatever is mentally painful. My concept of these destructive fantasies is similar to that of Bion (1957a), whose writings on "attacks on linking" I shall review in Chapter 4.

As Schafer (1968b) argues, defenses have a meaningful content, including unconscious fantasies and wishes concerning the self and object. I shall describe and illustrate the type of unconscious fantasies in denial and then explain the effects of these fantasies on the subject's cognitive processes. The major contents of this phase are the subject's unconscious fantasies of attacking, destroying, or rejecting some painful or threatening primary-process representation. For the purposes of this book I shall call these fantasies the "destructive attacks on the painful object." This is the critical phase of denial operations, and its psychic actions comprise the necessary and defining properties of denial.

Occasionally, aspects of these fantasy attacks may become conscious, as in states of deep regression or through the analyst's interpretive efforts. Usually, however, the attacks on the painful objects occur unconsciously, and the analyst infers the contents of this phase from an empathic study of the context in which it occurs and from the patient's behaviors in the screen behavior phase that immediately follows.

The term *painful object* is used in this book to designate the object of the subject's destructive attacks. In calling these objects painful, I mean either that they are viewed as pain engendering or that they are subjectively associated with some unpleasurable affect. From the objective observer's perspective, the object may be called an introject, a percept, an image, a memory, a primary-process presence, and so forth. But from the subject's point of view, these different kinds of psychic phenomena are not recognized or distinguished as such. Rather, they are viewed concretely as if they were threatening and dangerous *things*. The painful object may be experienced as being within or outside the subject's body. When the object is experienced as something inside the body, often the fantasies imagine expelling it by such riddance reactions as defecation, spitting, or vomiting.

To illustrate the significance and varied contents of these unconscious fantasies, I shall present clinical data from two cases.

Case One

The patient was a 34-year-old woman who had been in analysis for over two years. An important context for the following episode was her impending vacation and separation from the analyst. Her associations were bland, and she complained of feeling sleepy. She said that on a previous evening she had talked to a friend who was "so analytic" that it made her feel bored and tired. She wished she did not have to come to analysis. All of the above and much more was said in a disinterested and sleepy tone of voice.

I made the following interpretation: "You are wiping me out of your mind, and at the same time you are also wiping out the part of yourself that is related to me. You wish that our relationship would mean nothing so that you won't miss the analysis when you leave next week." ("Wiping out" was her phase, and it meant blanking out or destroying something in her mind. Considerable analytic work had been done previously to understand the reasons and motives for her defensive tendency to wipe out feelings and ideas that disturbed her.) She then became consciously angry and said, "I hate coming here and I hate depending on you. What good is it? When I leave analysis you won't care about me." Gradually her anger turned to sadness and crying over the impending separation from the analysis. She was then able to affirm that she would miss the analyst and that she was anxious about the break in the analysis.

At the beginning of the analytic hour, the patient was attempting to deny both her anxiety over the impending break in the analysis and her anger toward the analyst. The unconscious fantasy of her denial defense was one of destroying (or wiping out) any representation of the analyst as someone who was important to her. In wiping out the image of the analyst, she at the same time also subjectively destroyed the part of herself related to the analyst and any affects connected with that relationship.

Case Two

On her return from a brief vacation, a middle-aged analysand came to an analytic hour talking in a confused and fragmentary fashion. I told her that I did not understand what she was talking about and that I wondered if she had some wish to evoke feelings of helplessness and confusion to me. She replied that she also made herself confused and helpless. After a while, it became clear that she was envious of me and others for being able to have a longer vacation than she could afford. I said, "Your way of speaking in a confused and confusing way was done to avoid awareness of your painful envy. You are so uncomfortable with your envious feelings toward me that you have attempted to destroy any ideas that you have about my having more money than you." She was then able to speak in a coherent manner about her envy of me and of her widowed mother, who did not work because she was supported by a pension.

On another occasion, when I had interpreted her defensive need to reject and to destroy the meaning of one of my interpretations, she told me in a burst of hostility that she had had the fantasy of "spitting out of myself everything you said." Her fantasy of "spitting out" indicated that her thought processes regarding my interpretations were operating at a primary-processlike level in which she viewed what I had said as something concrete that she had taken into her body and that she then could spit out of her mouth.

Cognitive Arrest

As shown in the foregoing cases, the unconscious fantasy in denial is one in which the subject seeks to attack, destroy, or reject the painful object. Primary-process mentation is concrete; the painful object is viewed as a dangerous thing that somehow must be destroyed or rejected. The nature, origin, locus, and/or meaning of the object attacked are not determined, as these kinds of discriminations require the rational evaluations of the secondary process. Primary-process thinking does not discriminate between what is thought and what is reality, or among percepts, memories, and fantasies. The fantasy attacks on the painful object cause an arrest of the subject's capacities for rational thought and communication regarding the painful object.

Secondary-process cognition regarding the subject's relation with the painful object is inhibited and arrested at the point of mental pain. The employment of all of the ego and superego functions that could be used for understanding the painful object and the subject's actual or imagined interactions with the object is disrupted. Denial, then, is like a jury that renders a verdict before the evidence is presented. The "verdict" in denial is peremptory, arbitrary, and prereflective.

Another and related consequence of these attacks is that they prevent the conscious awareness of the painful object and the representations of the subject's self in interaction with it. In other words, denial leads to the subjective loss of some object relation, including the subject's representation of an interaction between the self and an object.

The unconscious fantasy attacks bring about the denier's loss of contact with the denied aspect of reality. Freud (1924b) raised the question of what the mechanism is that is analogous to repression by which the ego severs itself from the outside world. The answer, I believe, is that the denier's unconscious fantasy attacks on the painful object impair his or her capacities for symbolizing and understanding what in fantasy has been destroyed. Our relationship with reality is not directly experienced but mediated through the use of symbols. The destructive attacks on the painful object in denial reactions impair the subject's apperception of reality by blocking the formation of verbal thoughts required for representing the subject's relation to the painful object.

A skeptical reader might ask, "How can a mere fantasy have such powerful effects on the subject's thinking and perception? After all, one may have similar kinds of conscious destructive fantasies without any resulting impairment of one's cognitive processes." But an unconscious fantasy is not simply a fantasy that is not conscious. It is precisely because the fantasy attacks in denial are unconscious that they are associated with disruptions of normal thought processes. The term *fantasy* may indeed be a misnomer, or at least a misleading rubric, for this unconscious process. At the primitive level of psychobiological function involving unconscious fantasies, fantasizing is not differentiated or separable from other psychic functions such as unconscious perception and enactive memory.

A case in point are the unconscious fantasies implicit in conversion symptoms. Unconscious fantasies are the presymbolic aspect of a larger configuration, including sensorimotor activities, enactive memories, and unconscious perceptions. The neutral observer infers the occurrence of an unconscious fantasy from some observable overt behavior, for example, verbal or nonverbal communications and conversion symptoms.

In calling the unconscious content of denial a *fantasy*, I have followed, somewhat reluctantly, the psychoanalytic convention of referring to unconscious contents as *fantasies*. Actually, the processes that contribute to the unconscious content of defense reactions include unconscious perception, unconscious memory, projection, and introjection, as well as fantasy (Langs 1982b).

Chapters 10, 11, 12, and 13 discuss both the clinical and the theoretical significance of evaluating the interactional dynamics, including the processes of unconscious perception, projection, and introjection, in the unconscious content of denial responses.

Theories of Thought Formation

The unconscious fantasy attacks disrupt and abort the normal processes in the formation of thoughts, with the consequence that the subject does not form verbal representations of the painful object and his or her relation to it. In order to examine more closely these normal processes of thought formation, and to explain further both how and when the fantasy attacks disrupt cognitive processes, I shall briefly review the theories of thought formation and studies of the microgenesis of cognition.

The foregoing discussion of how denial causes an arrest of rational thinking implies a theory of how thoughts are formed, a theory I shall first summarize and then compare with theories of thought formation by Freud (1911a, 1912, 1915b), Bion (1958a) and cognitive psychologists. Verbal thought is formed from its more primitive primary-process precursors such as primary-process representations. This statement is in accord with Freud's (1911a, 1912, 1915b) concepts of thought formation. He held that every mental act begins as an unconscious one and that some remain so, whereas others attain consciousness. Freud (1915b) emphasized the importance of an object's hypercathexis to the attainment of consciousness.

These hypotheses regarding the stages of thought formation and the inhibitory effects of denial on verbal thought are congruent with Bion's (1958a, 1967) concepts. According to him, "embryonic thought" (in my terms, primary-process thinking) provides the link between sense impressions and consciousness. The concrete objects of embryonic thought, in his view, are normally transformed into verbal thought. "Attacks on linking" prevent this transformation and fragment the concrete objects which the subject then casts out in fantasy (via projective identification).

The Microgenesis of Cognition

Microgeny, as defined by Werner (1956), is the sequence of events inherent in a psychological phenomenon. Thoughts and percepts are believed to undergo a very brief but theoretically important microdevelopment. The word *microgenesis* refers to the rapid prestages of cognitive acts, for example, the processes in immediately perceiving a simple visual or auditory stimulus. In most people, this extraordinarily rapid formative process does not usually become an object of awareness.

The study of microgenesis is a potential avenue for the exploration of what is ordinarily called unconscious thought. Knowledge of the microgenesis of thought and perception comes from clinical studies of pathological conditions such as cases of schizophrenia, neurosis, and brain injuries and from experimental investigations of perception and cognition. Both clinical and experimental studies on the microgenesis of thought and perception support the hypothesis given earlier in regard to the formative processes in cognition. It is remarkable to what extent contemporary research on cognition has confirmed Freud's (1911a, 1912, 1915b) concepts of how thoughts are formed.

An important principle underlying the writings of Werner (1948) is that microgeny reproduces ontogeny and phylogeny; the early prestages of thought tend to be similar to the kinds of cognition that occur in childhood. A number of investigators, including Arieti (1955) and Flavell (1956), point out the striking similarity between microgenetically early cognition and pathological cognition. In conditions such as schizophrenia and aphasia, there may be an arrest at primitive forms of cognition. The microgenetic approach is useful in understanding not only normal thought and speech formation but also the psychopathology and neuropsychology of thought and language. Aphasia and related phenomena are viewed as interruptions at successive planes in the process of language formulation. According to Brown (1972, p. vii), this process is conceived as a hierarchic unfolding of levels in a path from memory through stages of cognition to articulated speech. The various clinical forms of aphasia relate to stages in normal speech production, and they have been classified by Brown (1972) and others according to their sequence in this process.

According to Werner (1948), thought in its early states is global, diffuse, and undifferentiated in structure. These prestages of thought seem to have the quality of what Rapaport (1951) has called "drive representatives." The normally unconscious early judgments of situations tend to be primitive, dichotomous affairs framed as good or bad, pain or pleasure, and the like. Differences between the early and late stages of cognition described by Werner (1948), Flavell and Draguns (1957), and Brown (1972) are similar to Freud's distinctions between the primary and the secondary process. Neisser

(1967), a cognitive psychologist, provided evidence for the hypothesis that cognitive activity (whether perception, memory, or thinking) is a two-stage mechanism in which the primary process precedes the secondary process. The first, or primary-process, stage is fast, crude, and holistic, and the second, or secondary-process, stage is deliberative and attentive. The first stage is a preattentive and prereflective stage in which holistic operations form the object to which the focal attention may then be directed.

The primary-process stage forms an array of crudely defined "objects." Then, in alert and waking subjects, the secondary process of directed thought selects among these objects and further examines and develops them. Rational thought is "secondary" in the same sense that it works with the objects previously formed by a "primary" process. The denier's fantasy attacks on the painful object block the final linguistic phase in the microgenesis of thought and thus arrest the cognition of the painful object.

Most studies of microgenesis and cognition do not consider the role of affects. Central to my hypothesis of the cognitive arrest phase of denial is the role of painful affects in triggering the defensive actions. Arieti (1978, p. 288) provided evidence for the hypothesis that each stage of cognition is accompanied by some affective response and that it is this unconscious affect that determines whether or not a given image of thinking will become conscious.

Screen Behavior

In the cognitive arrest phase, the denying subject has subjectively destroyed the kinds of information and representations that he or she could use to orient and adapt himself or herself to some actual or imagined threatening situation. The cognitive arrest concerning the painful object and the need to adapt to the dangerous or traumatic situation stimulate the need to create a "cover story" or screen to hide, as it were, the gap caused by the preceding phase.

The cognitive arrest phase is usually followed by some kind of screen behavior whose content is often the opposite from what has just been negated. An individual's unconscious disavowal of his or her weakness, for example, may be followed and supported by a boastful assertion of strength. A schematic formula for the relation between the cognitive arrest and screen behavior phases is (1) A is *not* true; (2) B *is* true. The negation of something or other is followed by an affirmation that contradicts what is negated. According to Anna Freud (1936), "The denial of reality is completed and confirmed when in his fantasies, words, or behavior, the child reverses the real facts" (p. 95). Defenses make both a negative and a positive assertion. The negative assertion—that something is not so—in denial belongs to the cognitive arrest phase, whereas the positive assertion occurs in screen behavior.

The negative assertion of denial is more often implicit than explicit. Often clinicians make the error of limiting the concept of denial to cases of explicit denial (or verbal negation). They are seemingly unaware that denial may be implicit as well as explicit and that implicit denial occurs far more frequently than does explicit verbal denial. As Weinstein and Kahn (1955) point out, denial reactions may be classified into explicit verbal denial and implicit denial. In their study of denial behaviors in brain-damaged patients, examples of explicit verbal denial were seen in paralyzed patients who said they were not paralyzed. Examples of implicit denial were seen in patients who used various maneuvers such as confabulation, rationalization, and delusion to defend themselves against the awareness of their disability.

"Screen behavior" refers to the ideas, fantasies, affects, and overt behaviors activated by the subject's need to fill in the gaps formed in the cognitive arrest phase and to support its defensive aims. From the need for this protective tactic emerge the many different masks, disguises, rationalizations, delusions, confabulations, and other forms of screen behavior. As Fingarette (1969) explains, the subject creates a "cover story" so as to render the story as internally consistent and plausible as possible. If someone else notes a discrepancy between the cover story and the true facts of the situation, the subject is moved to ever-continuing effort and skill to elaborate the cover story and to protect its credibility.

Greenson (1958) provides clinical data supporting the concept of screen functions. Screen *memories* are attempts to contradict a painful reality. Screen *affects* are used to prevent awareness of disturbing affects. Screen *perceptions* are painless perceptions used to conceal frightening perceptions.

Many of the different types of screen behavior judged by clinicians to be defensive may be understood as alternatives to the behavior, thoughts, and emotion that have disappeared as a result of the cognitive arrest. Screen behaviors are not only substitutes and alternatives but also diversions. The more completely an individual's focal attention and energy are concentrated on one activity, the more completely and efficiently can information concerning another potentially disturbing activity be excluded. Any kind of mental or physical activity can be undertaken defensively as a diversion from something else.

Another motive for screen behavior is restitutive: the subject seeks to substitute a wished-for object relation for the painful object relation destroyed in fantasy during the antecedent cognitive arrest phase. Freud (1924b) noted that in both neurosis and psychosis there is not only a loss of reality but also a substitute for reality. Such patients attempt to substitute a reality more in accord with their desires for the unsatisfactory real one that they deny. Melanie Klein (1975, p. 202) describes the relationship between the subjective annihilation of a frustrating object by means of denial and the subsequent need to idealize the object.

The relationship between the cognitive arrest phase and the screen behavior phase is similar to the relationship between repression and the "return of the repressed" in substitute formations such as neurotic symptoms. Freud (1915b) noted that the substitute idea in the return of the repressed played the part of an anticathexis (or countercathexis). Waelder (1951) extends Freud's concept of the countercathexis and the return of the repressed to denial reactions. He explains, "If the defense was denial, the return of the disclaimed has the form of a claim" (p. 173).

Waelder's concepts regarding the "return of the disclaimed" are in accord with my observation made earlier in this chapter that what is excluded from focal attention may nonetheless attain registration outside conscious awareness. Also, I noted that what is excluded from focal attention may be recovered by techniques such as hypnosis, free association, and dream analysis. The point of these remarks is that whatever is denied may "return" in a distorted or modified way in the screen behavior phase. The cognitive arrest in the cognitive arrest phase regarding the painful object is specific and limited to the inhibition of verbal thought. The subject's unconscious primary process operations continue to deal with the traumatic or dangerous situation and may provide some of the contents used to form the screen behavior.

As Waelder (1951) suggests, oftentimes the only clinical clue to a denial defense is the manifest counterclaim, or what I have called *screen behavior*. In such cases, the analyst infers the unconscious occurrence of an unverbalized or implicit denial from his or her observations of screen behaviors. The silent nature of most denial reactions may explain why so many clinicians, in my teaching and supervisory experience, do not notice most implicit denial reactions. Frequently they conceptualize and interpret the supplementary and specific defenses of screen behavior as if they were the whole defensive process.

Waelder proposes that paranoid ideas stem from denial and projection acting together. For example, an individual may deny his or her love for another person ("I do not love him") and then project the impulse onto the other person ("she loves me"). What Waelder observes about the relationship between denial and projection may be generalized to the relation between denial and the specific defenses such as undoing, isolation, reaction formation, and repression. These and other specific defenses function together with an antecedent denial, and their activity belongs to the screen behavior phase of defensive reactions. These auxiliary defenses are unconsciously used to bolster and support the defensive aims of the previous cognitive arrest phase.

Some clinical examples may further illuminate the relationship between denial and the operations of specific defenses in the screen behavior phase. A patient who tended to deny his hostility toward his wife became excessively and inappropriately solicitous over her well-being. His conflicts over his hostile feelings and his denial of his hostility were screened and supported by the reaction formation defense of inappropriate solicitousness.

Defensive identifications with lost objects are often used in conjunction with an earlier denial to defend against the painful awareness of loss. A young analysand who had not completed the "work" of mourning for her mother who had died of Parkinson's disease began to develop a shuffling gait. The unconscious fantasy underlying the symptom was "It is not true that I lost my mother; I have her inside me." Working through this conversion symptom entailed uncovering both the denial of her mother's death and her identification with her mother's pathological gait.

In depressive disorders, one may often observe the concurrent employment of denial and identification. Anxiety over an anticipated object loss leads the depressive to deny his or her anger toward the "bad" aspects of some need-fulfilling object and, at the same time, to deny his or her perceptions of those bad qualities. Typically, the depressive will then identify himself or herself with those "bad" qualities and turn the aggression inward.

The Concept of Defense as Implying Denial

So far, I have provided clinical examples supporting the hypothesis that the various specific defenses function together with an antecedent denial. In addition to reviewing the empirical evidence, one can also adduce logical evidence for the idea that the concept of defense implies denial. Defensive projection cannot (logically) occur without an implicit denial of whatever is projected. One cannot defensively ascribe to another person (projection) psychic contents linked with one's self-representation unless one has first denied that these contents are aspects of oneself. The unconsciously jealous person, for example, who ascribes his or her own jealousy to another person, first denies the jealous wishes and then projects them onto the other person. The converse occurs when identification is used as a defense. The subject denies something about another person and then unconsciously identifies with what was denied.

The idea that an implicit denial is part of all defensive functioning is derived from a conceptual analysis of what the term *defense* means. When psychoanalysts speak of an individual's defensive activity, they are implying that the subject is unconsciously negating, denying, or rejecting some psychic content in order to avoid becoming conscious of whatever is being repudiated. This property of disavowal or rejection is the generic feature of defense. Others who have maintained that denial (or its synonyms, disavowal and self-deception) is one of the essential and defining characteristics of defensive activity include Fingarette (1969), Hilgard (1949), Mischel (1974), and Weisman (1972).

This line of reasoning should not be misconstrued to mean, as Brenner (1981) claims, that the words *defense* and *denial* could be used as synonyms, because there are other aspects and meanings of defense not covered by the concept of denial.

According to Haan (1977), all of the specific defenses include some element of negating intersubjective and/or intrasubjective reality. *Isolation* denies the logically indicated connecting relationships among things. *Intellectualization* also denies the logically indicated connecting relationships among things, and more particularly the affective components of cognitive propositions. *Rationalization* denies the reality of a chain of causal events. *Doubt* denies a person's necessities and abilities to make decisions. *Regression* denies the reality of a person's age and time within his or her own time span. *Displacement* denies either the object or the situation concerned with a person's affective reactions. *Reaction formation* denies affective reactions felt to be undesirable or dangerous. *Repression* denies the reality of a person's affective reactions by erasing their cognitive representations.

The Cognitive Arrest Theory and the Consequences of Denial

The microanalytic method used in this chapter is best suited for explicating the immediate and short-range effects of denial. Other methods of study are used in later chapters to investigate and demonstrate the long-range effects, complications, and consequences of denial reactions. Psychoanalysis, following Freud's lead, emphasizes the role of unconscious motives and contents in defensive activity and in the psychopathology caused by or linked with defense. The cognitive arrest theory deals with another element that has been overlooked in the psychoanalytic and psychiatric literature on defense. Both the short-term and the long-term effects of denial should be viewed as resulting from the cognitive arrest.

The suspension of the *constructive, integrating,* and *regulatory* functions of focal attention and consciousness explains such consequences of denial as the "splitting of the ego," developmental defects, acting out, and the failures of higher-level functions, for example, perception, reality testing, and judgment. In Chapters 9 and 16 the dynamic functions of consciousness and the loss or suspension of these functions in denial reactions are investigated and explained.

Chapter 5 discusses the relationship between denial and unconscious perception. In perceptual processes, as in other cognitive processes, denial interrupts the normal process of percept formation, thus preventing the full development of conscious and accurate perception of the painful object. The second stage of perception, the stage involving conscious awareness of the object and the verbal representation of its meaning, is blocked. But the first stage of perception, involving the registration and unconscious perception of the painful object, does occur.

Denial and Psychic Defects

Long-standing and repetitive denial responses often bring about psychic defects and developmental arrests related to the failure to symbolize and assimilate whatever is denied. In brief, this is explained by the fact that denial blocks the formation of reality-syntonic, verbal representations of the self and objects. Studies of how the cognitive arrest theory explains psychic defects such as the loss of regulatory control (dyscontrol) for what is denied may be found in Chapter 9. The role of denial and dyscontrol in symptom formation is examined in Chpaters 9 and 13.

Memory pathology, including enactive memory, gaps in memory, and screen memories, is a long-range consequence of denial. Denial prevents the formation of accurate representational memories because permanent memory storage requires acts of focal attention. This failure to form representational memory for whatever is denied, and the relationships between denial and other kinds of pathological memorial activity are illustrated with case studies and investigated in depth in Chapters 14 and 15.

Developmental Considerations

The cognitive arrest theory includes a developmental perspective in positing primitive kinds of denial as the basic, primordial defense. Freud hypothesized a primitive defense, *primal repression*, that prevents preconscious derivations (verbal representations) from attaining conscious levels, and he believed that this primitive defense coexists in adults with repression proper. Chapter 6 reviews writings on primal repression and argues that primitive kinds of denial and primal repression are the same.

In Chapter 5, denial is viewed as undergoing a complex development out of its physiological precursors, sensorimotor avoidance behaviors—for example, eye blinking. Primitive forms of denial emerge in the second year of life and are followed by the formation of advanced kinds of denial. Chapter 5 provides an overview and integration of clinical and experimental studies on the ontogenesis of denial.

Negative hallucination, a form of denial involving perception, is the primary-process mode to protect against external stimuli and a clinical manifestion of the stimulus barrier. Chapter 7 presents clinical studies on the negative hallucination and proposes hypotheses regarding the role of the negative hallucination in the primary process and in the development of defense and cognition.

An object relations perspective on defenses is presented in Chapter 8, in which defenses are conceptualized as the structuralized derivations of internalized object relations. Case studies illustrate how defenses protect against pathological introjects.

Interactional Aspects of Denial and Defense

Psychoanalytic theory suffers from a poverty of concepts to describe the interplay between phenomena in the intrapersonal sphere and phenomena in the interpersonal sphere. A few analysts such as Ogden (1982) have used projective identification as one such bridging formulation, and in Chapters 11, 12, and 13 I shall attempt to demonstrate and explain some interactional aspects of denial reactions.

Defense is an important and, until recently, a neglected aspect of how individuals unconsciously communicate and relate with one another. Chapter 11 reviews and discusses the literature on interactional aspects of denial and defense. Chapter 12 includes a systematic investigation of an analysis's process notes and describes the development of a shared denial system in which the analyst and analysand denied certain of their interactions. Chapter 13 extends this study into the unconscious ways in which their shared denial contributed to the formation of symptoms manifested by the patient during analytic hours.

Brain Function and Denial

As shown in Chapter 16, the results and conclusions of studies on denial reactions in brain-damaged patients are consistent with the cognitive arrest theory. One of the important somatic causes of denial reactions are brain lesions that interrupt the transmission of information to the speech centers in the dominant hemisphere.

Summary

The basic concepts and terms used in the cognitive arrest theory of denial and defense were defined and discussed. Denial is an aspect of all defensive activity, and it is one of the essential and defining elements of defense. This chapter presented a microanalysis of the psychic actions and processes in the following four phases of denial: (1) preconscious appraisal of danger, (2) painful affect, (3) cognitive arrest, and (4) screen behavior. The subject's preconscious appraisal of some situation as actually or potentially dangerous or traumatic causes the formation of some more or less painful affect. The painful affect initiates a reaction in which the subject turns his or her focal attention from whatever is disturbing to something less threatening. This turning away from or rejection of what is disturbing arrests the subject's perceiving and/or thinking about the painful object.

Denial interrupts the normal process of thought formation and prevents the construction of verbal representations of the painful object and the denier's relation to it. Unconscious fantasies of destroying or rejecting the painful object produce the cognitive arrest.

The fantasy attacks on the painful object and the consequent cognitive arrest are followed by screen behavior. Screen behavior is defined as the ideas, fantasies, affects, and overt behaviors motivated by the need to fill in the gaps created by the cognitive arrest, to substitute a different object relation for the one subjectively lost, and to support the defensive aims of the cognitive arrest. The unconscious "return" of what is denied is often manifested in derivative form in screen behavior. Specific defenses (e.g., repression, isolation, reaction formation, undoing) function together with an antecedent denial, and their activity belongs to the screen behavior phase of defensive reactions.

Both the short-term and the long-term consequences of denial stem from two interrelated but distinguishable sets of dynamisms: (1) whatever is denied continues to be unconsciously active and has far-reaching effects on the denier's psychic functioning; (2) the cognitive arrest suspends the constructive, integrating, and regulatory functions of focal attention and consciousness regarding what is denied. Long-term consequences of denial include developmental defects, enactive memory, character malformations, affective and cognitive dyscontrol, and symptom formation. These topics will be taken up in later chapters.

2

Freud's Contributions

The goals of this chapter are to review Freud's writings on disavowal and to propose modifications and corrections in his theories of defense and disavowal.

This chapter is divided into three parts: the first reviews Freud's writings on disavowal; the second examines the clinical meanings of *decathexis* and *anticathexis* and compares them with the cognitive arrest theory of denial; and the third discusses Freud's theory of two basic defenses, repression and disavowal, and argues for the view of their being just one defense, disavowal.

Freud's Writings on Disavowal

From the beginning, Freud was concerned with what he thought were two different types of defensive activities—the defense against instincts and the defense against perceptions. Although he did not approach the defenses against perceptions as systematically as he did the defenses against instincts, he did have a continued interest in them from the time of the *Project* (1895) to the time of his final writings.

Freud's first reference (1923) to disavowal and the resulting split in the ego was made in his paper "The Infantile Genital Organization." In describing how small boys react to first noticing the absence of a penis in females, he noted that they disavow the fact and may insist that they do see a penis.

This disavowal may be supported by various fantasies—for example, that the female has a small penis and that it will later grow. The two coexisting attitudes—the young boy's denial of the woman's "penislessness" and the simultaneous recognition of the real situation—is described as a "split in the ego." The concept of ego splits was restated in similar language in "The Economic Problem of Masochism" (1924a) and in "Some Psychical Consequences of the Anatomical Distinctions Between the Sexes" (1925b).

In the latter paper, Freud (1925b) discussed little girls' disavowals of their sexual differences. The little girl's wish for a penis and her envy for the male's genital equipment may lead her to disavowal, to a refusal to accept her not having a penis. This idea may develop into the conviction that she does after all have a penis, and consequently, she may feel compelled to behave as though she were a man.

In "The Future of an Illusion," Freud (1927b) noted that religious beliefs require a disavowal of reality. Religion brings with it obsessional restrictions in much the same way as does an obsessional neurosis. Also, in Freud's view, religion comprises a system of wishful illusions together with a disavowal of reality.

In his paper "A Disturbance of Memory on the Acropolis," Freud (1936) linked the symptom of derealization to a disavowal of some part of reality. On visiting the Acropolis for the first time, Freud had a feeling of derealization. According to him, the essential nature of the thought was "By the evidence of my senses I am now standing on the Acropolis, but I cannot believe it" (p. 243). In his analysis of the derealization experience, Freud indicated that it served the purpose of defense, of disavowing some part of reality. He traced the childhood roots of his momentary symptom to a feeling of filial piety and to unconscious guilt for excelling over his father.

Freud (1938) returned to the topic of disavowal and the splitting of the ego in his unfinished paper "Splitting of the Ego in the Process of Defense," published posthumously in 1940. The paper is mainly a restatement of views expressed in his earlier papers. He described three possible responses to anxiety by a child faced with dangerous libidinal gratification. The child's ego is faced with either recognizing the danger and renouncing gratification or repudiating the reality in order to retain the satisfaction. In fact, Freud explained, the child attempts to follow both courses at the same time. On the one hand he or she rejects reality, and on the other hand he or she recognizes the danger of reality and takes over the fear of that danger as a symptom. The two contrary reactions to the child's conflict persist as the basis of a split in the ego.

Disavowal and Fetishism

In several papers Freud (1927a, 1938, 1940) discussed the significance of disavowal and the castration complex in fetishists. In his paper "Fetishism" (1927a), he stated that the fetish is a substitute for the woman's (the mother's) penis that the little boy once believed in and, because of his anxieties over being castrated, does not want to give up. To relieve his castration anxiety, the child disavows his perception of the penisless female genitals. In the phallic phase of development, such a boy may turn away from the reality of women's penislessness and strongly cathect (invest) the earlier fantasy of his mother's possessing a penis. The now heavily cathected "universal" fantasy of the phallic woman (Bak 1968) is unconscious, but its presence becomes apparent in the formation of a fetish. Clinical evidence indicates that two mutually contradictory fantasies must exist to explain the wish for a fetish: one is that of the phallic woman and the other is that she has been castrated (Jacobson 1957). According to Freud (1927a), the fetish becomes a token of triumph over the threat of castration and a protection against it.

If the disavowal defense consisted solely of the disavowal of reality and the conscious belief in the phallic woman, a delusion would result. However, the fetishist maintains intact reality testing at the same time that the fetish is formed. On the one hand, fetishists disavow their perception—that they see no penis in the female genitals. On the other hand, they maintain intact reality testing: they recognize that females have no penis, and they draw the correct conclusions from their observations. These two contradictory attitudes persist side by side throughout their lives without influencing each other. This, Freud claimed in his "Outline" (1940), is what may rightly be called a "splitting of the ego." The little boy who notes the absence of a penis does not simply contradict his perceptions and hallucinate a penis where there was none to be seen. Instead, he effects "a displacement of value —he transfers the importance of the penis to another part of the body" (Freud 1904, p. 277). According to Freud, this displacement of importance relates only to the female body, and nothing changes regarding the boy's own penis.

In fetishism the coexistence of both parts of the ego split is evident (Freud 1940). The fetish represents the observable manifestation of the disavowal of female penislessness, while at the same time there are some aspects of the fetishist's behavior that indicate the continued presence of castration anxiety. The latter observation, according to Freud, demonstrates that the female's lack of a penis was accurately perceived. Freud's opinion has been challenged by Stewart (1970), who credits Charles Fisher with the suggestion that the boy's fleeting look at the female genitalia does not attain full conscious awareness. Because of the physical difficulties in obtaining a clear view of the female genitalia and because of the boy's castration anxiety, he most probably does not obtain an accurate and conscious perception. Instead, he does have a subliminal or *unconscious perception* of the penisless state of the female genitalia. (See Chapter 5 for further discussion of unconscious perception.)

Disavowal in the Psychoses

In "Neurosis and Psychosis," Freud (1924c) indicates that psychosis is the outcome of a conflict between the ego and the outside world in which the ego is swept away by the id and thus is separated from reality. Freud raised the question of what mechanisms the ego uses in detaching itself from reality, and he suggested that this mechanism, like repression, consists of withdrawing the libidinal cathexis. Later contributions by both Freud and his daughter Anna suggested that the mechanism in question is disavowal: for example, in "The Loss of Reality in Neurosis and Psychosis," Freud (1924b) again discussed the decathexis of reality in the psychoses and used the concept of disavowal to describe this decathexis.

The idea of disavowal, without its name, was used much earlier by Freud (1911b) in his formula for the four types of paranoia: delusions of persecution, delusional jealousy, erotomania, and megalomania. The formulae for all of these begin with "I do not love him." This is followed by contradictory claims that uphold the denial and serve as a countercathexis (such as "I *hate* him" or "I love *her*"). In these studies Freud assumed that some process akin to disavowal was applied to a drive derivative. Clinical observations of this kind led Waelder (1951) to the opinion that denial can defend against drive derivatives as well as external perceptions.

Freud's ideas on the role of disavowal in the psychoses were modified in his "Outline" (1940) and in "Constructions in Analysis" (1937), where the psychoses are no longer described as a total detachment from reality. After their recovery from psychotic illness, patients stated that even during the height of their illnesses, some part of their mind was functioning normally. Also, Freud discussed a case of chronic paranoia in which after each attack of jealousy, a dream conveyed to the analyst a correct picture of the precipitating cause of the illness, free from any delusion. On the basis of these findings, Freud reasoned that psychotic patients do maintain some contact with the reality they disavow.

In "Construction in Analysis," Freud (1937) noted that psychotic delusions contain a historical truth insofar as they represent the return of the previously disavowed content in distorted form. He explained the delusions of psychotic patients as attempts at explanation and cure, even though they accomplish no more than a replacement of the fragment of reality that is disavowed in the present by another fragment disavowed in their distant past.

Freud (1937, 1940) recognized that the withdrawal from reality in psychotic patients is never a total one. By disavowing disturbing perceptions, the ego defends itself against some demand from the external world that it finds distressing. These disavowals are half-measures, incomplete attempts at detachment from reality (Freud 1940), which are supplemented by acknowledgments. Two contrary and independent attitudes are formed, with the result that there is a splitting of the ego: one attitude represents normal, reality-oriented thought, whereas the other one, under the influence of the instincts, detaches the ego from reality. When the latter attitude becomes stronger, the necessary condition for a psychosis is present.

Decathexis and Anticathexis

In this section my aim is to outline Freud's concepts of decathexis and countercathexis and to compare them with the cognitive arrest theory. The two major phases of denial and defense—the phase of cognitive arrest followed by the phase of screen behavior—were discussed in Chapter 1. Here, I propose to compare these two phases with the two mechanisms Freud hypothesized as occurring in defensive activity—decathexis (or with-drawal of cathexis) and anticathexis (also called *countercathexis*). It will be evident that the concept of the cognitive arrest in denial roughly corresponds to the decathexis concept and that the notion of screen behavior is similar to that of anticathexis.

As used by Freud and classical analysts, the terms *cathexis, decathexis,* and *anticathexis* have two sets of referents and meanings. One set stems from Freud's theories about psychic energy, and the other set comprises the clinical or experiential referents. My presentation will focus on the clinical referents. The energic referents and meanings will be omitted because I, along with many other psychoanalysts, believe that psychic energy concepts are neither valid nor useful (see Gill, 1977, G. Klein 1976, Rosenblatt and Thickstun 1977a). The clinical theory of defense has been obscured by the energic conceptions of cathexis, decathexis, and anticathexis.

In his paper "Repression," Freud (1915b) explained that a withdrawal of cathexis (or decathexis) is one thing that the mechanisms of defense have in common. Freud used the term *decathexis* to refer to the suspension of some function. For instance, in his discussions of the theory of sleep he viewed falling asleep as a process of decathecting the higher regulatory psychic centers and functions, with the result that the secondary process, which ordinarily has a regulatory function and predominates in waking life, is regressively subordinated to the primary process (1900, 1917).

In this book the terms *denial* and *cognitive arrest* refer to some of the same clinical phenomena that Freud referred to when he used the term *decathexis.* The concept of cognitive arrest in denial concerns the indivdual's suspension of focal attention from something actually or potentially dis-turbing.

After first relying on decathexis to explain defense, Freud (1915a, 1915b) in his later writings increasingly used the idea of anticathexis to explain the mechanism of repression and other defenses. In the obsessional neurosis the anticathexis against the repressed sadistic impulses is the reaction formation of kindness and gentleness (Freud 1915a, 1915b). Earlier, in his discussion of the Dora case, Freud (1905) observed that repression is often achieved by means of an intense reinforcement of the thought contrary to the one that is being repressed.

In anxiety-hysteric patients, the "substitute formation" or "substitute idea" (for example, the wolf in the case of the Wolf Man and the horse in the case of Little Hans) functions as an anticathexis (Freud 1915a, 1915b). The anticathexis in hysteria, according to Freud (1926), is predominantly directed outward and takes the form of a special watchfulness and avoidance of situations in which dangerous perceptions could occur.

Anticathexis, then, refers to an individual's wish to reinforce or to emphasize certain thoughts, affects, or actions in order to avoid becoming aware of other unconscious wishes or ideas. According to Schafer (1968a, p. 65), anticathexis pertains to the strength of certain motives not to see, feel, act, or experience the aims of other motives. Effective interpretations of defenses depend for their effect on their being formulated in terms of motives specifically opposed to other motives. Shorn of their energic connotations and meanings, Freud's concepts of anticathexis and substitute formation are similar to the screen formation concept used in this book.

Screen behavior is what individuals do to support their denial of reality and to provide a substitute for the portion of reality that is missing from consciousness as a result of their denial. There are an infinite number of different psychic contents and forms of behavior, including affects, memories, percepts, overt actions and the like, that persons may use defensively for their screening or anticathectic function. All of the specific mechanisms of defense—for example, repression, undoing, isolation, reaction formation, and projection—serve this screening function.

Denials betray themselves by voids: certain ideas, perceptions, and emotions an observer expects as a normal response to some event are missing. The cognitive arrest (or decathexis) in denial reactions creates this void, and the subject unconsciously attempts to fill the gap by screen behavior (or anticathexis). We infer the occurrence of an earlier denial from the various forms of screen behavior.

This formulation of an initial decathexis followed by an anticathexis in defensive reactions is similar to Rapaport's (1967, p. 322) hypothesis that repression proper begins with a withdrawal of cathexis of the conscious and preconscious systems from the idea to be repressed. This decathexis is followed by a countercathexis against those ideas in order to prevent their reemergence and the continuous conflict and anxiety that would otherwise ensue.

In summary, the *clinical* and not the energic meanings of the terms decathexis and anticathexis do contribute something important to the clinical theory of denial and defense. Decathexis refers to the suspension of some psychic function, and it corresponds to what I have called cognitive arrest. Anticathexis refers to the intense, defensively motivated reinforcement of some psychic content that is contrary to the content being defended against, and so the concept of anticathexis means essentially the same as do the ideas of substitute formation, substitute idea, and screen behavior.

Two Basic Defenses or One?

Freud's (1940) final conceptualization of the defenses was presented in Chapter 8 of his "Outline," in which he summarized his concepts of the major structures of the psychic apparatus and the basic defenses, repression and disavowal. His idea of two defenses was partly derived from his metapsychology of the psychic apparatus. He described the id as the core of our being and as having no direct communication with the external world. Within the id the instincts operate, and the processes taking place in the id he called the *primary process*. The other agency of the mind, the ego, developed out of the id's cortical layer, which, through being adapted to the reception and exclusion of stimuli, is in direct contact with the external world.

Freud's view of repression and disavowal was based on his spatial concept of the psychic apparatus in which the ego is in contact with the id "below" and with the external world "above." He presents a picture of the ego as mediating between the id and the external world. Disavowal is described as the defense operating against painful perceptions from the external world, and repression as a defense for dealing with forbidden instinctual demands. Thus, the ego is conceived as fighting on two fronts, as it must defend its existence against an external world that threatens it with annihilation and against an internal world that makes excessive instinctual demands.

Freud assumed that there are two different pathways by which stimuli attain consciousness. One is the direct, perceptual path from the external world to the ego and consciousness, and the second is the internal route in which drive derivatives from the id move to the ego and consciousness. Advances in understanding cognition and perception since Freud's time demonstrate one (not two) general pathways to consciousness, clearly indicating the mistake in Freud's assumption of two different pathways.

Because of his notion of two pathways, Freud's theory of the defenses required two different kinds of defenses: repression for the pathway from the id and disavowal for the pathway from the external world. The idea of two pathways to consciousness was based on two concepts in Freud's theory of the psychic apparatus that have been demonstrated to be fundamentally false. One was that the id or unconscious is not in direct contact with the external world, and the second was that perception is identical with consciousness. In the following sections I shall discuss the implications of these errors for Freud's theory of defense. Also, I shall present arguments for the hypothesis of there being one general pathway to consciousness and one (not two) basic defense, denial.

Perception and Consciousness

Some of Freud's mistaken ideas about the psychic apparatus and the defenses of repression and denial can be traced back to the false assumption he made (1900) that sensory stimuli, in contrast with endogenous stimuli (such as drive derivatives from the unconscious), have a direct access to consciousness. Freud believed it necessary to postulate different defenses for external and endogenous stimuli because of his error in thinking that perception is a sensory "given" and immediately known to the subject—that is, Pcpt = Cs (Freud 1900). Therefore, his theory posited one kind of defense, repression, for endogenous (instinctual) impulses, and another defense, disavowal, for protecting the organism against threatening external stimulation.

Several analysts, including Basch (1981), Fisher (1957), and Stewart (1970), examine Freud's error in equating perception and consciousness and the implications of this error for Freud's metapsychological theories. As noted in Chapters 1 and 10, many investigations in the fields of cognitive psychology and perception demonstrate that perception is a multistage process and that the perceptual process can be aborted at any one of several sequential stages before the percept becomes conscious. This total process from the time of sensory end-organ stimulation until there is a conscious perception of the stimulating object takes place in a very short period, and the subject becomes conscious only of the end products of this complex process. Consciousness is not a necessary or a regular feature of either an individual's perception of a stimulus object or the response to the stimulus. Most often reception, registration, and response to stimulating objects occur outside conscious awareness.

As discussed in Chapter 1, the cognitive arrest theory of denial postulates an arrest of perceptual and cognitive processes before the stage of conscious awareness. Hence, in denial reactions, the earlier phases of the perceptual process involving the unconscious and preconscious transformations of the sensory information remain intact and unaffected by the action of denial. To the extent that the denier of some stimulus object does unconsciously register the object, one can say that the denying subject does form a sub-liminal or *unconscious perception* of the object.

A further discussion about both clinical and theoretical studies of un-conscious perception may be found in Chapter 10, in which I shall present evidence for the hypothesis that perceptual input first goes through the primary process before attaining consciousness. The contents of unconscious perception are treated by primary-process mechanisms in much the same way as are unconscious memories and unconscious fantasies. Probably because he equated perception with consciousness, Freud was unaware of the existence of unconscious perception.

Fisher's (1956, 1957) experimental studies indicate that not only drive derivatives but also incoming sensory input are registered and transformed in the unconscious and preconscious before attaining consciousness (see also Stewart 1970). Both the drive derivative and the sensory input in this process come into contact with memory traces that give the percept meaning and the drive a psychical representation.

Fisher's conclusion (1956, 1957) that sensory input, like drive derivatives, are processed in the unconscious and preconscious before attaining con-sciousness is consistent with contemporary studies on perception (Erdelyi 1974, Neisser 1967). Cognitive psychologists conceive of perception as re-sulting from both inner (e.g., needs, wishes, drives) and external (e.g., information from receptors) determinants. Needs and wishes, according to Solley and Murphy (1960), determine how incoming information from sensory receptors is put into structured form. Schilder (1953) argues per-suasively that drives, wishes, and needs are necessary for the most elementary transformation of images into percepts.

All information, whether it arises from sources within the individual or from the outside world, first is treated by the primary process before it reaches higher levels, including consciousness. There is no need, then, to postulate, as did Freud, two different pathways to consciousness.

Relations Between the Id (or the Unconscious) and the External World

The clinical and experimental evidence cited earlier that perceptual input as well as drive derivatives are transformed in the unconscious and that drives, needs, and wishes help form concepts proves that Freud (1940) was mistaken in assuming that the id has no direct communication with the external world. Clinical studies such as those presented in Chapters 10, 11, 12, and 13 indicate that the so-called deep or unconscious regions of the mind are actually in more direct and immediate communication with other individuals than is conscious perception.

In both his clinical writings and theoretical studies on the topographical and structural models, Freud adhered to the view that the unconscious does not have direct access to the external world. There is, however, one passage that contradicts all his other assertions on this matter:

> It is a very remarkable thing that the *Ucs.* of one human being can react upon that of another, without passing through the *Cs.* This deserves closer investigation, especially with a view to finding out whether preconscious activity can be excluded as playing a part in it; but descriptively speaking, the fact is incontestable. (Freud 1915c, p. 194)

Freud's concept of the id and the unconscious as isolated from direct communication with the external world may have been one reason that his accounts of the instinctual drives tend to neglect or to minimize the important and complex ways in which sexual and aggressive wishes are activated by external stimuli (Holt 1976). Similarly, aggression is an innately determined (though modifiable) reaction to specific kinds of environmental provocations, frustrations, and threats (Holt 1976). I contend that phenomena such as sexual arousal and the activation of aggression that analysts have conceptualized in purely intrapsychic (or intraorganismic) terms should be accounted for in a way that takes account of the individual's mainly unconscious interactions with the environment.

Basch (1981) also argues against the view that disavowal defends against traumatic external percepts and that repression is the defense against forbidden instinctual demands. According to Basch, examination of clinical material, including Freud's, shows that this is not the case. In his view, repression defends against anxiety-provoking perceptions when disavowal fails to be effective—that is, when the self is threatened.

A Unified Theory of Defense

The foregoing arguments demonstrate errors in Freud's conception of the psychic apparatus and there being two basic defenses, disavowal and repression, protecting the two pathways to consciousness. The processing of information from the external world is similar to the processing of drive derivatives, inasmuch as information from whatever source must first pass through the unconscious before attaining preconscious or conscious levels. A major thesis of this section is that there is only one major pathway, or series of transformations, by which information stemming from diverse sources within and outside the individual's body attains consciousness. Contemporary concepts of this pathway are similar to the one Freud (1900, 1915b) himself posited in his theory of how thoughts are formed. As noted in

Chapter 1, Freud's (1900, 1915b) view on the microgenesis of thought is remarkably congruent with modern theories of cognitive psychology and the neurosciences. Briefly, all information, whatever its sources, goes through a series of rapid and complex unconscious and preconscious transformations before attaining conscious levels. Denial aborts this process, thereby preventing the explicit consciousness of whatever is denied, and denial blocks the consciousness of both endogenous and external stimuli.

Freud's concept of two different defenses, repression and disavowal, for what was "inner" and "outer," respectively, was based on his errors in his metapsychology of the psychic apparatus. His classification of two defenses was maintained by succeeding generations of psychoanalysts, including Anna Freud (1936), Sperling (1958), and others.

Conclusion

The dissolution of the two-pathway theory eliminates the necessity for postulating two different types of basic defensive operations, denial and repression. The extant clinical and experimental evidence cited and discussed in various chapters of this volume supports the hypothesis of a single, basic mechanism of defense. According to Freud (1915a), the essence of defense consists in rejecting and keeping something out of consciousness. The principal way that persons keep themselves from becoming conscious of something, whatever its source, is by unconsciously arresting their cognitive and perceptual processes concerning some disturbing content.

In place of Freud's model of two defenses, I propose that the basic model for all defenses is one that Freud (1915a, 1925a) postulated as the primordial defense of the infant against stress. The original pleasure ego tries to introject into itself everything that it deems good and to reject from itself everything that is bad. In infantile oral terms the generic mode of defense is to "spit it out" (Freud 1925a). In more everyday language, as used by Freud (1938), the generic aim of defense is to "disavow" or to "reject." This proposal to include the primordial mode of defensive function in a theory of defense is in the spirit of psychoanalytic theory construction, in which it is an accepted conceptual strategy to postulate the earliest form of any action as the enduring model on which later refinements and modifications are later built. These ideas on defense development will be elaborated on in Chapters 5, 6, and 7.

Freud's theories of disavowal and defense were constructed from both his clinical observations and his metapsychological assumptions regarding the nature of the psychic apparatus and the central nervous system. The clinical theory of disavowal and defense has been obscured by misconceptions and errors derived from Freud's now largely obsolete and mechanistic metapsychology. In this chapter I have attempted to disentangle the valid clinical meanings and facts concerning disavowal from the no-longer useful and disconfirmed metapsychological concepts. These modifications in the psychoanalytic theory of defense nonetheless do not detract from Freud's monumental contributions to answering questions about the how, what, when, and why of the ways human beings unconsciously defend themselves.

3

Further Analytic Contributions

In this chapter I shall review and discuss some of the major contributions to our knowledge of denial by psychoanalysts and others. This critique does not include the writings of the Kleinian school of psychoanalysis, which will be covered in Chapter 4. In his writings Freud gave more attention to repression than to denial. Since Freud's death, however, this trend has been reversed, in that contemporary writings on defense tend to be increasingly concerned with denial. As shown in the following review, this change has been associated with modifications in the definition and scope of denial.

Shlomo Breznitz

In his article "The Seven Kinds of Denial," Breznitz (1983) postulates seven kinds of denial, each related to a different stage in the processing of threatening information. These kinds of denial represent progressive attempts by the individual to protect himself or herself from danger by resorting to different cognitive strategies. The seven kinds of denial of stress that Breznitz proposes are denial of personal relevance, denial of urgency, denial of vulnerability or responsibility, denial of affect, denial of affect relevance, denial of threatening information, and denial of information. Their ordering reflects the amount of reality distortion involved, and in the last category, denial of information, there is the greatest amount of distortion.

Because individuals attempt to engage in the least reality distortion at any given point, the seven kinds of denial are stages in the same process. If the stress continues, the need to switch to a more primitive kind of denial is because objective reality makes it impossible to maintain the previous level of adjustment. Not all persons go through the entire sequence. The implications of threatening information may be so overwhelming that one can immediately move into the most primitive kinds of denial. For example, fainting, emotional shock, and the psychoses are states in which there is an attempt to deny all information.

Breznitz illustrates his seven categories with examples taken from studies of patients who have had a heart attack:

1. The *denial of personal relevance* is demonstrated in a study of a coronary care unit by Hackett, Cassem, and Wishnie (1968), who found that although 11 out of their 50 coronary patients witnessed a fatal cardiac arrest during their stay in the unit, none identified with the victim.

2. The *denial of urgency* is shown in the vast literature on the tendency of many individuals, including those who have experienced a personal emergency—either a heart attack or symptoms of cancer—to delay calling for help.

3. The *denial of vulnerability or responsibility* pertains to some cardiac patients who, because they follow medical advice regarding diet, exercise, and smoking, may deny their vulnerability by thinking that following the medical regimen will protect them against another heart attack. Other cardiac patients abdicate their responsibility for their fates and claim that heart attacks are totally outside their sphere of control. Often they state that heart attacks are due to luck, fate, or other such uncontrolled factors.

4. The *denial of affect* was found in a study of patients who had just experienced a coronary occlusion, in which it was observed that although most of them admitted to thoughts of death, only a few admitted feeling fear during that time (Hackett et al., 1968). This and similar findings indicate that cardiac patients often use the denial of affect as a coping device.

5. The *denial of affect relevance* can be explained by the fact that once an emotion, like anxiety, cannot be explained away or denied, it is still possible to attribute it to other causes. Although the signs of cardiac illness may be quite evident, and the person is familiar with them, he or she may attribute them to other causes and thus reduce the anxiety over having heart problems. The significance of anxiety itself may be dismissed as not stemming from a response to impending, actual danger.

6. The *denial of threatening information* can be seen in cardiac patients who may backslide and fail to exercise because the exercise itself may remind them of their vulnerability to more heart attacks. Even though a person may defensively block threatening information, there is much evidence from studies of unconscious perception and perceptual defense, reviewed in Chapter 10, that such a person does, on an unconscious level, register the threatening information.

7. The *denial of information* can be found in the severe depression and/or psychoses experienced by some cardiac patients who may have an unconscious wish to block the input of all information. Denial of all information is totally indiscriminate, and the psychotic person is a dramatic example of this final stage of denial.

Breznitz provides a much-needed comprehensive classification of the many different forms of denial, and his process-oriented conceptualization envisions the varied ways in which an individual's denial reactions change over time. His study should dispel the common misconception that denial is always and only a primitive defense. Only the last two categories (that is, denial of information and denial of threatening information) are primitive kinds of denial, and the other kinds of denial imply higher levels of reality testing and psychic development.

Anna Freud

Anna Freud's (1936) classic work *The Ego and the Mechanisms of Defense* was a milestone and a turning point in the history of psychoanalytic theory and technique. In her first five closely reasoned chapters, the theory of defense mechanisms is covered and illustrated. The following five chapters are devoted to case histories showing the use of defenses in children. The last two chapters discuss instinctual anxiety and defensive activity during puberty and adolescence.

Anna Freud makes the important observation that individuals use similar defense mechanisms in their resistances and neurotic behavior. She introduces a new idea: resistance is not merely to be overcome but represents a form of communication by the patient. When the patient is not resisting, he or she produces id material. When the patient is resisting, he or she is communicating his or her defensive structure. Before Anna Freud, resistances were not treated as being equal in value to id material. She shows that defenses are part of normal psychic development and structure, as well as of character structure and symptom formation. Another idea she introduces is that individuals have only a restricted repertory of defensive responses at their disposal.

Anna Freud does not include denial as one of the defenses. Instead, she describes it as involved in the "Preliminary Stages of Defense" (p. 71). Although she uses the term *preliminary stages* in the ontogenetic sense, she does not state whether or not she also uses that term in the microgenetic sense. The cognitive arrest theory of denial views denial as a preliminary stage of defense in both ontogenesis and microgenesis. Microgenesis repeats ontogenesis. In adult defense functioning, the ontogenesis of defense is repeated insofar as a defensive action contains an implicit denial in conjunction with some screen activity.

Anna Freud does not include denial in her list of defenses because she defines defense as the psychic processes whose purpose is "the protection of the ego against instinctual demands" (p. 46). She describes denial as a method for avoiding objective "pain" and objective danger. At the present time the term *defense* is usually used in a broader sense to cover unconscious self-protective responses to all kinds of unpleasure and mental pain, whatever their source.

Anna Freud includes the following ten mechanisms in her list of defenses: regression, repression, reaction formation, isolation, undoing, projection, introjection, turning against the self, reversal, and sublimation. These defense methods discovered by psychoanalysis all serve a single purpose—aiding the ego in its struggle with instinctual life. She describes three motives for the defense against instinct: superego anxiety, objective anxiety, and anxiety caused by the strength of the instincts.

Anna Freud proposes a developmental chronological classification of defenses and holds that repression and sublimation cannot be used until relatively late in development. The earliest mechanisms she lists are regression, reversal, and turning on the self, and she indicates that these methods develop as early as the instincts themselves do. The remaining methods develop somewhere between the earliest methods and the late appearance of repression and sublimation. Her statement that the developmental chronology of defenses is both debatable and obscure remains as true today as when she was writing.

Anna Freud describes the simultaneous defensive processes, directed respectively inwards and outwards, in the case of Little Hans. After writing about his defenses against the jealousy of his father and his castration anxiety, she tells of Hans's anxieties over objective dangers and frustration. In one fantasy, Hans imagined a plumber who took away Hans's buttocks and penis and replaced them with larger and finer ones. Anna Freud explains that Hans denied reality by means of this fantasy and that he could not "accept" reality until he had first transformed it to suit his own purposes and fulfill his wishes.

Such denying fantasies in childhood acquire their pleasurable character through a complete reversal of the real situation. Children refuse to become aware of some disagreeable reality. They turn their back on the painful reality, deny it, and imagine that the unwelcome facts have been reversed. Denial belongs to a normal phase in early childhood development, but if it occurs in later life, according to Anna Freud, it indicates an advanced stage of mental disease. The ego's capacity for denying reality is wholly inconsistent with its capacity for recognizing and testing reality.

The denial of reality is completed and confirmed when in their fantasies, words, or acts, the children reverse the real facts. Just as in a neurotic conflict, the perception of a prohibited instinctual impulse is warded off by means of repression, and so the infantile ego resorts to denial in order not to become aware of some painful impression from without.

Children's denials in word and act are subject to a restriction that does not apply to denials in fantasy that are not communicated to others. Dramatization of fantasies in word or act requires a stage in the outside world. Therefore, using denial in word or act is conditioned externally by the extent to which those around the child fall in with his or her interpretation.

Anna Freud's classification of defensive activities is similar to her father's, who, as I explained in Chapter 2, defined repression as defending against internal (instinctual) dangers, and denial as a protection against dangers stemming from the external world. Repression, according to both Freuds, abolishes awareness of instinctual derivatives, just as denial gets rid of unpleasurable external stimuli. Reaction formation, for example, secures the ego against the return of repressed impulses from within; whereas through fantasies in which the real situation is reversed, denial sustains the ego against an overthrow from without.

A number of analysts, including Basch (1974), Stewart (1970), and Sperling (1958), criticize Anna Freud's overemphasis on the pathological nature of denial. (She limits denial to the psychoses and to young children.) These and other authors describe neurotic as well as psychotic forms of denial, and they claim that denial does not always mean a gross distortion of reality.

In a number of places Anna Freud emphasizes the severe pathological implications when denial in act or fantasy continues beyond childhood:

> The defensive method of denial by word and act is subject to the same restrictions in time as I have discussed . . . in conjunction with denial in fantasy. It can be employed only so long as it can exist side by side with the capacity for reality testing without disturbing it. The organization of the mature ego becomes unified through synthesis and this method of denial is then discarded and is resumed only if the relation to reality has been gravely disturbed and the function of reality testing suspended. (p. 90)

In my opinion, Stewart (1970) is correct in criticizing Anna Freud's generalization that denial in adults is always pathological. In Stewart's view, denial and repression coexist in the normal as well as the neurotic, and denial expressions range from the normal through various pathological levels to the psychotic.

Similarly, in her discussion of denial in fantasy, Anna Freud exaggerates the pathological quality of denying, wish-fulfilling fantasies in nonpsychotic adults. Basch (1974) points out that it is only the exceptional person who faces painful reality and does not assuage narcissistic injury through compensatory wish-fulfilling fantasy. According to Basch, Anna Freud underestimates the universality and significance of denial in fantasy when she assigns it an, at most, trivial role in the psychic life of the nonpsychotic adult.

Probably some of the disagreement with the views of both Freuds on the degree of pathology and universality of denial reactions is a definitional issue concerning the scope of denial. Common usage today employs the term *denial* in a broader and more inclusive way than did both of the Freuds. They and other analysts before about 1950 focused on the types of denial using the greatest amount of reality distortion. Sigmund Freud's early papers on denial concern mainly the use of denial in psychotic patients, and only in his final papers does he begin to appreciate the universality of its occurrence in normal and neurotic patients as well as in psychotic individuals.

Of the seven kinds of denial described by Breznitz (1983), the two most primitive types (i.e., denial of threatening information and denial of information) are those that predominate in the studies of both Freuds. The five kinds of denial involving less reality distortion (i.e., denial of personal relevance, denial of urgency, denial of vulnerability or responsibility, denial of affect, and denial of affect relevance) are scarcely mentioned in the writings of the Freuds and other early analysts.

To the existing list of the ten defenses, Anna Freud adds two special forms of defense: identification with the aggressor and what she calls "a form of altruism." What is special about these defensive activities is their property of using another person for purposes of defense. In describing identification with the aggressor, she tells of a young patient who bitterly reproached her analyst for being secretive. It turned out that in fact the patient at times kept certain experiences secret from the analyst, anticipated the analyst's reproaches, and coped with this expectation by reversing the roles. She thus blamed the analyst for the very fault of which she herself was guilty.

The "altruistic surrender" or "form of altruism" is described as a combination of projection and identification for defensive purposes. By using this mechanism, the individual succeeds in relinquishing unconscious forbidden desires by assisting others in gratifying the same desires. The example provided by Anna Freud is that of an unmarried governess who came to analysis with little sign of any ambition for herself. She had a lively and affectionate interest in the love life of her women friends, and she was an "enthusiastic matchmaker." As Anna Freud indicates, "she lived in the lives of other people, instead of having any experience of her own" (p. 125).

In both of the two defensive constellations just summarized, Anna Freud emphasizes the patient's defensive projection onto others of some attitude, quality, or affect. What she does not explain about these special defenses is that whatever an individual projects onto another person, he or she also implicitly denies as part of the self. Another point that she omits about these defenses is that to some variable degree they are interactional (or transactional). That is to say, both parties in these defenses contribute to forming and/or maintaining the interactional defensive activity. These and other issues concerning interactional aspects of defenses are examined in depth in Chapters 11, 12, and 13.

Samuel Sperling

In his paper "On Denial and the Essential Nature of Defence," Sperling (1958) attempts to define more sharply the concept of defense and the basic defense mechanism of denial. Along with Glover (1947), Fenichel (1945), and Jacobson (1957), Sperling believes that the primitive process called denial is a forerunner and precursor of repression. The infantile defensive pattern of total rejection of external perception, when incorporated, becomes the prime defense mechanism (repression) of the unconscious ego against perceptions of intrapsychic origin.

Sperling divides defensive mechanisms into two types, *rejecting* and *countering* classes of defenses. The rejecting class ("not this") includes denial and repression, and the countering class ("not this but this other") includes the other types of defense mechanisms such as isolation, reaction formation, and projection. According to Sperling, the countering category comprises the overwhelming majority of defenses seen clinically, and they complete what denial and repression have left undone. In the countering class of defenses, the rejective component (repression or denial) is supported by a substitutive cathectic unit.

Sperling's concept of the rejecting and countering aspects of defensive activity is, in most respects, identical with the cognitive arrest theory. In my view, denial, and not repression, is involved in the rejecting or cognitive arrest phase; and repression, as well as other specific defense mechanisms, falls into the countering class—or according to the theory presented in Chapter 1, they comprise screen behaviors.

Sperling's differentiation between repression and denial is based on Freud's mistaken concept that instinctual strivings are dealt with by repression and external stimuli by denial. In Chapter 2 I demonstrated the errors in this conceptualization.

Sperling makes an important distinction between neurotic and psychotic forms of denial. The psychotic denies the existence of some part of reality, whereas denial in the neurotic is a defense only against the meaningfulness or emotional impact of a percept and reflects only a circumscribed impairment of the ego's integrative functioning. Freud (1924b) expressed this distinction as "neurosis does not disavow the reality, only ignores it" (p. 185).

Sperling's argument that all defensive activity is pathological is not validated by clinical experience or research on defensive reactions to trauma and stress (Beisser 1979, Breznitz 1983, Hackett et al. 1968, 1969; Horowitz

1976, Weissman 1972). These studies show that denial often is an expectable and normal, though temporary, response to overwhelming stressful and disruptive situations. In such contexts, denial may assist individuals in doing away with a threatening portion of reality in order that they may continue to contend with other problems. Studies by Hackett and associates (1968, 1969) show the survival value of denial in acute coronary patients. One study indicates that those patients on a coronary care unit who denied the most had better survival records (Hackett et al. 1968).

A judgment of whether a defensive reaction is normal or pathological should be contextual, because the person's circumstances need to be appraised in order to determine whether a particular defense aids or detracts from the individual's adaptation. Also to be considered in assessing the normality or pathological nature of a denial reaction is the kind of denial used and its intensity and duration.

Mardi J. Horowitz

Horowitz's (1976) outstanding contribution to our knowledge of denial reactions is his evidence from a comprehensive review of clinical studies, field studies, and experimental studies regarding the universality of denial responses to various kinds of stresses and traumas. His review of clinical studies indicates that major stress events are followed by involuntary "intrusions" in thought, emotion, and behavior. The term *intrusion* refers to the period of unbidden ideas and pangs of feelings that are difficult to dispel and that are direct or symbolic behavioral reenactments of the stress event complex. These repetitions of trauma tend to recur in phases and to alternate with periods of relatively successful warding off of the intrusions by ideational denial and emotional numbness.

Field studies (e.g., military combat, concentration camps, nuclear holocaust, bereavement, rape) show the same kind of general response tendency despite the variations in differences in personality or event. An overall pattern of alternating denial and intrusion phases can be found in responses in these various groups of persons. This pattern of response to stress and trauma can be summarized as an initial response of outcry, followed by denial, intrusion, working through, and finally completion.

Michael Basch

Basch (1974, 1981) holds that disavowal is what Freud (1900, 1915c) called the "second censorship," the censorship between the preconscious and the conscious systems. In Basch's view, the second censorship is a barrier to the transformation of thought into words and thereby into consciousness. In the event of conflict, a barrier can be erected between conceptual thinking and its translation into the subject-predicate language used by individuals to describe the contents and products of conceptualization. Disavowal bars the translation of thought contents into discursive verbal symbolism or inner speech. Basch believes that Freud's idea of the second censorship could not be understood theoretically until cognitive development was studied and the crucial experiments were performed by Vygotsky (1934) that demonstrated the separation of thought from speech and the distinction between inner speech and social speech.

Freud (1900) considered repression to be the censorship between the unconscious and the preconscious mind, but he did not indicate the name or the nature of the so-called second censorship between the preconscious and conscious systems. According to Basch, repression need not be thought of as a barrier between word and thing presentation, as Freud (1923) suggests, but, rather, as Freud (1895) earlier speculated in his "Project," as a barrier to thinking itself.

According to Basch, only content that can be dealt with by inner speech is acknowledged as belonging to the self. If the individual unconsciously blocks the transformation into inner speech, then it is the equivalent of disavowing the content—that is, it has no meaning for the self. The absence of inner speech means losing the self-regulatory function of speech over what is disavowed. The disavowed content cannot be processed by being subjected to the corrective action that the feedback system called consciousness initiates. Luria (1961) shows that the introduction of speech creates a self-symbolizing mechanism that is much more effective in controlling voluntary action than are the instructions of others.

In analysis, the self-regulatory function of speech, also called self-consciousness, is brought to bear on the newly acquired thought complexes and concepts that emerge in the treatment. This is a necessary step because only when self-conscious awareness has been developed sufficiently is the patient able to perform self-analysis. Conflict is then not only resolved unconsciously but also may present itself to self-consciousness for examination, approval, and recycling. What we call self, or acknowledge as being "me," is that aspect of our information processing activity that presents itself in the form of discursive symbols—especially, but not exclusively, those of speech. It is the activity of expressing our thought content in verbal symbols that we call *self* or, more properly, should call *selfing*.

Technical Implications

Basch holds that the task of interpretation is twofold: first, to raise past conflicted experiences to the cognitive level appropriate to the patient's present development and, second, to make them a part of his or her self-concept through inner speech. Once a repression is resolved, the second part of the task undoes the effect of the defense Freud termed *disavowal*. Disavowal, rather than repression, is the main defense of narcissistic character disorders, and the task of overcoming the second censorship through interpretation is the main one in the analysis of such patients.

Basch's view that disavowal blocks inner speech and that the therapeutic working through of disavowal is done by putting ideas into words is closely akin both to Fingarette's (1969) concept that the self-deceiver does not spell out in words what he or she disavows and to the cognitive arrest theory presented in Chapter 1.

In Basch's view, repression blocks thinking, and disavowal blocks inner speech, and he cites Vygotsky's (1934) studies to assert that secondary-process, conceptual thinking can be distinguished from inner speech. In other words, language is not a necessary part of conceptual thinking. Even if we assume that it is, we are left with the practical problem of how we are to distinguish between individuals' defending by not thinking about something and their defending by not translating their thoughts into either inner speech or spoken language.

As analytic observers, we infer the occurrence of some defensive activity by voids, because the patient does not express something that we have some reason to expect to be a reasonable response. And if the patient does not say something, how are we to know whether the void arises because the patient has not allowed himself or herself to think about it or because he or she has not transformed the thought into words? Basch does not provide evidence or arguments to support his thesis that repression blocks thinking, nor does he explain how one is to distinguish clinically between repression and disavowal.

Bertram Lewin

Lewin's (1950) classic monograph *The Psychoanalysis of Elation* emphasizes the role of denial as a basic defense in the elations, manic and hypomanic states. He extensively reviews the literature on depression and elation and describes the oral triad of wishes that occur in the elations: the wish to eat, the wish to be devoured, and the wish to sleep. These wishes generate the unconscious fantasies and memories underlying the denial reactions in mania, hypomania, and the elations.

Lewin notes that it is chiefly the denial of the emotional impact of reality that influences the elations' clinical picture. He recognizes and describes different degrees and kinds of denial. Denial may oppose the intellectual recognition of an external fact, say a death, and state that it did not occur. This may lead to a delusion. Or denial may oppose the affective impact of an external fact: although admitting that a death did occur, the denier would take the point of view that it did not matter.

In his discussion of the mild hypomania that may occur during part of a therapeutic analysis, he describes the case of a young woman who had an airplane phobia in which the motion of the airplane symbolically represented her experiences as a child when she shared an upstairs sleeping porch with her parents. During her analysis, when she became aware of the connection between her phobia and her childhood primal scene experiences, she became hypomanic for several days. Only after this brief period of elation could the patient begin to remember and work through the aggressive and erotic aspects of her childhood experiences on the porch. Lewin describes her hypomania as a *screen affect* because it was used to deny and conceal the affects linked with her primal scene experiences and fantasies.

As a resistance during analysis, elation represents a defense against reality and the effective admission and acceptance of known dangers, losses, rejections, and defeats. Mourning often appears in an analysis as part of working through, and elation may be used unconsciously to block the mourning process. Lewin views elation as an interruption of the analytic process, as an inappropriate substitution for working through.

Research confirms Lewin's hypotheses on the role of denial in the mourning process (Bowlby 1961, Gorer 1965, Lindemann 1944). These studies show that a variable degree of a usually temporary denial of loss is a prominent and early reaction to the death of a love object. A prolonged denial of loss, however, may lead to an arrest of the mourning process and various kinds of psychopathology, including depressive and suicidal reactions (Bowlby 1980, Dorpat 1972, 1973; Parkes 1970, Pollock 1978).

Lewin compares the function of denial in mania with denial in sleep. In mania the ego fuses with its superego in reproducing that fusion with the breast that takes place in nursing. Sleep and dream life include a normal split in the ego in which the denial of reality occurs. To be devoured into sleep in the nursing situation is a purely pleasurable wish fulfillment, but later it may become defensive so as to shut out disturbing stimuli. Sleep, then, is the deepest form of "denial" of the environment. Sleep gains protection from potential evokers and disturbers by dreams, the great guardian of sleep.

The psychological equivalents of biological sleep (stupors and hypomania) depend on the same mechanism of fusion with the breast or its later successors. In the elations, various fantasies, words, and deeds are used mainly for denial, and they resemble the denying secondary elaborations that come after the distortion of the latent dream thoughts. As a defense, sleep is subject to unconscius eroticization, according to Freud's formula, which states that those functions that originally serve to ward off impulses gradually become substitute expressions for the wishes against which they are defending.

Robert Waelder

In his article "The Structure of Paranoid Ideas," Waelder (1951) offers a closely reasoned and critical survey of various theories of the structure and formation of paranoid ideas. He maintains that projection is a form of implicit denial—that is, denial with a specific countercathexis. Through projection an individual may unconsciously fortify the denial of his or her own impulses or guilt by blaming somebody else. A two-year-old may disavow responsibility for having wet the bed; if he claims that the teddy bear is the culprit, he has made a projection. In this way the child has strengthened his denial ("I have not done it") by a particular form of countercathexis ("he has done it"). The child's fantasy functions as a countercathexis supporting denial and substituting for the reality that has been disavowed. What has been disclaimed returns as a claim, and because the denial consists in disclaiming, the countercathexis has the form of a claim. Denial is betrayed by its countercathexis, by its noisy counterclaims. An individual may deny his love for another of the same sex ("I do not love him"). Although the homosexual impulse is *disclaimed*, it "returns" in the form of a *claim* ("he loves me") through the mechanism of projection.

Waelder discusses the role of the return of the denied in the form of delusions. Freud (1937) held that delusions may contain a kernel of truth, albeit distorted, and it may be due to this content of truth that individual's tenaciously adhere to their delusions and cannot be dissuaded from them. The kernel of historical truth in delusions often is something that the patient disavowed long ago and that now returns and contributes to delusion formation.

Waelder makes a convincing analysis of the role of implicit denial in projection and the formation of paranoid ideas. One of this book's major hypotheses is that his conclusions about the significance of implicit denial in defensive projection and paranoid ideas can be extended to other defensive activities and the process of symptom formation. An implicit denial is an aspect of all defensive activities. The causal significance of denial reactions in symptom formation is discussed in Chapter 9.

Avery Weisman

Weisman's (1972) book *On Dying and Denying* is a study of denial reactions in 350 hospitalized patients who are seriously or terminally ill. He observes that the various interactions that give rise to denial are so fluid and diversified that it is impossible to catalogue all the forms in which denial expresses itself. Even when the manifestations of denying and denial are restricted to impending death, the scope of denial is never exhausted.

Weisman classified three orders or degrees of patients' denial of death. A *first-order denial* is the disavowal of the primary facts of the individual's illness. A first-order denial precludes second-order and third-order denials because when the patient denies facts it is unnecessary for him or her to consider their implications. Usually short-lived, a first-order denial is then replaced by a second-order or a third-order denial.

A *second-order denial* refers to the inferences that a patient draws, or fails to draw, about the implications and extensions of his or her illness. Patients with a second-order denial accept the primary facts of their illness, even the diagnosis, but they do not visualize its implications and possible extensions. A *third-order denial* pertains to the patient's image of death itself, the denial of extinction. Patients may come to accept their diagnosis and its implications but they still may resist the conclusion that incurable illness results in death.

Although denial usually evokes images of avoidance and aversion, its full meaning cannot be grasped without also understanding its opposite, *acceptance*. During the course of a threatening illness, shifts in the mixture of denial and acceptance are something like sand flowing down an hourglass. At first, there are both reasons for optimism and opportunities for denial. Then the first-order denial decreases and, falling to the bottom of the hourglass, becomes a first-order acceptance. There is a beginning recognition of painful reality. Time goes on, and with the progressive encounter with inexorable illness, the second-order denial passes into a second-order acceptance. Finally, when inimical forces exhaust the reasonable means of denial, even a third-order denial yields to acceptance, and the sand in the hourglass runs out. Weisman presents a valuable, moving account of the stages of steadily decreasing denial and concomitant increasing acceptance shown by patients in their attempts to adapt to serious illness and death.

Individuals who experience other kinds of major trauma, in my opinion, usually manifest a similar sequence of denial reactions. At first they deny the primary facts of the trauma. When this primitive and usually brief form of denial is resolved and they are able to accept the facts, they may still deny its implications and consequences. The gradual relinquishment of these denial reactions, whether occurring spontaneously or taking place in psychoanalytic therapy, is accompanied by a concomitant growing acceptance of the trauma's facts, implications, and personal meanings. Weisman's observations of denial responses in seriously ill individuals is consistent with the findings reported in studies of defensive responses to other kinds of trauma (Hackett et al. 1968, Horowitz 1976, Bowlby 1961).

Weisman's idea that denial is an aspect of defensive activity and not a discrete defense mechanism is essentially the same as the concept advanced by Fingarette (1969) and by me in Chapter 1. Weisman's *Dying and Denying* highlights the adaptive value and ubiquity of denial reactions in life-threatening situations. It is one of the few books about denial and defense that emphasizes the interactional elements in the initiation and maintenance of defensive activities, and a discussion of Weisman's studies on interactional factors in denial responses may be found in Chapter 11.

Edith Jacobson

In her article "Repression and Denial," Jacobson (1957) compares and contrasts repression and denial, and she views denial as a more archaic, more primitive, and historically earlier mechanism than repression is—in fact, it is its forerunner. According to her, all defenses serve to avoid anxiety, but in repression, signal anxiety mobilizes a defensive struggle against the sources of danger (i.e., the instinctual drives). In denial reactions, the ego reacts to the danger signal by immediately attempting to ignore this very signal itself.

Jacobson, like Basch (1981), believes that denial prevents ideas that have reached the preconscious from becoming conscious, and so denial acts as a second censorship between the preconscious and the conscious. Agreeing with Lewin (1950) and others, Jacobson holds that both inner reality and outer reality can be denied. Though she distinguishes between psychotic and neurotic forms of denial, her accounts of denial reactions tend to restrict denial to primitive and seriously pathological kinds of defensive activity.

Jacobson provides an excellent discussion on the relationship between denial and acting out. She concludes that the analyst's endeavors to help patients relinquish their acting out, in favor of remembering and reconstructing their past, must be directed essentially against their denial and distortion of reality.

She maintains that denial tends to affect the thought processes, to interfere with logical thinking and reality testing to a much greater extent than does repression:

> Denial works not in a selective, specialized manner, as does repression, but in a massive, global way which easily induces an indiscriminate, collective generalization of defensive processes, with displacements and transference manifestations expanding to all objects, areas, and activities. (pp. 81–82)

Jacobson's view that repression and denial may act concurrently and that denial can prepare and assist in the repression of memories is similar to concepts advanced by Stein (1965) and is consistent with this book's theory of denial. Ideas originating in a denial and distortion of reality, such as the concepts of the castrated or the phallic woman, may become truly and deeply repressed. Perhaps only after a memory of a traumatic experience has been relegated to the unreal, to the "It may never have happened," can effective forgetting be allowed to occur. Jacobson concludes that the defensive processes resulting in infantile amnesias normally utilize denial for a preparatory and supportive elimination from consciousness of those painful elements of external events and internal images in which unacceptable instinctual drives have found a concrete expression.

Jacobson has made an important contribution in her clinical formulations of developmentally low-level defensive functioning dominated by primitive kinds of denial, in contrast with more advanced forms of defensive organization marked by a predominance of higher-level defenses such as repression.

Kris Study Group

The monograph *The Mechanism of Denial* (edited by Fine et al. 1969) recounts the Kris Study Group's systematic exploration of denial from the metapsychological viewpoint, including genetic, dynamic, economic, structural, and adaptive aspects. Case studies are used to correlate the theories with clinical experience.

The members of the Kris Study Group disagree with Freud's concept that denial is limited to the defense against some threatening percept of external reality. They point out that Jacobson (1957), Lewin (1950), Waelder (1951) and others have extended and expanded the concept of denial. A consensus favored study group member Max Schur's summary of the broadened point of view, that "denial operates primarily against a danger. This danger can be an affect, an instinctual impulse, a superego command, or a percept, whether external or internal" (p. 6).

The group cites Anna Freud's idea (1936) that denial is a prestage of defense and suggests that perhaps denial can be considered a basic substrate of all defensive activity. According to some of the members, denial is usually observed in combination with other mechanisms and is seldom seen in pure form except in young children and sometimes in psychotic patients.

The "Return" of the Denied

What is denied may return in a distorted way, thus giving rise to symptoms such as delusions. The case of an exceedingly bright and gifted woman who referred to herself as a "coconut head" is an example. This supposed "defect," which the patient knew was not actual, enabled her to deny the more painful "real" defect, her lack of a penis. A return of the denied is often implicit in displacement reactions, as what takes the place of the denied, as in the above case of the gifted woman, represents it in a more acceptable way.

One of the study group members presents a case in which a conversion symptom, a pain in the abdomen, represented the introjection of the patient's dead brother. The patient's introjection had bolstered his denial of the death in unconscious fantasy. What was denied also returned and was present in the symptom, because the patient's brother also suffered from abdominal pain due to the appendicitis that had caused his death.

The terms *return of the denied* and *return of the repressed* mean that some unconscious content that has been defended against manifests itself in a derivative embedded in a dream, symptom, or verbal communication. Denied contents may "return" as derivatives of unconscious memories, unconscious perceptions, or unconscious fantasies. Writings on the return of the denied are in error when they imply or state that what returns was once conscious. This is true for the return of repressed contents, but it is not true of denied contents. Clinical evidence discussed in Chapters 9, 10, 14, and 15 indicates that what is denied has never been conscious but that what is repressed has been conscious at some past time.

The study group concludes that denial occurs in response to the ego's requirement that it reconcile reality to instinctual strivings and superego demands. By itself, denial is at best an ineffective defense, partly because denial endangers the individual's relations with reality. For adaptive as well as defensive reasons, ancillary support from other defenses is necessary, or else the organism may continue to operate solely at the behest of the pleasure principle—the outcome of which would be severe ego distortion.

The Kris Study Group Monograph provides an excellent review of the literature and some interesting discussions of case vignettes. There is virtually no consideration of interactional factors in the development or maintenance of denial reactions, and in this respect it is typical of the classical writings on denial and defense. Although it mentions the notion that denial could be a basic substrate of all defensive activity, this perspective's full implications are not investigated. Most often the study group members speak of denial as if it were a specific and discrete defense mechanism, such as isolation and reaction formation. This book focuses mainly on primitive forms of denial and says little about more developmentally advanced kinds of denial.

Sandor Feldman

Feldman (1959) offers many examples of denial in common mannerisms of speech and gestures in everyday life. The phrases "before I forget" or "by the way" may be used as denial when the person pretends that the matter is not important to him or her, even though he or she actually considers it of great importance. Phrases such as "to be perfectly frank," "to be honest," "to tell the truth," "frankly," and "honestly," *may* (but not necessarily) be used for denial.

Throughout Feldman's book there are many examples of ways in which individuals may deny their hostility to one another. Examples include "I was just kidding," "I'm only joking," and "I don't want to hurt you, but. . . ."

In *The Interpretation of Dreams* Freud (1900, p. 488) illustrated the use of denial in the word *only*. The dreamer's defensiveness against unpleasant ideas in the dream lies in minimizing their impact and denying their reality by saying, "It's only a dream."

A transient and defensive disbelief on hearing bad news may be expressed by "Oh, no!" or "I don't believe it!" or "I can't believe it!" The expressions "Really" and "I really mean it" often conceal the speaker's *not* meaning it. In Feldman's experience, and in my experience with two patients, the unconscious meaning of "I don't know" was "I do know, but I don't want to know." The explicit denial "I'm not boasting . . ." often precedes actual boasting, and "It's none of my business, but . . ." frequently prefaces an intrusion into someone else's private affairs. "Whistling in the dark" denies danger.

Some of the gestures that Feldman describes as expressing denial are also, in very young children, precursors of denial. They have in common some overt motoric action used to ward off, actually or symbolically, something unpleasant or painful. They include closing or blinking the eyes, putting something in front of the eyes or ears, and negative head shaking. The gestures of the three little monkeys statue—see no evil, speak no evil, hear no evil—may at times express the disavowal of painful reality. In their study of denial responses in brain-damaged patients, Weinstein and Kahn (1955) describe various nonverbal signs and gestures as expressions of implicit denial, which include indifference, inattention, neglect, and averting the gaze from the body's disabled side.

Compare these gestures that have symbolic meaning with similar avoidance behaviors in infants. There is, of course, an important difference between infants and adults in the meaning of these gestures, because these avoidance behaviors in infants (e.g., blinking, averting one's gaze, and covering one's eyes) serve a physically protective function in minimizing unpleasant stimuli. In Chapter 5 I shall discuss these sensorimotor avoidance behaviors as precursors of denial. In adults the same motor behaviors expressing denial have primarily a symbolic significance and express the need to defend against a threatening idea.

Edward Weinshel and Sander Abend

Weinshel (1977) recounts the analysis of a patient who presented a constellation of defensive reactions that were so pervasive as to impart a specific cast to her entire character structure. The essence of this defensive constellation is reflected in the phrase "I didn't mean it." Weinshel considers this phrase and other similar expressions as forms of what Freud (1925a) called *negation*, and he considers negation and denial to be different, though related, types of defensive actions. This phrase signified how the patient attempted to cope with unacceptable and potentially painful impulses, thoughts, and wishes. She attempted to disclaim responsibility for what were for her essentially forbidden but desired activities. She assumed little responsibility for the analysis, feeling that the analyst and circumstances had forced her into the treatment. Similarly, she avoided responsibility for sexual relations, thinking that she participated in this activity because her husband compelled her. Weinshel offers a credible account of the role of defense in character development, and he gives a convincing explanation of the genesis of the patient's defensive structure in early childhood trauma.

In another article, Abend (1975) also uses the term negation to refer to a similar kind of defensive reaction. He shows how some patients respond to unwelcome interpretations by an initial agreement followed by some reference to factors in external reality that the patients state also play a part in determining their reactions. These patients consciously believe that they agree with the interpretation, but their addendum emphasizing reality represents a method for defensively disclaiming the correctness and importance of the analyst's explanation. Abend called this defense the "Yes, but . . ." response.

Both Weinshel and Abend, in my opinion, are describing different kinds of denial responses. Weinshel's patient's defensive attitude could be called a denial of responsibility, and Abend's patients' "Yes, but . . ." responses could be called (using Breznitz's [1983] classification) a denial of affective relevance. These denials, and for that matter all kinds of defensive activities, contain an explicit or implicit negation. Because there are many types of cognition and communication involving negation that are not necessarily defensive, the term negation should not be used to describe some defensive activity. Both Weinshel and Abend cite Freud's (1925a) paper, "Negation," wherein Freud discussed negation from both a clinical and a theoretical point of view. It is quite clear that Freud distinguished the concept of negation from that of denial. The German word *Verneinen* is translated as "to negate," and the German word *Verleugnung* is translated as "denial" or "disavowal." Freud's clinical examples indicate that he was writing about a defensive activity no different from one that most analysts, including myself, would today call denial. In Freud's first vignette a patient says, "Now you'll think I mean to say something insulting, but I really have no such intention." Freud comments that the patient's statement indicates a defensive disclaimer of an idea that has just come up. Freud's second example is of a patient who says, "You ask who this person in the dream can be. It's *not* my mother." Freud amends this to "So it *is* his mother" (p. 235).

Why did Freud use the term negation and not denial for these defensive actions? Probably he did not label these defensive activities as denial because in his other papers he consistently restricts the concept of denial to defenses against external stimuli, and the clinical examples in his paper "Negation" do not concern external stimuli. Reasons for our no longer limiting denial to external stimuli are presented in Chapters 1 and 2.

Herbert Fingarette

A neglected but profoundly original and stimulating book, *Self-Deception*, was written by an American philosopher, Herbert Fingarette (1969), whose formulations concerning self-deception are derived in part from Freud and other psychoanalysts. "Self-deception" in philosophy refers to some of the same phenomena that psychoanalysis describes as disavowal, censorship, and defense. In Fingarette's view, the person in self-deception is one who persistently avoids spelling out some feature of his or her engagement in the world. Whenever there is a purposeful discrepancy between the way an individual is really engaged in the world and the story he or she tells himself or herself and others, we can suspect the presence of self-deception.

To become explicitly conscious of something is to exercise a certain skill that Fingarette calls *spelling out*. His concept of spelling out is expressing some action or engagement in language, whether in overt or inner speech. To spell out something is to be explicit, to think it or say it in a clearly and fully elaborated way. Self-deceivers are those who, on the basis of their tacit assessment of their situation, find an overriding reason for adopting a policy of not spelling out their engagement. They do not thereafter spell out the matter in question, and by means of this policy they are further obliged not to spell out the assessment or the policy. Fingarette's idea of a "tacit assessment" preceding disavowal is supported by contemporary studies on cognition and perception, which demonstrate the existence of complex preattentive analyzers or screening mechanisms making a preconscious assessment of information before consciousness (Neisser 1967).

Self-deceivers fabricate an elaborate "cover story" to fill the gaps created by their failure to spell out something. Out of this self-protective cover story emerge the masks, disguises, and rationalizations of self-deception in all its forms. Fingarette's concept of the cover story is essentially identical with what I described as screen behavior in Chapter 1 and similar to what classical analysts, beginning with Freud, call *anticathexis*.

Self-Deception reviews the philosophical writings on self-deception, including most notably the writings of Sartre and Kierkegaard. Fingarette compares his theory of self-deception with psychoanalytic theories and offers a lucid critique of Freud's concept of defense. According to Fingarette, the dynamic essence of defense and generic aim of defense is what Freud called disavowal.

Fingarette is mistaken in describing self-deceivers' defensive activity as an "incapacity to spell out" (p. 74) because their failure to spell out their actions is an unconsciously motivated and purposeful activity. The failure to spell out in disavowal stems from an unconscious wish to avoid spelling out one's actions in order to avoid psychic pain; it does not stem from an incapacity. Fingarette's view that there is an "incapacity" contradicts his other statements that the failure to spell out in self-deception is purposeful.

Avowal and Disavowal

A comprehensive understanding of disavowal requires an evaluation of its opposites, *acceptance* and *avowal*. Avowal is a central concept in Fingarette's theory of the formative processes of constructing the self. He conceptualizes the self as an achievement, a synthesis, and he views self-deception as a failure of this synthesis. As synonyms for *avow*, he uses the terms *to identify oneself as* and *to acknowledge*. The person, in Fingarette's view, is constituted by acts of avowal. The avow is to define one's personal identity for oneself. Fingarette's concept of avowal is broader than the psychoanalytic concept of identification, and he considers identification as an important but special case of avowal. In speaking of avowal, we are concerned with the person's acceptance that is constitutive, that has much power, and that establishes something, as *for* him or her.

Fingarette claims that avowal is the "missing link" in the doctrine of the self as synthesis. He sees the self as a creation that emerges in time, an achievement. In order to demonstrate how avowal is important to the development of the self, he briefly reviews child development, emphasizing the gradual development of a coherent and cohesive autonomous governing center, the self. To take some engagement into the personal self is an action that our notion of personal identity presupposes.

Avowal, Fingarette explains, is manifested in three ways: in assuming the authority to spell out, in integrating what is avowed into the achieved synthesis that is the personal self, and in accepting responsibility for the engagement avowed. Some of the prime characteristics and consequences of disavowal stem from the denier's failure to avow his or her actions. In place of assuming authority to spell out, the denier tacitly adopts a policy of not spelling out certain engagements. Instead of integrating what is avowed into the achieved synthesis that is the personal self, the denier isolates whatever is denied. Lastly, instead of accepting responsibility for the avowed engagement, the self-deceiver denies responsibility for whatever is disavowed. In short, isolation, nonresponsibility, and the failure to spell out—with the effects and consequences attendant upon them—constitute three dimensions of dis-avowal and three significant defects of personal integrity.

Fingarette's idea that the disavowed becomes isolated is akin to the Freudian concept that denial causes a splitting of the ego or the self. One mark of disavowal is the high degree to which the disavowed is isolated from the influence of everything that is avowed. The continuous and mutual influence on one another of the elements of the avowed is necessary for the cohesiveness and harmony of the personality. What is disavowed remains relatively static and primitive because it is isolated from this system. The rigidity and irrationality of the disavowed engagement are familiar manifestations of this isolation.

Disavowal and Dyscontrol

Though Fingarette does not use the term *dyscontrol*, he does appreciate that disavowal is closely associated with the individual's loss of control over denied actions and engagements. The failure to spell out, to articulate one's actions, because of its importance to sophisticated planning and assessment of complex engagements, leads to a profound loss of control over the self and its functions. (See Chapter 9 for a more comprehensive discussion of the relationships among denial, dyscontrol, and symptom formation.)

Three manifestations of disavowal that either imply or lead to dyscontrol are (1) the surrender of that special authority to spell out the engagement that is disavowed; (2) the rejection of personal responsibility for the engagement and its consequences; and (3) a certain irrational persistence in pursuing the disavowed engagement, this by virtue of its estrangement from the highly organized, evolving system of engagements that constitutes the person. Fingarette's last point resembles Freud's concept of the repetition compulsion, the intense unconscious need to repeat traumatic experiences.

The Splitting of the Ego

Fingarette reviews Freud's concepts of ego splitting and adds some clarifying modifications. From the beginning, defense has been conceived psychoanalytically as causing a kind of split in the psyche. Before the development of ego psychology, the split was conceived to be between the conscious and the unconscious, each eventually conceptualized as a system. In the 1920s when the structural theory was developed, the split was conceived to be between the ego (goaded by the superego) and the id. In both versions, the conflicting entities are viewed as quasi-autonomous, incompatible, and alienated systems. What is split off operates according to the primary process: logical, temporal, and causal relations are ignored; part stands for whole; and so on. The other systems operate according to the more rational secondary process.

The result of defense is to split off from the more rational system that is being defended, a "counterego nucleus." This split-off ego nucleus is a complex of motive, purpose, affect, perception, and drive toward actions. The concept of the counterego nucleus is a generalization in structural terms of the economic concept of anticathexis. Isolated as it is from the learning and experimentation constantly engaged in by a healthy ego, the split-off nucleus remains relatively static and rudimentary, as compared with the maturing ego. The ego treats this unassimilable split-off nucleus as "outside" rather than "inside," and in effect the ego says, "This is not me." According to Fingarette, the generic mode of operation of defense—the ego's splitting off from itself a counterego nucleus—was not appreciated by Freud (1938, 1940) until the last months of his life.

Discussion

As far as my review of the literature has been able to determine, Fingarette is the first to have suggested that disavowal is the generic feature of defense. Weisman (1972) later made a similar assertion, and this viewpoint is implicit in the book *Denial of Illness* by Weinstein and Kahn (1955).

A promising project for interdisciplinary research would be to compare and integrate Fingarette's concept of avowal as a formative process with classical psychoanalytic writings on the place of identification in the construction of psychic structures. His views on the role of avowal in the formation of the self are consistent with psychoanalytic theories of the role of internalization processes in the development of psychic structures (Loewald 1980, Meissner 1981, Schafer 1968a).

There is one important difference between Fingarette's concept of avowal and psychoanalytic theories of internalization. Psychoanalysis views internalization subprocesses such as introjection and identification as predominantly unconscious, with only occasional and minor aspects available to awareness (Schafer 1968a). In contrast, Fingarette and, before him, Kierkegaard emphasize the decisive role of conscious acts of avowal and choice in the formation of the self. The truth, I suspect, rests somewhere in between. A comprehensive psychological theory of either avowal or internalization must take into account both conscious and unconscious factors. Philosophers, like most educated persons before Freud, have overestimated the role of consciousness in psychic activities, and psychoanalysts have not offered a systematic theory of the role of consciousness in internalization and other psychic functions. George Klein (1959) writes about the neglect of consciousness in psycho-

analytic theory, and Habermas (1971) points out the need for a psychoanalytic theory of self-reflection (a concept allied to that of avowal).

Fingarette's theory that the self is created and structured by acts of
avowal omits the important role, particularly in early childhood, of interpersonal interactions in the development of the self. In his view, the self is an
achievement, a psychic formation in which the person is, all at the same time,
the architect, the contractor, and the building. Psychoanalytic theories of the
development of self-representations and object representations focus on the
central importance of internalized interactions with others, most notably
the parents, in the development of the psyche (Loewald 1980, Meissner 1981).

Psychoanalysis needs to aim for an integrated and more comprehensive
theory of psychic structure formation—a theory that would take into account,
as Fingarette and Kierkegaard do, the self as the agent and architect of its
own construction, as well as the role of interpersonal and social factors. To
what degree and in what ways disavowal either inhibits psychic structure
formation or leads to pathological structures and unintegrated divisions
(e.g., splits) in the psyche is another area for further research.

The psychoanalytic literature on psychopathology, to a considerable
degree, has described the effects of unconscious conflicts and defenses on
symptom formation and psychic development. Very little has been written
about the pathological consequences of the denier's failure to become conscious of and to avow what he has disavowed. Fingarette makes a challenging
and novel contribution in his explanations of the effects and implications of
the denier's failure to avow what he or she has disavowed. A further
discussion of this topic and its clinical implications may be found in
Chapter 9.

Fingarette's theory of self-deception explains how individuals disavow
their engagements and actions, but it does not solve old puzzles and para-
doxes regarding the relationships between defense and perception. The
cognitive arrest theory presented here incorporates some of the best features
of Fingarette's contributions and in Chapters 1 and 10 goes beyond Fingarette
in attempting to resolve conceptual and empirical issues surrounding the
problem of perceptual defense. Humans do not deny only their overt actions
and engagements; they may and often do also deny aspects of the perceptual
side of their reactions. Neither perception nor the response to perception is
identical with consciousness. And as we shall show in Chapters 10, 11, 12,
and 13, individuals often deny both what they perceive and how they have
responded to the perception. Conscious awareness of what we perceive and
how we respond to a perception is only an occasional and fugitive quality of
our psychic life.

Fingarette's monograph on self-deception is presented in lucid everyday
language; he avoids philosophical and psychoanalytic technical terms and

clichés. The very absence of technical language gives the reader a fresh and thought-provoking approach to disavowal and defense.

John Bowlby, Emanuel Peterfreund, Allan Rosenblatt, James Thickstun—Information-Processing Theories of Defense

Several psychoanalysts have used the concepts and tools of information-processing theories to examine defensive phenomena from a new point of view. They claim that these theories enable psychoanalysts to collect data more systematically and to formulate hypotheses in a language shared by other behavioral scientists.

John Bowlby

Bowlby (1980) bases his theory on advances in neurophysiology and cognitive psychology that demonstrate the central control of sensory input. This input, deriving from the environment through exteroceptors and from the organism itself through interoceptors, goes through many stages of selection, interpretation, and appraisal before it attains conscious levels. Most of the information reaching central levels is routinely excluded from further processing in order that the individual's capacities not be overloaded. Most selective exclusion is both adaptive and necessary. In childhood the selective exclusion of certain sorts of disturbing information may be adaptive. Later, when in adult life the situation changes, the persistent exclusion of the same sorts of information may become maladaptive. Psychoanalytic concepts of defense belong in this category. Defense refers to the individual's self-protective exclusion of information from processing.

Allan Rosenblatt and James Thickstun

According to Rosenblatt and Thickstun (1977), the processing of information input via normal channels requires *gating*, inhibitory mechanisms that inhibit the transmission associated with lower-priority motivational systems in favor of what is appraised as relevant to higher-priority systems. This screening is initiated by preattentive appraisal processes and is necessary for the organism's efficient functioning.

This inhibition may occur at any stage of the information-processing activity. It may occur during the perceptual organization of input, memorial storage or retrieval, or appraisals of either external or internal input. When information is evaluated as portending danger, inhibitory processes (similar to those used in normal screening) may be initiated. Such inhibition prevents the relevant information from reaching a felt phase (i.e., prevents the information from becoming conscious) and is called repression.

Emanuel Peterfreund

Peterfreund (1971) claims that the organism will defend itself against any source of information, whether internal or external, that produces significant stress. The "mechanisms of defense" of classical analytic theory refer to the defensive activation of information-processing programs that are less stressful or less disequilibrating. Simultaneously, there is a deactivation of those programs or systems that are sources of disruptive information. As a result of these defensive activities, information is lost or filtered out.

Peterfreund argues that there are extensive sources of information, including sexual and aggressive impulses and associated fantasies, and the outer world, that impinge on the organism and may become objects of defense.

Discussion: The Cognitive Arrest Theory and Information-Processing Theories

The information-processing theories proposed by the above authors are similar to the cognitive arrest theory insofar as they all describe an arrest or inhibition of cognition (information processing) before the stage of consciousness. Though the cognitive arrest theory emphasizes the arrest at the final stage of the information processing of verbal thought, it does not rule out the possibility that inhibition may also occur at lower and earlier levels of the process.

The cognitive arrest theory advanced in this book is consistent and congruent with knowledge about central nervous system functioning, but it is not an information-processing theory. Rather, it is a psychoanalytic clinical theory derived from observations and inferences made in the psychoanalytic situation.

Some elements (such as hypotheses regarding filters, programs, and gating) of the information theories of defense advanced by the authors reviewed earlier are not testable by psychoanalytic methods. Their validity and usefulness may be later demonstrated by the research methods of the neural sciences. But until more clinical and experimental research has been completed, it will remain uncertain how successful the information-processing theory approaches will be. It is not clear whether these new theories will be able to do justice to the wide range of defensive phenomena seen clinically.

Further Contributions

Many clinical articles describe denial as either a prime component or a part of the defensive mechanisms and operations in a wide variety of syndromes, symptoms, and psychiatric illnesses. Fenichel's (1945) encyclopedic work on psychoneurosis is grounded on the idea that denial permeates the entire range of psychopathology. His underlying assumption appears to be that denial is always available whenever a person is threatened. Fenichel's treatise gives the reader the impression that denial can be set in motion by any stress or conflict and that most defensive activities and many symptoms depend on denial.

Early writings on denial by both of the Freuds limit the action of denial to the perception of external reality. A later generation of analysts claims that elements of internal reality may also be denied (Fenichel 1945, Hartmann 1964, Jacobson 1959). Both the facts and the meanings and implications of those facts may be denied, and issues concerning what is inside or outside are not necessarily relevant to concerns about the denial of meaning.

Somatic sensations and organs may also be denied. Stunkard (1959) describes a group of obese women who denied hunger and other sensations caused by gastric emptiness. According to Horney (1933), some women, because of infantile fears of genital injury, may deny the existence of the vagina.

As I indicated earlier in the review of Breznitz's (1983) article, affects may be denied. Jacobson (1959) gave examples of patients who denied various affects whose existence in the patient was readily observable to others. Fenichel (1954) writes about patients who denied anger and anxiety, and several analysts have discussed the denial of guilt and superego injunctions and prohibitions (Jacobson 1959, Waelder 1951, Fenichel 1954).

Jacobson (1959) describes denial's being directed toward aspects of the self-image in depersonalization. Greenson (1958) tells of patients who used one self-image as a screen against other, more painful self-images. Finally, Siegman (1967) writes about the denial of threatening object images.

4

Kleinian Concepts of Primitive Defenses

Kleinian analysts have made important contributions to our knowledge of defenses, and this chapter provides a critique and a selective overview of their writings on the primitive defenses, splitting, and projective identification.

The term *paranoid-schizoid position*, first used by Melanie Klein (1975) to describe the early months of life, reflects the persecutory anxiety that afflicts both the infant and the earliest defenses used against anxiety.

Projective identification, an explicitly interactional concept and distinct from projection, Klein first described in 1946. In projective identification, the self's split-off parts are projected onto an object with the aims of injuring, controlling, and possessing it. (A study of the interactional aspects of projective identification may be found in Chapter 11.)

Klein (1935, 1952, 1975) wrote about the split between the good and bad internal objects during the phase of the paranoid-schizoid position. With the later development of the *depressive position* and the formation of whole internal objects (both good and bad), splitting—through processes of neutralization and sublimation—undergoes a change of function and becomes repression.

Grotstein (1981) equates primal repression with splitting, and in his view, splitting and projective identification are the common denominators of all defense mechanisms. Higher-level defenses such as repression are derived from splitting and projective identification. According to Bion (1967), the psychotic personality or part of the personality uses splitting and projective identification as a substitute for repression.

Kleinian analysts such as Grotstein (1981) and Klein (1975) view splitting and projective identification as occurring in sequence. What is split off (e.g., hunger as a bad breast) is then projected outward onto an external object.

Splitting requires the auxiliary participation of projective identification in order to translocate the self's split-off aspect.

Grotstein (1981) defines splitting as the activity by which the ego discerns differences within the self and its objects or between itself and objects, and he indicates that there is both normal and defensive splitting. Splitting, he claims, is a basic mental mechanism and includes perceptual, cognitive, and defense operations.

Unconscious Fantasies in Defense

Kleinian analysts have emphasized the importance of unconscious fantasy to defensive operations and, for that matter, to all ego mechanisms. Isaacs's (1952) idea that fantasy underlies all ego mechanisms has been supported by Schafer (1975), who also avers that unconscious fantasies are always latent features of ordinary ego functioning.

One of the most important contributions made by Kleinian analysts to theories of the primitive defenses is their explanation of the disruptive effects of certain unconscious fantasies on thinking and verbal communication (Bion 1967, Grotstein 1981). Their writings on this subject provide a much-needed integration of object relations, interactional, cognitive, and communicative approaches.

Bion's Concept of Attacks on Linking

My views expressed in Chapter 1 on the unconscious fantasies in denial and their effects on the subject's object relations and thinking functions are similar to what Bion (1958a) called "attacks on linking." According to Bion, these attacks on linking constitute the unconscious fantasies underlying the primitive defenses of splitting and projective identification. The patient's defensive aim in splitting and projective identification is to rid himself or herself of the awareness of reality, and he or she accomplishes the maximum severance from reality with the greatest economy of effort by launching these destructive attacks on the links connecting sense impressions with consciousness. Bion's formulations concerning attacks on linking are the most comprehensive and illuminating studies available about the unconscious fantasies underlying primitive defenses and their pathological effects on cognition, communication, and object relations. By attacks on linking, Bion refers to the destructive attacks that some patients make on anything felt to have the function of linking an object with another. Bion's (1958a, 1967) clinical vignettes of splitting and attacks on linking make it clear that he is describing the same general type of unconscious fantasy that I labeled in Chapter 1 as "the destructive attacks on the painful object." For example, he made the following interpretation to one patient: "You have split my word 'penis' into syllables and now it has no meaning" (p. 28). His descriptions of his patients' fantasy attacks on the analyst's interpretations are similar to what I pointed out in the second case study in Chapter 1, in which a patient destroyed the meaning of my interpretations through her fantasies of spitting them out of her mouth.

Bion tells of how patients, by means of fantasy, attack or "split" into fragments, their object representations and at the same time attack those parts of their mental apparatus that would make them aware of the reality they hate. According to Bion, these attacks are directed against such psychic functions as the apparatus for perception and conscious awareness and the subject's capacities for curiosity, judgment, and verbal communication. The attacks on linking are followed by the projective identification onto external objects of the fragments produced by the attacks.

Bion used the term *link* to signify the organs and functions connecting different objects. Symbols of the breast and penis are especially important in this regard because of these organs' functions in connecting one object with another. The most primitive link between infant and breast or patient and analyst is the mechanism of projective identification. Bion describes a developmental series of links ranging from the most primitive (i.e., projective identification) to the most sophisticated forms of verbal communication and the arts.

Bion uses an implicit object relations model for his formulations of attacks on linking. The attacks are directed against those functions and relations that join different objects. Attacks on links subjectively destroy the relations or links between the subject and his or her human and nonhuman objects in the environment. In the state of mind characterizing attacks on linking, emotions are hated because they are felt to link objects and because they give reality to objects that are not self.

The attacks on linking concept applies to unconscious attacks on the communications of others as well as on the subject's own cognitive and communicative functions. What Bion names as the attacks on the communications of others is the same kind of defensive activity that I report in Chapter 7 as the patient's negative hallucination of others' communications.

Attacks on Verbal Thought

Fantasy attacks on linking are directed against either the prototypes and precursors of ideas or the verbal thought itself. Bion shows that an awareness of psychic reality depends on the development and maintenance of the capacity for verbal thought, whose foundation is linked with the depressive position. Verbal thought synthesizes and articulates impressions and is therefore essential to an awareness of internal and external reality. Attacks on linking destroy, by means of splitting and projective identification, both verbal thought and the preverbal precursors of thought.

The ability to form symbols and use formal thought is dependent on the ability to grasp whole objects, the abandonment of the paranoid-schizoid position with its attendant splitting, and the joining of splits and the ushering in of the depressive position. The emergence of verbal thought is intimately associated with the depressive position, which is a phase of active synthesis and integration.

Bion's accounts of attacks on linking and the central significance of verbal thought should not be misconstrued to mean that such fantasy attacks necessarily and completely destroy language functions. Many schizophrenics, for example, are able to speak fluently. However, close examination of their use of language reveals that they frequently employ words as *things* and not as *symbols*. Words are used concretely as if they were things to create barriers to interpersonal relatedness and communication. Emotionally charged spoken language can be used as a weapon to destroy symbolic communication. Though the most primitive kinds of attacks on linking are observed in the schizophrenic disorders, more subtle and limited forms are found in less disturbed patients.

Segal (1964) speaks of unconscious fantasies in primitive defenses that are similar in content to the ones Bion (1958a, 1967) describes and the ones I wrote about in Chapter 1. The denial defensive process was experienced by one of Segal's patients as an extremely vivid fantasy in which he cut off one of the analyst's breasts and threw it out into the street. Another patient's unconscious fantasy of denial was expressed in a dream. In the dream a little girl, who represented the patient, was cutting out paper figures with a pair of scissors. The cut-out figures, which represented the good parts of the analyst, she kept for herself, and the discarded bits of paper, which represented the bad parts of the analyst, were left for the other children.

Critique of Bion's Concepts

One point at which my formulation differs from Bion's (1958a) concerns what the subject attacks in fantasy. Bion claims that the subjects attack their psychic functions, such as the capacity for verbal thought. In my view, the object of the subject's unconscious fantasy attacks is what I have termed the *painful object*, a concrete or primary-process representation. The painful object, a primary-process representation, is attacked *before* the denier can use verbal thought to symbolize either the painful object or his or her relation with it. I disagree with Bion's contention that the subject necessarily intends to destroy or impair his or her own cognitive capacities. In my clinical experience with analyzing primitive defenses, I have found no instances in which patients consciously or unconsciously intended to damage their own psychic functions. In my view, the denier's fantasy attacks on the painful object have the *unintended consequence* of arresting his or her cognitive capacities for understanding the painful object and his or her relation to it.

Though we differ somewhat in our conceptions of what is attacked in fantasy, our formulations do agree on the effects of these attacks. Both of us hold that the attacks lead to serious disruptions of the subject's capacities for rational, verbal thought and communication about whatever is disturbing him or her. As an unintended consequence of the fantasy attacks on the painful object, the denier is not able to use veridical or rational thought processes regarding the painful object and his or her relation to it.

My theory of primitive defenses differs somewhat from the Kleinian concept in that I view denial, rather than splitting, as the earliest and basic defense. The unconscious psychic contents and actions that Bion calls attacks on linking and that Bion (1967), Segal (1964), and Grotstein (1981) as well as others term splitting are best described as the unconscious fantasies in primitive kinds of denial.

Splitting As a Defense

In my opinion splitting is not a defense, and my aim is to show why it is not. I shall review the literature on the splitting defense, and I shall try to demonstrate with case material that there is no specific splitting defense different and distinguishable from denial.

In his comprehensive view of the psychiatric and psychoanalytic literature on the concept of splitting, Pruyser (1975) discusses the ambiguity of the verb *to split*. Not only can it be used transitively and intransitively and in an active as well as a passive voice, but it also can be used as an adjective or a noun. With such a multipurpose word, it is often unclear who or what is doing the action of splitting and who or what undergoes the action. Pruyser reviews Freud's writings on splits and splitting and demonstrates that Freud was neither consistent nor clear in his use of these terms. In Freud's writings, it is not clear which psychic parties did the splitting and which were victimized by it. Pruyser recommends banning split and splitting from the psychological vocabulary because they create worse problems than they solve. As he indicates, these words have become bits of jargon used indiscriminately to hint at some alleged psychic process or activity that, when scrutinized, may not be there at all.

Those who believe that there is a splitting defense use the words split and splitting as active transitive verbs to denote a defensive process in which the subject or the ego splits psychic contents such as affects and representations.

The terms split and splitting are also used as *descriptive* nouns and adjectives to designate the coexistence of organizations of ego states, dispositions, attitudes, and representations that are contradictory or antagonistic to one another (see Schafer 1968a, p. 99). When the words split and splitting are used in this descriptive way, they do not refer to a defense or any other activity or process. Freud (1924c, 1972a, 1938, 1940) conceptualized this kind of ego splitting to be the consequence of the ego's defensive activity. Kohut (1971) also uses the words split and splitting descriptively to denote disparate attitudes, and his concepts of vertical and horizontal splitting follow Freud's conception that splitting of the ego may result from either repression or denial. Horizontal splits are maintained by repression, and vertical splits are maintained by denial. In his discussion of vertical splits in the narcissistic personality disorders, Kohut (1971) writes:

> In the narcissistic personality disturbances (including, espe-
> cially, certain perversions) we are not dealing with the isolation of
> circumscribed contents from one another, or with the isolation of
> ideation from affect, but with the side-by-side existence of dis-
> parate personality attitudes in depth; i.e., the side-by-side existence
> of cohesive personality attitudes with different goal structures,
> different pleasure aims, different moral and aesthetic values.
> (p. 183)

Although Freud's and Kohut's use of the terms split and splitting as descriptive terms is valid, it is best to follow Pruyser's (1975) recommendation and avoid these terms altogether, because of the widespread ambiguity and confusion in their usage. For these reasons I shall use the phrase *contradictory attitudes* in place of descriptive terms such as ego splits and splitting of the ego. With case vignettes from the psychoanalyses of two patients with narcissistic personality disorders, I shall present clinical evidence for the proposition that contradictory attitudes are brought about by denial and not by defensive splitting. Later I shall discuss the concept of the splitting defense and the evidence for its existence.

Denial and Contradictory Attitudes

The relationship between denial and contradictory attitudes is illustrated in the following vignette in which the analyst was able to observe and study a denial defense and the consequent formation of contradictory attitudes *in statu nascendi*. The analyst was ten minutes late for the hour, and the 25-year-old patient anxiously wondered aloud if he had been mistaken about the time for the analytic hour or if his watch was fast. Then, in a different tone, he said, "But I don't care." The analyst asked for his associations to "I don't care." Gradually and painfully the truth emerged, as the patient reluctantly admitted that he *did* care about the analyst's lateness. Just before the session began he had felt frustrated and angry about the tardiness, but he had attempted to defend himself against the anxiety engendered by his hostile feelings by assuming responsibility for the event. In thinking that he had come at the wrong time and that his watch was fast, he had attempted to deny his anger toward the analyst. This denial was supported by a defensive identification with the analyst's responsibility for the tardiness. In saying, "I don't care," the patient was denying that he did care about the analyst's lateness. Through denial he could bar from consciousness any representation of the bad, tardy analyst and of himself as angry at the analyst. Also, denial aided him in maintaining a sense of well-being, through affirming his relation with the good, idealized object. His denial resulted in two contradictory attitudes: his idealization of the analyst and his anger over the analyst's mistake.

This episode occurred in the second year of the analysis, when the analysand was first becoming aware of his need to idealize the analyst and to defend himself against his angry feelings toward the analyst. The patient's associations to his "I don't care" statement centered on his relations with his mother and grandmother. His mother was an emotionally unstable woman, prone to temper tantrums and to yelling at her children. When he was very young he had been troubled by her outbursts, but as time went on he defended himself by denying her importance to him by means of adopting an attitude of indifference to her.

He remembered when his grandmother became abruptly and unexpectedly angry with him when he was seven. It seemed to him that her face changed into that of a different person. "It couldn't be my grandmother!" he thought to himself. (Note the explicit denial in his statement.) Previously he had considered his grandmother a very good person who loved him. From then on he had two contrary images of her, and his image of an idealized grandmother was incompatible with his image of an angry, bad grandmother.

His denial defense affected his self-representations as well as his object representations. He recalled being scolded by a grade-school teacher and feeling indifferent and untouched by her remarks. He felt that the teacher was talking not about him but about some sort of bad guy. In this account of his memory, one can note his need to deny that what his teacher had said about him had anything to do with him. He denied the bad, criticized aspects of himself.

The second patient was a 30-year-old divorced woman who, at the onset of her analytic hour, reported a recent telephone conversation with Bob, a man with whom she had recently ended an affair. He had been intoxicated and verbally abusive; he asked her how many men she had been "screwing" lately. As she related the conversation, her affect and demeanor alternated from laughing to barely perceptible, nonverbal signs of irritation and discomfort. From her description of the event and from the nature of her forced, somewhat inappropriate laughter, I inferred that the experience had been a most frustrating one, in which she had felt humiliation and anger. When I called attention to her rapid fluctuation between laughing and signs of irritation, she became anxiously reflective. She spoke blandly of her displeasure with her ex-lover, but then she went on to blame herself, saying that she had been "slightly promiscuous," as he had surmised.

The defensive aspect of this kind of laughing had been interpreted previously, as I had learned to recognize this particular mode of laughing as a denial of her anger at some idealized object, including myself. I interpreted her laughing as an unconscious need to pretend to me and to herself that she was not angry at Bob and that there was nothing in what he had said that was a cause for anger. Her associations went to memories from age seven, when she lived with her mother and stepfather. She was intensely angry with them because they "never listened" to her and because it seemed to her that they were always either fighting or drinking. I said, "You are doing to yourself here what your parents did—not 'listening' to yourself. You did not 'listen' to your angry feelings toward Bob." She confirmed the interpretation with an account of what had happened to her the previous evening. Her current boyfriend wanted to go out, but she wanted to stay home. They went out for the evening, and she stated that she had not even thought about her wishes to stay home until after she had returned and gone to bed. "Come to think of it, I'm not very good at listening to my own feelings," she said reflectively.

In denying, the subject negates and refuses to reflect on some aspect of painful reality. This *negation* is followed and supported by an *affirmation* (or screen behavior) expressive of some wish-fulfilling fantasy. The patient's laughing meant: "It is *not* true that I am troubled by angry feelings about Bob's insults. It *is* true that he is good and that he will care for me." Her rapidly alternating attitudes, or ego states, of irritation and laughter had different and contradictory contents. When she felt irritated, she saw herself as an angry and anxious little girl. Bob and her parents were represented as bad persons who had abandoned her and would not listen to her. In the laughing ego state, she represented herself as a happy person who was cared for by some idealized figure such as Bob. Her conflicts over these affects, relations, and self and object representations were repeated many times in the transference situation.

Freud was the first to propose that ego splitting results from denial, and he referred to fetishism (1927a) and the psychoses (1924c) as examples of ego splitting. In a later paper (1940) he suggested that ego splitting occurs in both the neuroses and the psychoses:

> Whatever the ego does in its efforts of defence, whether it seeks to disavow a portion of the real external world or whether it seeks to reflect an instinctual demand from the internal world, its success is never complete and unqualified. The outcome always lies in two contrary attitudes, of which the defeated, weaker one, no less than the other, leads to psychical complications. (p. 204)

Let us compare Freud's formulation of a fetish with our study of the two case vignettes. In his paper on fetishism (1927a), Freud said that the main mechanism in the genesis of fetishism was that of disavowal. The young boy who later developed a fetish perceives that women do not have a penis, but he refuses to accept the meaning and implications of his perceptions. Then, in order to relieve his castration anxiety, he constructs an imaginary penis substitute, the fetish.

The fetishist's denial leads to what Freud (1927a, p. 156) described as a "divided attitude" toward the facts of the female anatomy. On the one hand the facts of female genital anatomy are affirmed; on the other hand the subject denies the meaning of the female's lack of a penis by constructing a symbolic female phallus, the fetish. Freud (1927a) did not limit himself to a discussion of fetishism but went on to describe two male patients who as children had lost their fathers. Both patients had denied the meaning of their father's death. Two "mental currents" were created: one took cognizance of death, but the other, in the service of defense, denied the loss's significance. Denial may be directed against the recognition of facts or the meaning of facts. For example, a psychotic patient may deny that his or her parent has died, whereas a neurotic patient like those described by Freud (1927a) may deny various meanings of the parental death.

One of the most common clinical configurations of contradictory attitudes is the one presented in the case vignettes in which the patients were unable to tolerate their ambivalence toward a need-fulfilling object. By denying that the object had done anything to evoke their anger, these patients were able to relieve their anxieties over losing the object. Through their denial they could maintain in fantasy a relationship with the idealized object. The concept of a splitting defense of Klein (1946), Kernberg (1976), and others has been used erroneously to explain such situations in which the subject is said to split at the same time both self and object representations. According to Segal (1964), "The earliest splitting is between the good and the bad self and the good and the bad objects" (p. 128). Careful examination of these vignettes and other similar case material will demonstrate, I think, that denial—not defensive splitting—is the crucial defensive activity in the formation of contradictory attitudes.

The same basic formulation made by Freud in his explanation of how denial leads to divided or contradictory attitudes in the case of fetishism also applies to situations such as those in the case of vignettes. Unconscious conflicts over aggressive wishes regarding need-fulfilling objects were the proximal stimuli for the denial defense in both patients. Their denial led to contradictory attitudes in which the self and object representations linked with each attitude were discordant and unintegrated with the self and object representations of the other attitude. The first subject did perceive that the analyst was late, but because of his conflicts over feeling angry toward the analyst, he attempted to deny that the analyst was late and that he was angry with him. Similar needs and defensive operations obtained in his formation of two contradictory and unintegrated images of a good and a bad grandmother. In the second case, Bob's insults evoked a conflict within the patient that she avoided by denying their meaning. She perceived the insults, but she would not reflect on them or her angry feelings. Denial was used to escape her anger and to maintain an image of her ex-lover as an idealized, need-fulfilling person.

Because denial alone is not usually sufficient to ease the subject's distress, the denier unconsciously calls into operation various screen defenses to augment the denial. In addition to the antecedent denial, the subject may also employ one or more of the following specific defenses: (1) He or she may *displace* the anger from the need-fulfilling object onto someone else. It is a common clinical observation that young children who are physically separated from their mothers may displace their anger onto others, who then come to represent the "bad" mother. A schematic formulation for this defensive constellation of denial plus displacement would be "It is not my mother who is bad, but it is so-and-so." (2) After denying the bad aspects of the object, the subject may *identify* with those bad aspects and turn the anger against himself or herself. This combination of denial followed by identification with the object's bad aspects was observed in both of the above patients, and it frequently plays a central role in depressive disorders. (3) In addition to denying the good or bad aspects of himself or herself, the subject may also *project* either good or bad self representations onto object representations. As Klein (1975) indicates, the denial and then the projection of the good aspects of the self contribute to the idealization of the object.

The Splitting Defense

Splitting words—that is, split, splits, splitting—have different and confusing meanings and usages in psychoanalysis. Lichtenberg and Slap (1973) review their various meanings, including splitting as a general organizing principle in psychic development and splitting as a process connected with the organization of mental contents in infantile life. In his review of Kernberg's and M. Klein's concepts of different splitting processes, Robbins (1976) concludes that splitting terms have value only when used descriptively to refer to divisions in the mental apparatus. Some of my criticisms of the concept of defensive splitting often apply to other usages of splitting words as well. Although the following discussion is limited to defensive splitting, I believe that there are many reasons for abandoning altogether the use of splitting words in systematic psychoanalytic discourse.

My major disagreement with the concept of defensive splitting centers on the supposedly explanatory concept that contradictory attitudes and ego states are formed by the splitting of affects and the splitting of self and object representations (see Kernberg 1976, M. Klein 1946, Lichtenberg and Slap 1973, Masterson 1976, and Volkan 1976). How should we interpret their explanation that defensive splitting acts through the splitting of representations and affect? Is splitting being used in the metaphorical or the literal sense? One who uses splitting literally is committing the fallacy of reification. Affects and representations (ideas) are abstractions, and abstractions cannot (logically) be split. Physical things (e.g., a piece of wood) can be split, but it does not make sense to say that ideas and affects can be split. One who uses splitting in a metaphorical rather than a literal sense should specify what the clinical referent is of splitting. I assume that the proponents of defensive splitting have used it in the literal sense, because none of them has described the activity or process that is the metaphor's clinical referent.

It seems to me that there are two possible and different clinical referents of splitting words. When used as verbs, these terms can be used to refer to the subject's more-or-less unconscious fantasies of splitting, cutting, or dividing himself or herself or others. Although it is not logically possible to split ideas and affects, one can in *fantasy* split apart oneself and others. Later, in my discussion of Melanie Klein's (1946) concept of the splitting defense, I shall consider the role of unconscious fantasy in defensive splitting and denial. The other clinical referent of splitting words is the occurrence of contradictory attitudes. When used as nouns or adjectives in this descriptive sense, splitting words, as I previously explained, do not refer to a mechanism, a process, or a defense.

Perhaps proponents of defensive splitting have committed an error similar to one I noted on a road sign that read "Do not herbicide." "Herbicide" is a noun and should not be used as a verb to designate an activity. Could it be that the advocates of defensive splitting have mistakenly interpreted the descriptive noun and adjective uses of split and splitting as a verbal designation of activity?

Kernberg (1976) and Lichtenberg and Slap (1973) distinguish defensive splitting and denial as different defenses. Lichtenberg and Slap claim that denial acts through the disavowal of whole percepts, whereas defensive splitting "separates along affective lines the self and object representations involved in a disturbing percept" (p. 781). They are unique in their assertion that denial acts through the disavowal of *whole* percepts, because it is commonly thought that denial may affect either whole percepts or some aspect of a percept. One may, for example, acknowledge the death of a loved one deny some meaning that the death has for one. Or one may acknowledge the fact that someone is talking but deny that the speaker is talking angrily.

Kernberg (1976) claims that introjections as well as affects, object-images, and self-images are defensively split. In his discussion of borderline patients, Kernberg (1976) writes of their successive activation of contradictory ego states. As he aptly indicates, some of these patients are conscious of the severe contradiction of their behavior; "yet they would alternate between oppositive strivings with a bland denial of the implications of this contradiction and showed what appeared to be a striking lack of concern over this compartmentalization of their mind" (p. 20). According to Kernberg (1976), the contents of these contradictory ego states are "internalized object relations," which include "a self-representation; an object-representation in some kind of interaction with the self-representation; and an affective state, usually of a strong, diffuse, overwhelming quality (rage, fear, idealized love, etc.)" (pp. 65–66).

What follows in this paragraph is a synopsis of Kernberg's (1976) theory of the developmental aspects of the splitting defense. He argues that splitting is the crucial mechanism for the ego's defensive organization before the development of object constancy. Splitting occurs with other related defenses such as projection, omnipotence, denial, primitive forms of idealization, and devaluation. Some time in the third year, splitting is normally replaced by repression and related mechanisms such as isolation, undoing, and reaction formation. The young child first establishes disparate and unintegrated good (libidinally invested) and bad (aggressively invested) self and object representations. Object constancy is achieved when the good and the bad object representations are integrated and when the corresponding good and bad self representations are integrated. The splitting defense involves the active separation of the good and bad self and object representations, thereby maintaining or restoring the unintegrated state of the self and object representations that existed before the attainment of object constancy.

Mahler (1968) also believes that libidinal object constancy is reached when the splitting defense is no longer readily available:

> By "splitting" I mean the clinically observable phenomenon that, when both longing and anger occur at the same time (our definition of ambivalence), the child, in order to preserve the good object image, will (during the mother's absence) separate the longed-for image of the love object from the hated image of it. (p. 224)

What is at issue here are not the clinical observations and developmental concepts of Mahler (1968), M. Klein (1975), Kernberg (1976), and others, but the formulations of what kind of defensive activity the young child is using. Kernberg's concepts of the developmentally early and late defensive organizations are, in my opinion, essentially correct—except that denial, not splitting, is the basic and earliest defense. The same phenomena in childhood that have been ascribed to the splitting defense can, I believe, more correctly be ascribed to primitive kinds of denial and the resulting formation of contradictory attitudes.

Kernberg (1976) tells of a patient who became anxious when the analyst confronted the patient with the unrealistic nature of his alternating episodes of idealization and denigration of the analyst. From this, Kernberg inferred that the

> splitting of the ego in this case served an essential function of protecting the patient against anxiety. . . . *Splitting, then, appeared to be not only a defect in the ego but also an active, very powerful defensive operation.* (p. 23, Kernberg's italics.)

This inference is not justified, because a patient's anxious response to a confrontation of his or her behavior does not necessarily mean that the behavior in question was defensive. Even if the inference is warranted that the analyst's confrontation affected or impaired some defensive behavior, it does not logically follow that this defensive activity was one of splitting rather than denial. Kernberg's theory of defensive splitting is based on a questionable and problematic inference and not on clinical evidence showing how patients bring about contradictory ego states or attitudes through some sort of previously unexplained defensive process of splitting psychic contents.

Revealing conceptual problems and fallacies in the theoretical formulations does not disprove the existence of a splitting defense. In order to determine whether or not there is a defense of splitting, one needs to examine the clinical evidence. Toward this end I examined the case studies of Bion (1967), Grotstein (1981), Kernberg (1976), M. Klein (1946, 1975), Mahler (1968), Masterson (1976), Volkan (1976), and others who have written about a splitting defense. I was not able to find an example of the so-called splitting defense that could not, in my opinion, be better explained as an illustration of contradictory attitudes resulting from an antecedent denial. Of all the writings reviewed, only Bion's (1967) described the unconscious dynamic content in the so-called splitting defense, and I summarized his concepts of attacks on linking earlier in this chapter.

Fenichel (1941) recommended that when interpreting defenses, analysts demonstrate to the patient "that he is defending himself, how he defends himself, why he does it, and what the defense is directed against" (p. 18). Writings on the splitting defense do not systematically describe, clarify, or explain the *how, why,* and *against what* of the splitting defense. By way of contrast, one can, as I did in the first section, answer such questions about denial.

As Schafer (1968b, 1976) demonstrates, defenses have meaningful content, including wishes and fantasies concerning the self and objects. Defenses are unconsciously intentional, complex actions with the aim of warding off some unpleasurable affect. What wishes, fantasies, and other psychic actions are included in defensive splitting? What are the clinical referents of splitting words when they are used to denote a defensive activity? Does splitting refer to an unconscious fantasy in which the subject imagines cutting or dividing others or himself or herself? Most of the writings on defensive splitting neither ask nor answer these questions. One author, Melanie Klein (1946) does state that it is in *fantasy* that the subject splits the object and the self, but she does not describe or offer clinical examples of the fantasy.

Klein (1946, 1975) links the process of denial with that of splitting. In my view, her description of denial is essentially correct, but she errs in postulating that both splitting and denial defenses, rather than denial alone, are operative in the formation of contradictory attitudes. In her explanation of the process of idealization, she (1975) writes:

> The persecuting breast is kept widely apart from the ideal breast, and the experience of being frustrated from the experience of being gratified. It seems that such a cleavage, which amounts to a splitting of the object and the feelings toward it, is linked with the process of denial. Denial in its most extreme form . . . amounts to an annihilation of any frustrating object or situation. (p. 202)

In another paper, she (1946) advances a similar formulation, again linking the defenses of splitting and denial. There she adds the important concept that it is not only the object that is denied but also the part of the self related to the object:

> The denial of psychic reality becomes possible only through the feeling of omnipotence which is characteristic of the infantile mind. Omnipotent denial of the existence of the bad object and of the painful situation is in the unconscious equal to annihilation by the destructive impulse. It is, however, not only a situation and an object relation which suffers this fate; and therefore a part of the ego from which the feelings toward the object emanate is denied and annihilated. (p. 102)

In her formulation of denial, Klein describes the crucial defensive actions in the formation of contradictory attitudes.

In order to preserve the image of the idealized object, the above two patients denied the behavior of the object that elicited their anger. They defensively obliterated from consciousness recognition of the bad, frustrating aspects of the object, and they also, at the same time, prevented themselves from becoming conscious of their anxious and angry responses to the object. Therefore one may conclude, in accord with Klein, that their denial barred from consciousness recognition of the frustrating object and the subject's angry object relation with the object.

Kernberg, Klein, Lichtenberg and Slap, and others wrongfully infer that contradictory attitudes and ego states are caused by the subject's splitting of affects, relations, and representations. My study of the pertinent literature and my analytic cases reveal no evidence for the existence of a splitting defense. Klein's own formulations of the action and effects of denial can account for the formation of contradictory attitudes without the need to postulate an additional splitting defense.

Summary

Kleinian analysts describe splitting and projective identification as the primitive defenses that have their onset in the paranoid-schizoid position phase of infantile development. During the depressive position phase that follows, these primitive defenses are gradually supplanted by higher-level defenses such as repression.

Bion contributes an illuminating description and explanation of the unconscious fantasies (i.e., attacks on linking) contained in the primitive defenses, and he explains their destructive effects on verbal thought and communication. In my view, the attacks-on-linking concept correctly applies to denial and not to defensive splitting.

This chapter examines two ways in which the terms split and splitting are used in psychoanalytic discourse. First, they are used as descriptive nouns and adjectives to designate the coexistence of organizations or attitudes, ego states, and self and object representations that are contradictory to each other. Freud and others show that such contradictory attitudes (or ego splits) are brought about by denial. When used in this descriptive way, splitting words do not refer to a defense or to any other psychic action or process. Second, split and splitting are also used as active, transitive words to denote a defensive activity in which the subject splits various psychic contents such as affects and representations. Published formulations of the splitting defense have committed the error of reification, because it is logically impossible to split psychic contents.

A review of the literature on the splitting defense demonstrated the paucity of empirical evidence for the existence of a specific splitting defense, different and distinguishable from denial. Freud's studies of fetishism and two case vignettes were used to demonstrate that contradictory attitudes can be explained as the consequence of the subject's denial. Because of the widespread ambiguity, confusion, and reification in the usage of split and splitting, it is recommended that these terms be dropped from systematic discourse.

5

Developmental Studies:
The Ontogenesis of Denial

This chapter summarizes and discusses studies made by child analysts and others on the precursors of denial and defense and on the development of denial in the first few years of life. One of the major propositions advanced is that denial is the basic or primordial psychic defense. The relevant literature on precursors of defense, the stimulus barrier, the chronology of specific defense development, and the ontogenesis of denial will be reviewed and integrated with the cognitive arrest theory.

Developmental Stages

The development of denial in the schema proposed here goes through four stages: (1) precursors of denial, (2) primitive kinds of denial, (3) advanced kinds of denial, and (4) verbal thought. This sequence is proposed as a general schema that embraces both progressive and regressive denial manifestations in childhood and adult life. In addition to covering the chronology of denial development in infancy and childhood, it is also applicable to adult psychic life in which an investigator, such as an analyst, may observe progressive developmental transformations from Stage 1 to Stage 4 and regressive changes from Stage 3 to Stage 1. It seems unlikely, if not impossible, for an individual to regress from Stage 4 (verbal thought) to lower levels. Once a person has avowed some previously disavowed content, I doubt that he or she can ever again disavow the same thing in the same way.

Strictly speaking, verbal thought is not a stage of denial. It is included in the above schema because verbal thought, as I shall demonstrate in Chapter 7, is the next-higher developmental step beyond the advanced kinds of denial. In psychoanalytic therapy and sometimes in everyday life, denied contents are lifted to a higher level of mentation when the subject articulates and avows what he or she had previously disavowed. The stages of denial development presented here are an ideal model, and it is doubtful if anyone in all areas of his or her psychic functioning has developed to the level of Stage 4. Some severely ill psychiatric patients are fixated at Stage 2 level, and many less disturbed individuals use as a substantial part of their defensive organization the more advanced kinds of denial, that is, those of Stage 3.

Freud's Concepts of Defense Development

The above developmental line for denial is consistent with Freud's (1905, 1925a) concepts of defense ontogenesis and with Piaget's (1937) theory of cognitive development. Freud (1905) established the position of defense in a genetic and functional context, and he suggested that defenses can be described as the intermediate stage between the defensive reflex and conscious acts of judgment or repudiation. He viewed defensive processes as the psychical correlative of the flight reflex, and he told how they prevent the generation of unpleasure from internal sources. This automatic regulation turns out to be detrimental and has to be subjected to conscious thinking.

Defense Precursors

Child psychoanalysts, such as Spitz (1961), who investigate early defenses via the direct observation of infants, trace a continuous series beginning with physiological prototypes and ending in familiar defenses. Greenacre (1958) shows that physiological activities such as respiration, defecation, and eating are some of the precursors for the later development of psychic defenses. Knapp (1967) describes somatic riddance reactions (e.g., coughing, sneezing, vomiting, defecation) as the models for the development of defenses. Hartmann (1939) explains that the newborn infant is not wholly a creature of drives; he or she has inborn perceptual and protective mechanisms that, after the differentiation of the ego and id, we attribute to the ego. Among the inborn apparatuses Hartmann includes perception, motility, thinking, and the laying down of memory traces. The inborn somatic apparatuses influence the ego's development and function and constitute one of the ego's roots. The ego and its defenses depend on the somatic apparatuses not only for their inception but also for their mature functioning. Both ego and drive development are based on somatic maturational processes, and the developmental rhythm of these apparatuses is one of the determinants of the sequence in which defenses arise.

Defenses as such are not innate; what is innate are the infant's capacities for using neurophysiological givens to cope with environmental conditions. According to Spitz (1961) and others, defense mechanisms are created, or at least decisively influenced, as a result of mother-child relations. Sensorimotor activities provide the prototypes for the development of psychological mechanisms. These prototypes represent what is available to the child in the first year or two of life; the nature of the mother-child relations as they unfold will govern the choice of the particular prototype suitable for a given situation. The significance of mother-child and other object relations in the formation and maintenance of defensive actions is taken up in Chapters 8, 11, 12, and 13.

The following lists some of the somatic prototypes noted in the literature and the developmentally related derivative defenses: vomiting-repression, defecation-projection, eating and respiratory inspiration-introjection, dreaming-undoing, stimulus barrier–repression and/or denial, and eyelid closing–denial (Greenacre 1958, Hartmann 1950, Spitz 1961, 1965).

The Internalization of Sensorimotor Reactions: Piaget and Erikson

Piaget's (1937, 1969) theories of cognitive development and Erikson's (1950) concept of organ modes provide a method for formulating the processes in the development of psychic defenses from their physiological precursors. Both Piaget (1969) and Erikson (1950) demonstrate the displacement in childhood development of action patterns or modes, first from one organ activity to another and later from organ activities to cognitive operations. Thinking, according to Piaget, develops by the internalization of overt sensorimotor actions. For example, the child's visual imaging of an object is an imitation of his or her overt sensorimotor action of perceiving (looking at) an object. In the development of the imaging and symbolic capacities, the young child imitates in fantasy many such sensorimotor actions.

Psychic defenses are developed through this gradual process of imitating in fantasy various sensorimotor activities. The closing or blinking of the eyes as a sensorimotor avoidance reaction against noxious visual stimuli such as bright lights has been considered to be one of the precursors of defense (Hartmann 1950, Spitz 1961). Over time and through many imaginary imitations of closing or averting the eyes, this self-protective reaction becomes internalized and transformed into denial. The subject's more or less unconscious idea expressed in the defense may be represented as "I will not look at, imagine, or think about this painful matter. Because I do not 'see' it, it does not exist."

The Stimulus Barrier

In my view, the negative hallucination (a type of denial used against disturbing perceptions) and sensorimotor avoidance reactions are clinical manifestations of what Freud (1920) called the *stimulus barrier*. After reviewing the literature on the stimulus barrier, I shall discuss the development of negative hallucination out of its precursors, sensorimotor avoidance behaviors.

One of Freud's most prescient and imaginative ideas was that of a stimulus barrier. The concept of the stimulus barrier has been widely used in the psychoanalytic literature in both literal and figurative senses, first by Freud and subsequently by many others. Freud's concept of the stimulus barrier was mentioned in several papers and foreshadowed in passages in his *Project* (1895, p. 367, 374): "Protection against stimuli is an almost more important function for the living organism than reception of stimuli" (1920, p. 27). In *Beyond the Pleasure Principle* Freud first delineated the stimulus barrier under that name (*Reizschutz*) and identified its function as one that would be taken over by the ego (1920).

In several papers he conceives of the stimulus barrier as an ego root or ego nucleus (1933, 1940). In *The Ego and the Id* he indicates that "the system *Pcpt-Cs* alone can be regarded as the nucleus of the ego" (1923, p. 35), and in *The Outline* he suggests that the ego is developed out of the cortical layer of the id which, being adapted for the reception and exclusion of stimuli, is in immediate contact with the outside world (1940). Studies by academic psychologists, psychoanalysts, and neurophysiologists support Freud's concept of an innate protective shield against noxious stimulation.

Benjamin (1965) reviews the psychoanalytic writings on the stimulus barrier and its theoretical significance as a precursor or prototype for the ego's later adaptive and defensive functions. Through the direct observation of infants, he concludes that an active form of the stimulus barrier develops at about the eighth week of life when infants first show some capacity for shutting out unpleasant stimuli. Before the formation of the active form of the stimulus barrier, there is a passive type of stimulus barrier—the latter the result of neural immaturity. Hence, many stimuli do not reach the central nervous system.

Shevrin and Taussieng (1965) investigated disturbed children with conflicts over tactile stimulation manifested clinically by periods of body numbness and anesthesia. These children dealt with conflict over tactile stimulation by a defensive raising of sensory thresholds for all stimuli emanating from the environment or the body. The authors relate the raising of thresholds to denial and maintain that the stimulus barrier is manifested by a raising of sensory thresholds to protect the organism from unpleasurable stimulation. They suggest that the persistence of this raised protective threshold in some children could account for such symptoms as apathy, withdrawal, ignoring of reality, depersonalization, and fear of death.

Lustman (1957) postulates a primitive "defense of imperceptivity" from findings that neonates exhibit diminished responsiveness to auditory, tactile, and electrical stimuli while nursing or suffering from colic. Klein (1949) and others suggest that the sensory apparatus's protective or stimulus barrier function is mediated by changes in the sensory threshold.

Emde and Robinson (1979) and Brazelton (1980) have made major contributions to our knowledge of the neonate's capacity to receive and regulate sensorial experiences. These studies show that just as infants can make avoidant responses to disturbing stimuli, they also can find and follow a stimulus that appeals to them.

According to Esman (1983), the stimulus barrier is best viewed not as a barrier or shield but as a screen admitting those stimuli consistent with adaptive needs and excluding others. Esman defines the stimulus barrier as "an innate, selective, maturing screening mechanism that admits stimuli of certain types and intensities under certain conditions, but excludes others on the basis of either quantitative or qualitative considerations" (p. 204).

Experimental studies of the neurophysiological and anatomic aspects of the regulation of sensory stimuli have attained prominence in recent decades. The physiologist Bekesy (1967) reports on sensory inhibition in the peripheral parts of the nervous system. Broadbent (1958) presents evidence from psychological experiments for a theory of a *filtering* mechanism through which the central nervous system can block the input of some information. Studies of *perceptual defense* by psychologists indicate higher perceptual thresholds to noxious stimuli (Brown 1961, Erdelyi 1974).

Central regulatory mechanisms are capable of modifying sensory input all the way from the receptor to the sensory cortex. Formerly it was thought that the sensory impulses' transmission to brain centers from peripheral receptors was a one-way or "centripetal" system. Neuroanatomical and neurophysiological studies reveal another system, a "centrifugal" system, by means of which the brain regulates the input of the sensory information it receives from the periphery by sending efferent impulses to the receptor-afferent system. This centrifugal activity, or feedback, can be negative, reducing the input of stimuli, or it can be positive, thereby increasing the input to higher centers (Granit 1955, Livingston 1959, Hubel et al. 1959).

Without some form of stimulus barrier, we would have no way of handling the great amount of information we receive from the environment. Our perception of reality is constantly filtered, and incongruent or disturbing sights, sounds, and bodily sensations are screened out. Such phenomena suggest a variable "gate" or sensory threshold for incoming information (Melzack and Wall 1965).

Some clinical and experimental findings support the notion that attention to certain information may lower the gate or threshold for relevant information at the same time as the threshold is raised for competing or distracting information (Buchsbaum 1976, Horn 1976). In threatening situations we may become hyperalert and attentive to specific stimuli. Such vigilance and lowered sensory thresholds for selective stimuli have obvious protective value in times of danger.

In order to provide a framework for integrating these physiological studies of perceptual inhibition with psychoanalytic concepts of defense and perceptual inhibition, I will define the stimulus barrier from an *organismic* point of view. The term *stimulus barrier* designates the hierarchical organization of somatic and psychological structures for the regulation and inhibition of stimuli from peripheral sensory receptors to the higher neural centers and consciousness.

At the lowest level, at the level of reflex functioning, are those sensorimotor reflexes and other sensory-inhibitory mechanisms that protect us from painful or excessive stimulation, for example, the blinking reflex. At higher levels of the stimulus barrier system there is denial, which is psychologically regulated by learned meanings. Lower levels are to some extent regulated by and under the dominance of the higher levels. This view of a hierarchical organization of psychological defenses and perceptual inhibitory mechanisms is in accord with Hughlings Jackson's model of the nervous system, which views the nervous system as consisting of a hierarchy of integrations and regulations in which the highest ones inhibit and control the lower ones.

Problems with the Stimulus Barrier Theory

Cohen's (1980a, 1980b) criticisms of the stimulus barrier concept are justified insofar as no one as yet has been able to translate the concept into psychoanalytic observational variables. Up to now there has been no consensus on what kinds of conscious or unconscious psychic actions are correlated or in other ways related to the raising or lowering of the stimulus barrier. Knowledge of the neurophysiological basis for the stimulus barrier has moved far ahead of that of the psychic aspects. The clinical referents of the stimulus carrier concept have been as uncertain and lacking in detail as has been the primal repression concept discussed in Chapter 6.

At what point or phase does the stimulus barrier interrupt or block the perception process? In Chapters 1 and 10 I have emphasized the blocking in denial reactions of cognitive and perceptual processes before the final verbalization phase. However, as Erdelyi (1974) and others demonstrate, the perceptual process is a multistage process that can be blocked (in principle, at least) at any one of several successive phases.

Because the microgenesis of thought recapitulates the ontogenesis of thought (Werner 1948), it appears reasonable to hypothesize that a cognitive arrest could occur at the sensorimotor level, the iconic level, or the level of symbolic thought. According to Brunner (1964), following Piaget and Werner, thought develops from enactive, through iconic, to symbolic representation—first being closely tied to overt action, then plastic representation, and finally verbal status.

Sensory Regulation or Attentional Regulation?

Cognitive psychologists who study perceptual defense and subliminal perception formulate two different sets of theories to explain the control of perceptual input to higher centers of the brain and to consciousness. These different sets of theories are based on the idea that the control of information to consciousness can be exercised in two ways: by either a drastic reduction of sensory inflow or a variable restriction of entry into consciousness. The first set of theories I shall call *sensory regulation theories* and the second set *attention regulation theories.*

Sensory regulation theories postulate different kinds of sensory regulatory mechanisms variously described as "thresholds," "gates," "sensory inhibition," "filters," "negative feedback," and the like. All of these theories hypothesize some type of process whereby informational input is actively blocked or inhibited at some place or places extending from the peripheral sensory receptors to centers in the brain. As I indicated earlier, there is much neurophysiological evidence for such a theory of sensory regulation.

The attentional regulation theories concern the employment of attentional mechanisms for providing a variable restriction of entry into consciousness (Dixon 1971, Neisser 1976). Neisser disagrees with other cognitive psychologists, who see an active exclusion or blocking of perceptual input. Rather, he maintains that the selection of stimuli is a positive process, not a negative one in which some stimuli are actively filtered or blocked, and he argues that we perceive what we consciously or unconsciously choose to perceive, not by shutting out its competitors. According to Neisser, perceivers pick up what they attend to and ignore the rest.

Though there is probably some validity in both the sensory regulation and attentional regulation theories, the available clinical and experimental evidence favors the attentional regulation theories as the best-known and best-understood psychophysiological mechanisms controlling the access to consciousness. There is no agreement in the literature on what the psychic referents of the sensory regulation theories are, and little is known about the psychological factors linked with the central control of sensory input to the brain. In contrast, the clinical referents of the attention regulation theories are conscious or unconscious acts of attention and/or inattention, and both clinical and experimental studies reveal much about how attentional mechanisms regulate access to consciousness (Dixon 1971, Neisser 1967, 1976).

Denial and sensorimotor avoidance reactions are, in my opinion, the most important clinical manifestations of the stimulus barrier, and their protection reaction is explained by the attentional regulation theories. In what follows I shall discuss the concept that the gradual development of symbolic functions and psychic representations, such as wishes in the second year of life, are necessary for the development of the basic defense, denial (negative hallucination) from its precursors, the sensorimotor avoidance reactions. Additional discussion of clinical and theoretical aspects of negative hallucination may be found in Chapter 7.

The Transformation from Needs to Wishes in the Transition from Precursor to Defense

The stimulus barrier operates initially on a reflexive basis and functions to reduce painful or excessive stimulation. With development, these innate sensorimotor avoidance responses come increasingly under the control of higher centers in the central nervous system until finally they become regulated by the highest centers for symbolic (ego) regulation. At some time in the second year of life, organized memory traces of the actions of sensorimotor avoidance reactions are established, together with memory traces of tension reduction and relief obtained by the successful action of these reflex activities. The development of the *wish* to avoid painful stimuli is formed from the preceding biological *need* to avoid painful stimuli, and it marks the beginnings of psychic defense. Ontogenetically, the progression from sensorimotor reflexes to a wish—mediated by the beginnings of psychic representations and memory traces of tension relief—is the function of maturation and development.

We may surmise that the infant links memories of the relief obtained from sensorimotor avoidance behaviors with the idea that he or she has magically done away with the noxious stimulating object. For the infant, it no longer exists because he or she has not matured to the stage of *object permanence*, in which something can be conceived that is not in the immediate range of the subject's perception. The saying "out of sight, out of mind" applies to this situation. Assume, for example, that infants who gain relief by closing their eyes or averting their gaze from a bright light discover that he or she has eliminated the noxious light source. From experiences of this sort, the fantasy of doing away with painful reality by not perceiving it is created. Other chapters of this book have described variations of this unconscious fantasy in adults who, in an ostrichlike manner, use denial to avoid the conscious recognition of painful reality.

At the primary-process level, *percipi = esse* (perception equals essence or being). The converse also applies: not to perceive is equated with the nonbeing or nonexistence of the object not perceived. Piaget found that considerable learning and maturation must occur before children can believe in the existence of objects that they do not perceive (Piaget and Inhelder 1969). The wish to *not* perceive or attend to threatening stimuli is formed by repeated experiences of relief obtained from the effective functioning of sensorimotor avoidance behaviors. This wish will then begin to serve as a signal for displacing focal attention away from painful stimulation and for initiating avoidance behaviors. This transformation from need to wish marks the dividing line between reflex avoidance behaviors and the development of the basic psychic defense, denial. Or more precisely, the earliest psychic defense is negative hallucination, a type of denial used against disturbing external stimuli.

Memory traces of experiences of need gratification provide the matrix for the development of the wish, and the emergence of the wish marks the beginning of the psychic structure functioning (Schur 1966). Considerable development of perception and memory ego structures is required before the biological need to withdraw from danger or pain attains psychic representation and assumes the status of a wish. The development of the wish implies some development of representational structures, because the concept of a wish includes representations of the self, an object, and some kind of interaction between the two.

Another of my studies cited clinical and experimental evidence for the hypothesis that the negative hallucination mechanism also functions as an unconsciously motivated regulatory control over involuntary physiological reactions to external stimuli (Dorpat 1968). The basic concept developed in that study is that the absence of sensation—that is, the negative hallucination—brings about a decreased motor and secretory response to external stimuli that ordinarily elicit the sensation. Thus the ego may use the negative hallucination mechanism not only for *perceptual* inhibition but also for *motor inhibition.* Along with de Monchaux (1962) and Rubinfine (1962), I propose that the functions of the primary model of cognition should be extended to include the *negative* hallucination as well as the positive hallucination (Dorpat 1968).

Negative Hallucination and the Primary Process

The negative hallucination may be considered to be the primary-process model for protection against disturbing external stimulation. Denial is the basic defense, and it includes the automatic avoidance of the unpleasurable that is characteristic of the primary mental processes. The observations and arguments in this section are intended to extend the model of the primary process to include both the negative and the positive hallucinations. Freud's (1900) theoretical model of primary-process thinking includes the positive hallucination:

> An impulse of this kind is what we call a wish. . . . Nothing prevents us from assuming that there was a primitive state of the psychical apparatus in which the path was actually transversed, in which wishing ended in hallucination. Thus the aim of this first psychical activity was to produce a "perceptual identity"—a repetition of the perception which was linked with the satisfaction of the need. (p. 566)

Dahl (1965) uses Helen Keller's recollections of her childhood sensory experiences as evidence for Freud's theoretical model of the primary process. As a child, before she could understand language or speak, Miss Keller would actively experience a taste hallucinatory sensation on her tongue when she wanted to eat something she liked.

The primary model of cognition was formulated by Freud in 1900 (pp. 509–510, 533):

> Mounting drive tension $\rightarrow$ Absence of drive
> object $\rightarrow$ Positive hallucination

We can add to this formula the primary model of cognition that includes the negative hallucination:

> "Painful" external stimulation $\rightarrow$ Negative
> hallucination $\rightarrow$ Inhibition of perception and of involuntary
> motor or secretory activity

This model includes two mechanisms in the primary process, one using the positive hallucination and the other the negative hallucination. The negative hallucination should play as central a role in the conceptual model of psychoanalysis as does the positive hallucination. The positive hallucination is brought about by the wish to repeat experiences of libidinal need gratification, and the negative hallucination is derived from wishes to repeat the relief of tension brought about by the sensorimotor avoidance reactions.

Basch (1981) argues that Piaget's studies on the ontogenesis of cognition make obsolete Freud's concept of the primary model of thinking as positive hallucination. In Piaget's system, cognition begins with and develops out of the sensorimotor stage in infancy. The two theories can be reconciled and integrated in this way: sensations in the infantile period include both those initiated by external stimulation and those of endogenous origin, that is, positive hallucinations. Both kinds of sensory experiences are associated with motor activities; for example, the hallucinatory visual images in dreams are accompanied by rapid eye movements (REM).

The primary model of cognition using negative hallucinations was not explicitly formulated by Freud, but it is consistent and congruent with his concepts of primary defense (Freud 1900), the unpleasure principle, and his speculation about the stimulus barrier as a prototypic homologue for the later development of some of the ego's defensive and adaptive functions. In *The Interpretation of Dreams*, Freud (1900) uses the concept of a primary "experience of an external fright" as a model for the response of withdrawal from painful stimuli and for the later development of psychic defense:

> Let us examine the antithesis to the primary experience of satisfaction—namely, the experience of an external fright. Let us suppose that the primitive apparatus is impinged upon by a perceptual stimulus which is a source of painful excitation. Uncoordinated motor manifestations will follow until one of them withdraws the apparatus from the perception and at the same time from the pain. If the perception re-appears the movement will at once be repeated . . . till the perception has disappeared once more. In this case, no inclination will remain to recathect the perception of the source of pain, either hallucinatorily or in any other way. On the contrary, there will be an inclination in the primitive apparatus to drop the distressing memory-picture immediately, if anything happens to revive it, for the very reason that if its excitation were to overflow with perception, it could provoke unpleasure. . . . (p. 600)

As Schur (1966, p. 134) indicates, the model for Freud's unpleasure principle is the *necessity* for withdrawal—physical withdrawal if the apparatuses for this are available, withdrawal of the cathexis of the percept, and, later, withdrawal of the memory trace of a disturbing excitation. Concern with the individual's need to master or withdraw from excessive or painful stimulation preoccupied Freud in both his clinical and theoretical writings.

This model for psychological defense mechanisms has not only biophysiological but also evolutionary implications. Schnierla (1959) describes the evolutional development from "biosocial" to "psychosocial" patterns, from "approach" and "withdrawal"—which are biophysiological concepts—to "seeking" and "avoidance," which are biopsychological concepts.

On first examination the reader may object to the concept of the primary process's including both the *negative* and the positive hallucination, as we know that the primary process contains no active form or symbol of negation. This difficulty is apparent and not real; it is a semantic problem caused by the term negative hallucination. The unconscious negation in the negative hallucination is presymbolic and preverbal. Actually, we do not change the concept of the primary process's lacking any symbol for negation when we include the operation of the negative hallucination in its functioning.

We shall turn now from experimental and theoretical writings on defense precursors to clinical studies on the development of primitive kinds of denial from their precursors, the sensorimotor avoidance reactions.

Avoidance Behaviors in the First Year: Precursors of Denial

One class of sensorimotor behaviors occurring in infants under one year of age that is believed to be a precursor of denial is the sensorimotor avoidance reactions used to protect the infant against noxious stimulation. Averting the gaze and closing the eyes are examples. Avoidance reactions occur most dramatically in the "anaclitic syndrome," a disorder that occurs in infants who have been deprived of their care objects for an appreciable period during their first years of life (Spitz and Wolfe 1946). These infants become increasingly withdrawn until contact with them becomes impossible. They lie or sit with wide-open expressionless eyes, frozen immobile faces, and a faraway expression as if in a daze, apparently not perceiving what goes on in their environment. Spitz and Cobliner (1965) also describe a more transient kind of avoidance behavior associated with eighth-month stranger anxiety. Infants with eighth-month anxiety anxiously refuse contact with strangers and turn away from them.

Mahler and associates (1975) observed avoidance behaviors in an infant develop later into the defense of denial *in statu nascendi*. Sam at age four or five months would protect himself from his overstimulating mother by looking away from her and using his arms to push her away. His particular denial defense later developed out of these self-protective avoidance behaviors.

Primitive Kinds of Denial

Primitive kinds of denial first develop in the second and third year of life concommitant with the child's development of symbolic functions. New cases of primitive denial seldom occur after the superego is formed except under two exceptional sets of circumstances: (1) in patients with severe superego defects—for example, patients with borderline disorders and psychoses—and (2) in patients in traumatic states. Primitive forms of denial include the denial of facts and gross distortions of reality. These primitive kinds correspond to what Weisman (1972) describes as "first-order denial" and to what Breznitz (1983) classifies as the two kinds of denial in which there is the greatest reality distortion—for example, "denial of threatening information" and "denial of information."

A number of different investigators, using direct psychoanalytically oriented observation of young children, have described the development of denial reactions in the second year, and they state or imply that these denials are the earliest kinds of psychic defensive reactions (Mahler and McDevitt 1968, Galenson and Roiphe 1980, Robertson 1953). Mahler and McDevitt (1968) describe the formation of denial reactions in a 14-month-old child. In Peter's relations with his mother they observed the beginnings of his denial of his mother's presence. He would veer away from her when he had seemingly started out to go to her, and when her name was mentioned, he did not appear to listen. The authors indicate that Peter's denial of the disappointing image of his mother hampered him in working through the experience of separateness.

Robertson (1953) reports that young children (18 to 24 months old) who were separated from their mothers and cared for in a hospital or sanatorium progressed through three phases of emotional responses which he calls the phases of protest, despair, and denial. He finds two kinds of denial responses: (1) denial of the need for mothering by the child's own mother and (2) denial of all need for mothering. If no substitute for the absent mother is made available, such children will become more self-centered and transfer their need for people onto material things such as sweets, toys, and food. Specific behaviors that Robertson names as denial include not responding emotionally to the parents' visits, withdrawal of interest in the parents, and looking away from the parents or other need-satisfying objects.

Denial of Sexual Differences in the Second Year

One of the most extensive and systematic studies of the development of denial is found in the longitudinal ten-year investigation by Galenson and Roiphe (1980) of children in their second year. Nearly all of the 35 boys in their series reacted to their first awareness of the sexual difference with a denial of it. This denial was supported by the visible and actual presence of the boy's own penis, as well as his increasing identification with his father. The authors believe that some boys' extensive use of denial interfered with their capacity for symbolic elaboration in fantasy and ongoing body schematization.

One of the behavioral signs used by Galenson and Roiphe as evidence for the denial defense was the avoidance of the boys' confrontation with their mothers' and their female peers' genitals. The authors present observational evidence of the young child's gradual awareness of sexual organs and sexual functions. In their study, the boys discovered their penises usually somewhere between the seventh and the tenth month. One subject, Andy, became aware of his own urination at 13.5 months, and at 14.5 months he became interested in his mother's urinary stream. Shortly afterward he avoided confrontation with the female genitals. At 17 months he became interested in his father's urination but not his mother's. Andy's attempt to deny the sexual difference was supported by his avoidance of confrontation with female genitals.

Another subject, Jeff, showed an inhibition of masturbation and various signs of castration anxiety concommitant with his initial acknowledgment of the sexual difference. The emergence of his denial was reflected in his avoidance of further confrontation with his mother's genitals. Whenever Jeff accompanied his mother to the bathroom, he would become involved with different objects there. Sometimes he would follow his mother to the bathroom, snatch some article from there, and dart from the room, waiting for his mother to retrieve the stolen object.

With the emergency of curiosity about the sexual difference, there occurred a definite divergence between the reactions of most of the boys and those of the girls. Initially, both girls and boys had a shocklike reaction which consisted of a rather ubiquitous denial of the sexual difference accompanied by a displacement of interest to the mother's breasts, umbilicus, and buttocks. Compared with the girls, nearly all of the boys showed some degree of preoedipal castration anxiety and more extensive denial of the sexual difference.

Advanced Kinds of Denial

By "advanced kinds of denial" I mean the five kinds of denial in Breznitz's (1983) classification system that have the least reality distortion (i.e., denial of personal relevance, denial of urgency, denial of vulnerability or responsibility, denial of affect, and denial of affect relevance) and that are more advanced developmentally than are the more primitive kinds of denial. Because child analysis and psychoanalytically oriented child observation studies of defenses have not included observations of these advanced kinds of denial, it is not possible to indicate precisely when they first develop. Because they have a greater capacity for reality testing, it seems most probable that they develop after about age three, when they gradually replace the primitive kinds of denial. Primitive kinds of denial are associated with the most primitive low-level defenses such as projection and introjection, whereas the advanced kinds of denial are linked with higher-level specific defenses such as isolation, undoing, and repression.

Chronology of Defense Development

A specific chronology for the emergence and formation of the typical specific defenses for the different phases of development has not been worked out in detail, although provisional and tentative efforts in this direction were made by Anna Freud (1936), Gedo and Goldberg (1973), and Glover (1937). The construction and validation of a timetable for defense development will depend on systematic longitudinal infant and child observation. There appears to be, however, a consensus among child psychoanalysts on Anna Freud's (1936) outline of a defense developmental line. She enumerates the various early defenses that had been described in her father's work, and they include introjection and projection, reversal into the opposite, turning against the self, and displacement of instinctual aims. At an intermediate level there are the defenses of undoing, isolation, and reaction formation. The highest-level defense, repression, belongs to the era following oedipal resolution and formation of the superego (Gedo and Goldberg 1973).

There is also a consensus on the view that the most serious psychiatric disorders are associated with low-level defenses and that the least disturbed patients tend to have predominantly higher-level defenses. Intermediate-level and high-level defenses of undoing, isolation, reaction formation, and repression are the most common defenses in the neuroses and neurotic character disorders. Low-level defenses such as introjection and projection are associated with the most serious psychiatric disorders, the borderline conditions and the psychoses (Beres 1956, Hartmann 1953). Some analysts consider the relative failure in schizophrenics to develop the repression defense to be an ego defect (Eissler 1953). For patients in the middle range of psychopathology, such as the narcissistic personality disorders as described by Kohut (1971, 1977), one typically finds admixtures of low-level and intermediate-level defenses.

Each defense uses a typical or predominant mode of defense only for a particular phase (Gedo and Goldberg 1973). In infancy and afterward, mental mechanisms used as defenses may also serve other functions. For example, after the phase in which projection is a typical defense, it further differentiates and serves other ends, as it does in the capacity for empathy. Neatness and cleanliness begin as reaction formations against anal-aggressive wishes to soil or to make messes. Over time, there is a *change in function* of these reaction formations so that they become character traits and habits relatively dissociated from their original defensive aims.

All of the specific defense mechanisms function together with some kind of either primitive or advanced denial. The basic defense of denial, whether primitive or advanced, is a fundamental substratum of all defensive activity. As demonstrated in Chapter 1, all defenses include an aspect of denial involving a cognitive arrest of whatever is disturbing plus some kind of screen behavior that contains the various specific defenses. In contradistinction to the atrophy of certain physiological systems or organs, the earliest psychic systems continue to function throughout life alongside more developed organizations. Sandler and Joffe (1967) formulated this concept as the "principle of persistence," according to which early psychic structures do not dissolve; rather, they continue to function, even though their functioning is inhibited, controlled, or overlaid by more recent structures.

The Developmental Line for Defenses: Gedo and Goldberg

In their excellent review of defense development, Gedo and Goldberg (1973) formulate a developmental line for the defenses, beginning with primal repression, followed by projection, then disavowal, and ending with the highest-level defense, repression. The theory of defense development proposed here differs from theirs in four ways. First, they define disavowal as one of several different and specific defense mechanisms, whereas I have argued in Chapters 1, 2, and 3 that disavowal should be considered an aspect of all defense rather than a specific mechanism of defense.

They are mistaken in placing the emergence of disavowal as a typical defense at a later time and developmental phase than the empirical evidence from child analysis and child observation studies indicates. In their hierarchical model, the phase in which disavowal predominates as a typical defense corresponds to the phallic phase, or Phase III in their model. (Phase III extends from the consolidation of the cohesive self to the formation of the superego.) The empirical evidence from the studies of Galenson and Roiphe (1980), Mahler and associates (1968, 1975) and others demonstrates that disavowal emerges in the second year and before the phallic phase. Gedo and Goldberg do not cite any evidence for their claim that disavowal develops as the typical defense in Phase III.

Gedo and Goldberg incorrectly state that projection emerges before disavowal. Observational evidence obtained from child analyses and direct child observation indicates that projection develops soon after the development of disavowal. Also, as I indicated in Chapter 1 and as Waelder (1951) argues, defensive projection occurs in conjunction with denial. Because an implicit denial is an integral aspect of defensive projection, projection cannot (logically) be formed before denial.

A fourth point of disagreement with Gedo and Goldberg concerns the nature of primal repression. Whereas they view primal repression as the earliest defensive activity and distinct from disavowal, I shall argue in Chapter 6 that primal repression and disavowal are identical.

The Ontogenesis of Denial: Retrospective Studies

Thus far this chapter has reviewed studies on defense development using the methods of child analysis and direct child observation. Study of data gathered from the psychoanalyses of adults is another method that can be used retrospectively to construct theories concerning defense development. This latter method is used by Stolorow and Lachmann (1980) in the psychoanalytic case study of an adult patient who had lost her father when she was four years old and had denied his death. In their investigation of "the ontogenesis of denial," they argue that there is a developmental line for each defensive process, with precursors or prestages of the defense occurring before the consolidation of self and object representations. They use case studies to "illuminate the distinction between the defensive denial of an event and the prestages of denial which occur when the psychological structures necessary for accurate perception and assimilation of an event have not yet been consolidated" (p. 45).

When the patient was four years old, her father had been taken to a Nazi concentration camp and died. The authors argue that the patient at age four had not yet developed the cognitive capacities that would have enabled her to comprehend the meaning of her father's disappearance and death. According to them, a four-year-old child has not yet attained the abstract concept of death as a final and irreversible cessation of life. To the extent that a death is acknowledged at all, it is typically conceived to be a reversible departure to a distant place.

Their case study is a fascinating account of how a denial in fantasy provides the dynamic nucleus of a patient's personality disorder. While exploring the ways in which she kept repeating aspects of her relationship with her father in her current experiences with men, the patient made the startling discovery that proved to be pivotal in her analysis. She suddenly realized that she had never accepted the fact of her father's death, and she recognized a feeling of absolute conviction that her father was still alive. According to the authors, the patient's discovery and dissolution of her "denial-in-fantasy system" were crucial to her successful analysis and made possible a belated mourning reaction and lasting structural change.

When her father left, the patient had developed fantasies in order to make sense out of the loss. She felt as if she were to blame for the loss and that her father had abandoned her because she was a defective person. The authors claim that such explanatory fantasies should not be described as denial fantasies. Instead, they assert, these fantasies represent attempts by a four-year-old child to adapt to a state of cognitive and structural insufficiency. Therefore, they refer to these fantasies as a prestage of denial. According to the authors, when cognitive and emotional maturation had enabled the patient to register and to comprehend the realities of her father's incarceration and death, she began to construct in her latency years an elaborate "denial-in-fantasy system." In forming this denial system, she made ample use of the ready-made fantasies by which she had originally explained her father's absence.

Stolorow and Lachmann present an enlightening explanation of why an unconscious denial system can have profound consequences on an individual's personality development. Their case report vividly describes the amazing and complex ways in which the patient's original fantasies about her father's death were later extended and amplified, with far-reaching consequences on her identity and object relations. However, I believe that their account of the ontogenesis of denial is flawed on several counts.

They erroneously claim that a four-year-old child could not have denied the death of a father because that young a child has not attained an abstract conception of death. Even though we agree that a four-year-old's conception of death is not the same as an adult's, it does not follow that four-year-old children are not capable of understanding, fearing, and denying death.

Yalom (1980) writes persuasively about the pervasiveness and intensity of death concerns in children as young as 18 months, and he offers convincing evidence that very young children fear and think about death and erect defenses such as denial against anxiety over death. Others, such as Rochlin (1967) and Furman (1974), also show that very young children both understand and deny death. Children, sometimes before their second birthday, are capable of denying some of the meaning and facts of death, even though they are not yet capable of comprehending the full range of meanings of death.

The authors state that the patient's denial defense did not begin until after she had entered the latency phase and had attained sufficient maturation to comprehend the realities of her father's death. They incorrectly assume that to deny something, the denier first needs to have a conceptual knowledge of whatever he or she is denying. In Chapter 9 I shall label this error the "fallacy of unconscious knowledge." The facts are that denial is an unconscious defensive activity and that it is a cognitive arrest of whatever disturbs the denier *before* he or she has formed a verbalized, conceptualized knowledge of what is denied.

Stolorow and Lachmann, in my view, are also mistaken in distinguishing between clinical phenomena that stem from a developmental arrest and clinical phenomena that function as a defense. As I shall demonstrate in Chapter 9, denial and developmental arrest are often different aspects of the same phenomenon. The authors claim that it is clinically important to distinguish between mental activity that functions as a defense and superficially similar mental activity that functions as a remnant of a developmental arrest arising at a prestage of defense development. Because they view the original trauma of the father's death and the consequent developmental arrest as antedating the patient's denial of the parental loss, they incorrectly assume that the developmental arrest is associated with a kind of mental activity different from denial.

Clinical data from their case study supports the conclusion that *both* the original trauma and the subsequent protracted denial of the father's death contributed to the patient's developmental arrest and personality disorder. The clinical evidence for the causal relationships between denial and developmental arrest has been presented in studies of children's long-term denial reactions to parental death (Altschul 1968, Dorpat 1972, 1973, Fleming and Altschul 1963), and it is reviewed in Chapter 9. The literature on trauma and stress demonstrates conclusively that it is not simply trauma alone that causes developmental arrests and psychopathology but also psychic reactions to trauma in which prolonged denial of the trauma blocks mastery and recovery.

Using their own clinical data, one can reconstruct a somewhat modified account of the more significant events and psychic reactions in the patient's case history. At age four the patient denied her father's death and elaborated denying fantasies of his eventual return. As the years went by she continued to use this defense and amplified her conscious and unconscious fantasies about him and her relationship with him. The trauma and the patient's persistent denial brought about a developmental arrest in which representations of her self and her father were frozen, so to speak, at the four-year-old level. The patient's denial at age four and thereafter prevented her from forming and accepting reality-appropriate meanings of her father's death. Not until this defense was worked through in her analysis could she undergo a belated mourning reaction, master the trauma, and resume her previously arrested development. The formulation differs from that of Stolorow and Lachmann in that it traces the beginnings of the denial reaction to the time of the trauma and holds that the patient's denial, as well as the trauma, caused her developmental arrest and personality disorder.

Summary

The literature on the precursors of defense, the stimulus barrier, the chronology of defense development, and the ontogenesis of denial was reviewed and integrated with the cognitive arrest theory. Denial was conceptualized as going through four developmental stages: (1) precursors of denial, (2) primitive kinds of denial, (3) advanced kinds of denial, and (4) verbal thought. A major hypothesis presented was that denial is the basic or primordial defense.

Freud's theory of a stimulus barrier is supported by studies in the fields of neurophysiology and academic psychology as well as psychoanalysis. Sensory regulation theories of the stimulus barrier deal with the central regulation of sensory input to higher centers, and attentional regulation theories concern the use of attentional mechanisms for restricting entry into consciousness. Denial and its somatic precursors, sensorimotor avoidance behaviors, are a self-protective turning away of focal attention from something disturbing to less threatening objects.

Sensorimotor avoidance reactions and the negative hallucination are probably the most important clinical manifestations of the stimulus barrier.

The development of the wish to avoid painful stimuli is formed from the biological need to avoid such stimuli, and this transformation marks the emergence of the basic defense, denial (negative hallucination). The negative hallucination is the primary-process model for protection against external stimulation, and it includes that automatic avoidance of the unpleasurable characteristic of the primary psychic processes.

Sensorimotor avoidance behaviors are internalized in the second year of life to form primitive kinds of denial, and the advanced kinds of denial probably develop after about age three. Both primitive and advanced kinds of denial function together with specific defense mechanisms that serve as a screen function.

6

Primal Repression or Denial?

This chapter reviews psychoanalytic writings on primal repression and attempts to demonstrate that primal repression is equivalent to primitive kinds of denial.

The Problem with Primal Repression Theories

Freud found that his theory of repression required the prior existence of a more primitive type of defense, one that had an earlier ontogenetic origin and that coexisted in adults with higher-level defenses. He called this primitive defense *primal repression*, and he distinguished it from the higher-level defense, *repression proper*. Unlike the psychoanalytic theories of repression proper and disavowal, the theories of primal repression proposed first by Freud and later by others are not grounded in clinical observations. Writings on primal repression do not give the clinical referents, and they do not state what is and is not primal repression. Freud's speculations about primal repression appear to have been derived deductively from his theories of defense, repression, and the psychic apparatus. The problem with hypotheses of primal repression is that their failure to include clinical referents has caused them to remain isolated and unintegrated with the psychoanalytic theory of defense. As it now stands, theories of primal repression lack clinical relevance and usefulness. One of the aims of this chapter is to integrate the valid aspects of theories of primal repression with the theory of denial presented in this book.

The unspecified clinical phenomena that Freud subsumed under the term primal repression are, in my opinion, the same phenomena that I have described in Chapters 1 and 5 and elsewhere in this book as denial. In both children and adults, the clinical referents of theories of primal repression are the same as the clinical referents of the cognitive arrest theory of denial.

The cognitive arrest theory of denial proposed in this volume is in most respects similar to the theories of primal repression advanced by Cohen (1980b), Frank (1969), Frank and Muslin (1967), and Freud (1915a, 1915c, 1926). For example, their theories indicate that new cases of primal repression occur only in early childhood, in the psychoses, and in traumatic states. With these exceptions, primal repression in adults is said to occur in combination with other defenses such as repression. The same linkage between denial and specific defenses is part of the cognitive arrest theory of denial. Specific defenses are secondary, both in the developmental sense and in the sense that they supplement an antecedent denial.

A common explanation for the absence of clinical referents in primal repression theories is that hypotheses of primal repression refer to events very early in a child's life. Therefore, any hypotheses are highly speculative, and the investigation can make only unverifiable inferences about what goes on in an infant's mind. But this argument dissolves in the face of the fact that the term primal, as first used by Freud, does not refer simply to what occurs in early childhood. Freud was considering the mind of the adult as well as the child when he wrote about primal repression (Pearson 1953). Specifying the clinical referents of primal repression in both adults and children is an important and thus far unfulfilled challenge for psychoanalysis. The cognitive arrest theory of denial fulfills this task in stating that an implicit denial in adult defensive reactions is the remnant of the basic primordial defense and that this infantile component in adult defensive reactions coexists with the specific defenses.

In my view Freud was correct that a primordial defense is operative in conjunction with higher-level defenses in older children and adults. However, the ambiguities and problems with the primal repression theory have prevented its assimilation into clinical theory and practice. Consequently, few analysts are aware of the requirement for recognizing and, at appropriate times, interpreting the underlying primitive aspect of defense, implicit denial, and the more easily discernible screen behaviors containing specific defenses such as repression, isolation, and reaction formation.

In what follows I shall first review and discuss psychoanalytic writings on primal repression and second argue that the cognitive arrest theory provides a coherent solution to old problems and puzzles concerning both the nature and the clinical referents of primal repression.

Freud's Writing on Primal Repression

Freud always maintained a developmental perspective in his theory of defense, and he held that ordinary repression, or repression proper, is a secondary phenomenon in the nature of an "after-pressure" which depends on the prior occurrence of a primal repression.

In the paper "Repression" he clearly states this hypothesis:

> We have reason to assume that there is a *primal repression*, a first phase of repression, which consists in the psychical . . . representative of the instinct being denied entrance into the conscious. With this a *fixation* is established; the representative in question persists unaltered from then onwards and the instinct remains attached to it. . . . The second stage of repression, *repression proper*, affects mental derivatives of the repressed representative, or such trains of thought as, originating elsewhere, have come into associative connection with it. (Freud 1915b, p. 148)

Freud (1915b, 1915c) believes that primal repression is, if not synonomous with fixation, intimately connected with it and directly responsible for it. He distinguishes primal repression from repression proper in this way: infantile experiences that precede the development of the preconscious are primarily repressed, whereas repression proper bars from consciousness preconscious derivatives. In primal repression the infantile urges and forces that are barred from consciousness have never been cathected by the preconscious system. In other words, early experiences that have been defended against by primal repression have never but put into words; primal repression prevents the conscious symbolization of experience. Some analysts believe that the theory of primal repression explains the infantile amnesia that quite regularly extends up until about the sixth year.

Freud (1900) argues that there exist in the unconscious some "infantile memories" and "wishful impulses" that are inaccessible to later conscious recall. These early memories and impulses never had preconscious ideational representation, and they are necessary for later repression proper to occur. In "Three Essays on Sexuality," he indicates that a "primarily repressed" instinct or derivative is fixated as a result of some "inhibition in its development" and lacks access to the preconscious system (Freud 1905). Freud associated the establishment of the secondary process, the beginnings of the adult preconscious, and the onset of primal repression with the development of language functions.

A number of analysts have specifically linked primal repression with the preverbal period (Basch 1976, A. Freud 1965, pp. 31–32, Eissler 1962, pp. 36–38, Glover 1939, chap. 5, Whitman 1963). Anna Freud (1965) describes the preverbal elements under primal repression as having never formed part of the organized ego. They cannot be remembered, only relived within the transference. Most authors use the primal repression concept to refer to those contents in the unconscious that have never been conscious (Basch 1976, Cohen 1980b, Eissler 1962, Frank 1969, Freud 1915b, 1915c, 1926, Whitman 1963).

Freud held different views on repression proper and primal repression at different times, and since his time there has been little agreement on either the nature or the significance of primal repression. In their article reviewing Freud's writings on primal repression Frank and Muslin (1967) state, "its significance has become blurred, its limits and definitions ambiguous, its importance subject to debate" (p. 55), and they illustrate their point with widely contrasting views from Freud's and others' writings.

In their review of Freud's concept of primal repression, Frank and Muslin (1967) distinguish between an earlier hypothesis of "passive primal repression" (circa 1900–1915) and a later hypothesis, "active defensive primal repression" (circa 1926). According to the first hypothesis, primal repression is unmotivated and results from the deferred development of the secondary process. Because of this, certain early unconscious impressions, urges, and forces are left lagging behind. Although these urges and drives continue to exert an indirect effect on mental life, they are inaccessible to consciousness because of their lack of preconscious (verbal) representations.

The occurrence later on of associatively connected impulses, even impulses that have attained verbal representation as wishes, is subject to the same defensive forces. Therefore, primal repression is a necessary precondition for later repression proper, and the defense of repression in older children and adults is a result of both repression proper (after-pressure) and primal repression, acting together. Frank and Muslin (1967) convincingly argue that superego formation marks the dividing line between primal repression and repression proper in normal development.

The second hypothesis (i.e., "active defensive primal repression") is the familiar stimulus barrier concept in which primal repression is the prototypical defense, and it occurs as the result of unpleasure associated with overstimulation of the immature mental apparatus. In contrast with the first hypothesis, the second hypothesis includes a motive, the unpleasure associated with overstimulation. Frank and Muslin (1967) contend that the second theory represents an addition rather than a correction of the first theory and that these two processes continue side by side in the developing psyche.

Cohen's Theory of Primal Repression

Cohen (1980b) criticizes both the passive and the active defensive primal repression theories, stating that the first (or "developmental lag") hypothesis does not explain why in some young children and not in others certain features of preverbal experience are excluded from further development when secondary process thinking is acquired. The second (or "stimulus barrier") hypothesis, he claims, is also unsatisfactory because it relies solely on a quantitative notion that thus far has not been translated into observable phenomena. (In Chapter 5, I defined the stimulus barrier and included in my definition the clinical psychological variables.)

Cohen (1980b) formulates a theory of primal repression based on the concept that trauma prevents the normal development of drive and object representations. He defines primal repression as a faulty structure characterized by an inadequacy of drive and object representations that results from trauma at all stages of development, preoedipal and postoedipal. Primal repression is a failure of the developmental step from need organization to wish organization in a given segment of development. In normal development the memory traces of satisfying experience with an object come to symbolize the need. In this representational process the need, which requires actual satisfaction, is transformed into a new psychic entity, a wish, which is a structure at a higher level of organization.

The structuring of needs into wishes, according to Freud (1915a), requires repetitive satisfactory experiences that not only do away with the need but also create the mental representation of the need as a connection between the need and the mental representation of the experience of satisfaction. It is this connection between needs and mental representation that Freud (1900, pp. 565–566) defines as a wish.

Cohen corrects errors in previous theories of primal repression and develops a coherent theory of primal repression that is consistent with contemporary knowledge of child development. His criticism that Freud's second (or stimulus barrier) theory of primal repression has thus far not been translated into observable phenomena is partly true of his own formulation, because he does not describe the clinical referents of primal repression.

Consequences of Primal Repression

In this section I shall briefly review and discuss what various authors have considered to be the consequences of primal repression. One clinically recognizable consequence of primal repression is mental functioning of a particular form, which Cohen (1980a) calls "repetition compulsion functioning." It could also be described as "protosymbolic," referring to the idea that it is typically an enactive memory form of a solitary painful state, as opposed to a wish (object interaction), that is the dominant type of representation. Cohen (1980b) conceptualizes the action of analytic therapy as the repair of primal repressions and the transformation of traumatic registrations into normal forms of representation.

Primal repressions, according to Cohen (1980a, 1980b) tend to undermine the capacity for wish-organized functioning at any regressive level. Experiences defended against by primal repression cannot be remembered or recalled; they exist as pathological memory forms, protosymbolically organized. Their mnemic content is functionally unconscious and organized as a function of the original mode of registration. Cohen's formulation of the relationships between primal repression and memory formation is similar to the one that I shall propose in Chapter 15 for the relationships between denial and memory pathology.

A central feature of Cohen's theory of primal expression concerns the developmental failure of transforming experiences of need into psychic entities such as wishes. In recent years there has accumulated evidence in the psychoanalytic literature for the existence in both children and adults of a primitive mode of psychic functioning in which basic human needs have not been transformed into mental representations such as wishes (Basch 1976, Dorpat 1971, Frank 1969, Gedo 1979). These analysts have examined primitive modes of psychic functioning that are presymbolic modes that characterize the psychic organization before the development of wishes.

The false assumption that *all* forms of experience (e.g., thinking, dreaming) stem from conscious or unconscious wishes so pervades psychoanalytic thought that it may come as a surprise to realize that some types of experience are so primitive that they do not emerge from wishes and are not regulated by the pleasure principle. The saying "The wish is father to the thought" is not always true. A study of patients who develop phantom symptoms following the surgical removal of a body part concludes that unconscious wishes do not bring about the phantom hallucinatory sensations (Dorpat 1971).

At first I made the common error of believing that all psychic activity was initiated by wishes. But my repeated efforts to make sense out of the phantom symptoms according to Freud's wish-fulfillment theory of hallucinations were unsuccessful. Because the patients' phantom sensations did not have symbolic content or psychological meaning and were not manifestations of unconscious wishes, I concluded that some more primitive and presymbolic factor was responsible for them.

Basch's Concept of Primal Repression

Basch (1976) translates Freudian ideas on the differences between primal repression and secondary repression into Piaget's and Inhelder's (1969) model for cognitive development. In this system, cognitive development proceeds through the following phases: sensorimotor (presymbolic), 0 to 18 months; preoperational, 18 months to 6 years; concrete operational, 7 to 11 years; formal operations, 11 years onward. Basch places the primal repression barrier at the division between the sensorimotor and the preoperational phases, and the repression proper barrier between the preoperational and the concrete operational phases.

According to Basch, primal repression involves sensorimotor schema that have never been given symbolic representation, that have not participated in cognitive transformation in the preoperational developmental phase. Primal repression is universal and the result of external sanctions and deficits, whereas the secondary repression barrier is the result of the child's own internal conflicts. Secondary repression refers to symbols already formed but subsequently barred from attaining the level of operational thought.

Prepsychological Modes of Psychic Functioning

Gedo (1979) reviews the clinical evidence for a primitive prepsychological mode of functioning that occurs sometimes in chronologically adult individuals. In his description of patients who regress to this primitive mode, he underscores the point that many of their needs never had and never could have attained psychic representation as wishes. Hypochondriacal and similar symptoms, according to Gedo (1979), often include the loss of symbolic capacities and a regressive return to the sensorimotor mode of infancy. A convincing argument has been made by Rubinfine (1973) that conversion symptoms mean a regression to a sensorimotor form of psychic functioning. Symptoms derived from this primitive mode are instances of what Frank (1969) calls the "unrememberable and unforgettable" repetitions of infantile experiences.

According to Frank (1969), primal repression refers to the unrememberable memories of childhood that can be inferred through altered states of consciousness and "contents of these stages; certain 'screen' phenomena; certain symptoms; symptomatic behavior and alterations; and the reproduction of early impressions by reliving them in the psychoanalytic situation" (p. 62). Cohen (1980b) and Frank (1969) present case illustrations that describe the revival during regressed analytic hours of highly charged primally repressed "memories." These memories all were of the *enactive* type, as contrasted with the more normal *representational* type (see Chapter 15 for a discussion of enactive and representational memory).

Isakower (1938) and later others describe an altered state of consciousness (called *hypnagogic*) characterized by the dissolution of boundaries between the self and external percepts. During these regressed states, the subjects experience various bodily sensations in their mouth and skin and have a visual impression of something round that approaches them. Isakower proposes that these phenomena constitute a revival of experiences of feeding at the breast and falling asleep. Anthony (1961) compares the screen sensations of a schizoid adolescent patient with those described by Marcel Proust in his *Remembrance of Things Past.* In both instances, the revived sensory impressions date from the early months of life, roughly the same period as do the phenomena that Isakower (1938) writes about.

In several papers Freud (1900, 1918) indicates that the earliest memories of childhood are not remembrable, as such, and that these experiences are repeated in transferences in dreams and in enactive forms. In "Remembering, Repeating, and Working Through," he notes that at times something is "remembered" that could never have been "forgotten" because it was never at any time conscious (Freud 1914). In the unrememberable category Freud includes certain experiences of early childhood that are later revealed and understood through dreams.

Repetition Compulsion

As I indicated earlier, these various examples of revived sensorimotor experiences Cohen (1980a) describes as "repetition compulsion functioning." Schur (1966) argues that Freud (1920) was mistaken in postulating a psychic regulatory principle, the repetition compulsion, as more basic and primitive than the pleasure principle. In my view, Cohen (1980a), Lipin (1963), and Loewald (1980) present cogent arguments for the validity and merit of Freud's (1920) hypothesis of the repetition compulsion as a basic regulatory principle. Freud's theory of the repetition compulsion was founded on clinical observations that have been repeatedly confirmed. For example, one set of Freud's observations was that posttraumatic dreams are exceptions to the rule that dreams are fulfillments of wishes and therefore exceptions to the pleasure principle.

These ideas about presymbolic form of mentation as repetition compulsion or pre-pleasure-principle functioning are consistent with Piaget's (Piaget and Inhelder 1969) theory of cognitive development. Piaget found that the sensorimotor period, which extends to about 18 months, precedes the development of symbolic thinking and the capacity to form mental representations. His concept of mental representation is defined as the capacity to evoke the image of the absent object. In sum, one clinically recognizable consequence of primal repression is repetition compulsion functioning. The activities that typify this mode are manifestations of enactive memory, the revival and repetition in sensorimotor reactions of infantile experiences that had been primally repressed. Experiences defended against by primal repression cannot be recalled; they exist as pathological memory forms, protosymbolically organized. Piaget and several psychoanalysts have contributed to our knowledge of a primitive, prepsychological mode of psychic functioning in which basic human needs have not been transformed into mental representations such as wishes.

Primal Repression or Denial?

Though the clinical referents of the primal repression concept are obscure, there is some consensus in the literature on the consequences of primal repression, including its effects on psychic development and memory formation. Below are summarized the major consequences of primal repression that have been described by different authors, and the chapters in this book that demonstrate that the cognitive arrest theory of denial accounts for the consequences previously ascribed to primal repression.

1. Primal repression prevents the formation of preconscious representations; what is primally repressed has never been verbalized. As discussed in Chapters 1, 3, 14, and 15, the cognitive arrest theory of denial explains the failure to create verbal representations.

2. Experiences defended against by primal repression cannot be remembered or recalled; they exist as pathological memory forms. The mnemic content is unconscious and organized as a function of its original mode of registration. The unrememberable "memories" of early childhood can be inferred from various clinical phenomena, including altered states of consciousness, screen sensations, acting out, and so on. Chapters 14 and 15 will present arguments for the hypothesis that denial prevents the formation of representational memories. Whatever is denied cannot be remembered or recalled in representational form; experiences defended against by denial are repeated as enactive memories.

3. Primal repression is associated with or brings about developmental defects, for example, fixations, developmental arrests, and developmental lags. The nature of the developmental defects linked with denial are discussed in Chapter 9.

Empirical Evidence

There also is empirical evidence that the primitive defense postulated by the primal repression theory is primitive forms of denial. Theories of primal repression proposed by Freud and Cohen posit a primitive defense that occurs in early childhood and that new cases of this defense normally do not occur following superego formation. New cases of primal repression occur only (1) in early childhood, (2) following trauma, and (3) in conditions in which there are gross superego defects, for example, borderline states and the psychoses (Cohen 1980b, Frank and Muslin 1967).

There is an overwhelming amount of clinical evidence that the most prominent and common type of primitive defensive activity found in the three conditions noted above is some kind of primitive denial. In assessing the clinical evidence for the nature of the defensive activity in these three conditions, I have assumed that the term *new cases* means instances of a primitive defense that is not overlaid with repression proper or another higher-level defense.

Both Cohen (1980b) and Frank (1969) indicate that trauma, even in adult life, constitutes a theoretically important exception to the normal period of closure of new primal repressions and that the destructive impact of trauma can overwhelm the ego structures involving secondary-process mentation and can evoke active primal repression. Horowitz's (1976) review of studies of defensive reactions to trauma demonstrates both the ubiquity and the predominance of denial reactions.

The evidence from analytically informed child observation and child analysis reviewed in Chapter 5 shows the prevalence and dominance of primitive kinds of denial in children under three years of age. Primal repression theories indicate that a third set of circumstances in which new cases of primal repression occur is found in chronologically adult individuals who have severe superego defects. Clinical evidence from studies of border-line and psychotic patients show that the defensive organization of such patients is marked by a relative lack of higher-level defenses (e.g., repression) and a predominance of primitive kinds of denial (Beres 1956, Eissler 1953, Hartmann 1953, Jacobson 1957).

Summary

Studies of primal repression were critically reviewed and arguments presented for the idea that primal repression is identical with denial.

Freud postulates the existence of a primitive defense, primal repression, that functions together with the developmentally more advanced defense, repression proper. Although writings on primal repression make important contibutions to the theory of primitive defense, they fail to provide the clinical referents or explain the clinical relevance of these theories. In this chapter, I proposed that the clinical referents of these theories of the primordial defense are the same as the clinical referents of denial. The primitive defense that analysts have called primal repression is, in my opinion, the basic defense of denial. One argument for the equivalence of primal repression and denial is that they have the same consequences, namely: the primitive defense prevents the formation of verbal representations; the content of what is defended against is unrememberable, and when it is later repeated, it occurs in the form of enactive memory; and developmental defects are consequences of the defense.

New cases of primal repression are said to emerge in early childhood, in traumatic states, and in the psychoses and borderline conditions. Clinical evidence obtained from studies of young children, traumatic states, and the psychoses and borderline conditions indicate that denial, and not primal repression, is the basic defense on which developmentally later and higher-level defenses such as repression and reaction formation are developed.

7

Clinical and Theoretical Studies of
Negative Hallucination

Both the clinical and the theoretical importance of negative hallucination have been overlooked in the psychoanalytic literature. This chapter, first, reviews the clinical studies on negative hallucination and, second, offers three brief theoretical investigations: a study of the relationship between negative hallucination and positive hallucination, an outline of the developmental levels of negation, and a hypothesis of the role of negative hallucination in the development of the secondary process.

Basic Concepts and Definitions

The negative hallucination is a type of denial used against a disturbing perception. In clinical writings the terms *denial* and *negative hallucination* are often used interchangeably. A review of the published clinical writings and my own clinical observations has revealed no differences in the essential dynamics, structures, or mechanisms. However, I do not suggest that denial and negative hallucination be used as synonyms, because negative hallucination should rightly be limited to denials pertaining to perception. My view of this essentially agrees with that of Bourguignon and Manus (1980), who state that disavowal is equivalent to negative hallucination.

Interpreted literally, negative hallucination is a misnomer, because the phenomenon it refers to is not an hallucination. Negative hallucination refers neither to a percept of an actual object nor to an hallucinatory object but to the *absence* of all or part of the usual and expectable perceptual response to a stimulus. Negative hallucination is defined as the unconsciously and defensively motivated loss of a perceptual response to some stimulus. In the negative hallucination, the subject unconsciously displaces his or her focal attention from a threatening stimulating object in order to avoid the recognition of the object and the generation of unpleasure and conflict. The positive hallucination is a percept of some object that does not exist, whereas the negative hallucination pertains to the absence of perception of something that does exist. The content of this perceptual absence is the loss of the sense of reality normally subjectively linked with the stimulating object.

De Monchaux (1962) defines the negative hallucination as a "subjective perception *that* something does not exist" (p. 312). Her definition is not quite right because the reality that is negated in negative hallucination is *implicitly* and *unconsciously* negated. The subject with a negative hallucination of something will seldom say (unless asked, as in hypnosis experiments) that something does not exist. Patients are rarely aware of their negative hallucinations. A diagnosis of negative hallucination is most often made by the observer. It is my impression, from teaching and supervisory experience, that negative hallucinations usually are not noticed by the therapist either. One reason is that little has been written about the negative hallucination in the literature, and another reason is that it is much easier to attend to and analyze something that *does* happen than it is to recognize and analyze an absence, something that does *not* take place.

In Chapter 1, I discussed experiments cited by Neisser (1967) in which hypnotized subjects formed negative hallucinations of a chair. Although they maintained that there was no chair, they did avoid bumping into it. From these and similar findings in other negative hallucination hypnosis experiments, it may be inferred that hypnotized subjects do register objects for which they have a negative hallucination. Negative hallucinations do not prevent the registration and unconscious perception of the negatively hallucinated object. The mechanisms by which denial or negative hallucination block conscious perception of an object are discussed in Chapter 10.

Several analysts have proposed that negative hallucination is either a precursor or a primal form of denial. Fenichel (1945) and Peto (1964) describe the negative hallucination as an "archaic denial," and Rubinfine (1962) views the negative hallucination as a prototype of denial. Hoffer (1952) writes about negative hallucination as a sort of sensory and affect deafness and suggests that it may be a primal form of repression.

What Is Negatively Hallucinated?

Either the sensorial or the meaning aspect of perception, or both, may be affected by the negative hallucination. Investigators of perception conceptualize two aspects of a conscious percept—the simple sensorial configuration and the more complex qualities of meaning, recognition, and affective significance. Percepts contain an awareness of the characteristics of what we are perceiving, a component of meaning that accompanies the bare sensory experience (Allport 1955). Ego functions such as memory, the synthetic function, and reality testing, acting conjointly, form the meaning component that normally blends with the sensorial configuration to form a conscious percept.

With some patients, both the sensorial and meaning aspects are blocked by negative hallucination. A borderline patient often asked me to repeat my interpretations because he claimed he had not heard what I said. A systematic exploration of this symptom revealed that his unconscious need to "scramble" and deny what I had said made it impossible for him to hear me. Sometimes his not hearing the analyst was accompanied by the sound of a roar in his ears. When his radio first announced President John F. Kennedy's assassination, he had shut out the announcer's voice by causing himself to hear a continuous noise like a roar in his ears. The patient claimed he could do this whenever he started to hear something he did not want to hear or thought he should not hear. The destructive unconscious fantasies underlying his negative hallucination were similar to those Bion (1958a) describes as "attacks on linking."

Other patients are able to hear what their therapists say but negatively hallucinate the therapist's interpretation. Such patients may distort interpretations as directives, criticisms, seduction, and so forth.

In negative hallucinations of the exteroceptors—that is, vision or hearing—either sensorial or meaning components, or both, may be affected. Breuer and Freud (1893–1895) provide detailed clinical descriptions of negative hallucinations in regard to the meaning component of perception in their classic case study of Anna O. Anna complained that she could not recognize her relatives, and the people she saw seemed like wax figures without any connection with her. They call the symptoms "hallucinatory absences."

Both the sensory and meaning aspects of perception are absent or markedly diminished in negative hallucinations of the somatic sensory systems, for example, smell, touch, pain, and taste. A clinical example is the conversion symptom of sensory anesthesia. Though the negative hallucination concept is generally restricted to the exteroceptors (vision and hearing), I find no reason that this concept should not be extended to instances of the defensive perceptual inhibition of somatic sensory channels.

Freud's Writings on Negative Hallucinations

Although the literature contains many brief references to the negative hallucination, there are few articles about this specific subject. This is surprising, in view of the frequency and importance of this symptom in clinical work and the theoretical significance of negative hallucination in the development of symbolic processes and defenses. Bernheim (1884) coined the expression "negative hallucination," and Freud used it from 1895 until 1917, when he discarded it. Freud's few brief references to negative hallucination were mainly descriptive rather than explanatory or theoretical.

In *The Psychopathology of Everyday Life*, Freud (1901) uses the term to explain two occasions of apparently "remarkable coincidence." The first instance was meeting a married couple he had been thinking about. Previously they had refused Freud's offer to treat their child. Freud tells of thinking that he would get revenge on them by refusing to treat the daughter if they returned and asked him to treat her. Just at the moment Freud was thinking of getting revenge on them, he heard a loud "Good day to you, Professor!" He looked up, saw the couple walking past him and then remembered that he had seen them a few moments earlier when they were about twenty paces away. Because of his conflicts over his feelings about them, he had set aside his perception of them.

A second example Freud obtained from Otto Rank had to do with meeting an acquaintance named Gold just after Rank had indulged in fantasies of acquiring some gold at a bank. Freud accounts for these seemingly remarkable coincidences as a negative hallucination whereby the subject had first defensively set aside his original perception of the individuals that he finally came to recognize fully. Similar occurrences were noted by Freud in the case of the "Rat Man" (1909, pp. 230–231, 270).

Freud provides another example of negative hallucination gathered from his observations of Bernheim's demonstrations of negative hallucinatory phenomena in a patient with somnambulism (Breuer and Freud 1893–1895, pp. 109–110). Bernheim gave the woman a negative hallucination suggestion to the effect that he was no longer present, and he then endeavored to draw her attention to himself in a variety of ways. He did not succeed. After she awakened, he asked her to tell him what he had said to her while she thought he was not there. Apparently surprised, she replied that she knew nothing of it. Bernheim insisted that she could remember everything and laid his hand on her forehead to aid her remembering. She was then able to describe everything that she had ostensibly not perceived during her somnambulism and ostensibly not remembered in her waking state.

In a paper called "Delusions and Dreams in Jensen's *Gradiva*," Freud (1907) examines the novel *Gradiva* from a psychoanalytic point of view. According to Freud, the protagonist of the novel, Norbert Hanold, suffered from an hysterical delusion that expressed his conflict over forbidden unconscious sexual wishes for a childhood girlfriend, Zoe. Hanold, an archaeologist, became infatuated with a statue of a woman. What fascinated him most was the particularly graceful gait depicted in the position of the lady's feet in the stone relief. He passionately sought to find the object of his desires, Gradiva, in the ruins of Pompeii. The hero's neurosis is cured by his confrontation with Zoe, the actual object of his repressed desires, the girl with the graceful walk who had been his childhood friend and who still lived across the street from him in his home town. Zoe complained to him that he had not noticed or recognized her after they had become teenagers. She had been the model in Hanold's unconscious mind for the imaginary Gradiva of antiquity. Freud comments:

> Hanold, who, according to the girl's accusation had the gift of 'negative hallucination', who possessed the art of not seeing and not recognizing people who were actually present, must from the first have had an unconscious knowledge of what we only learned later. (1907, p. 67)

Negative Hallucination in Hysteria

In hysterical patients, the negative hallucination is used to ward off stimuli that could evoke sexual conflict. The negative hallucination should be distinguished from those symptoms that are compromise formations arising from and symbolically expressing unconscious conflicts. Negative hallucinations are formed from the need to avoid unpleasure and conflict. The hysterical patient's tendency to ward off potentially disturbing stimuli is illustrated in Freud's (1907) study of Jensen's *Gradiva* and in a case vignette presented by Basch (1974).

Basch describes a negative hallucination in a hysteric patient who had previously denied any transference feelings for him. One day the patient and the analyst found themselves entering an otherwise empty elevator. Several moments later they were joined by a man who knew the analyst and greeted him. The threesome reached the street level and went their separate ways. The next day the patient reported a dream that expressed in thinly disguised form the patient's anger at the interruption of their privacy in the elevator the previous day. Her associations led to her rage at being excluded by her parents on several occasions. Basch mentioned to the patient that her dream seemed to have been in response to the interruption of their elevator ride by a third party. She matter-of-factly replied, "No, that couldn't have been so; no one else got on the elevator. We were alone." The patient had defended herself against jealousy by negatively hallucinating the third party in the dream. Her unconscious perception of the event in the elevator and her conflicts over this experience were expressed in her dream.

In the analysis, the patient's sexual conflict found transferential expression, but the anxiety associated with such a development was absent because of the patient's massive disavowal of the analyst's significance for her. The negative hallucination of the third party in the elevator supported this disavowal. Basch indicates that analytic progress was facilitated when her disavowal was systematically confronted.

Negative Hallucinations in Depersonalization and Derealization

In depersonalization and derealization symptoms, negative hallucinatory phenomena mean the loss of both the meaning and the sensorial aspects of perception. Certain stimuli have assumed a threatening meaning; consequently the patient unconsciously blocks, by the negative hallucinatory mechanism, the conscious recognition of such stimuli. According to Levitan (1969) and Stamm (1962), in such symptoms there is a reduction of incoming stimuli from the outside world of such a kind that could be used by the ego to validate its sense of self in a physical and/or emotional sense. In depersonalization and derealization states, the same kind of perceptual inhibitory mechanisms that individuals normally use in going to sleep are used against external stimuli. These inhibitory mechanisms are activated by the need or the wish to avoid and turn away from potentially disturbing stimuli. Stamm (1962) draws our attention to the similarity between states of estrangement and the wish to sleep. Individuals in these states tend to perceive reality as a dream. Levitan (1969) also relates the depersonlizing process to the blocking of sensory impulses, to sleep, and to negative hallucination.

Denial in the estrangement states is manifested in both perception and fantasy. The underlying unconscious fantasy in depersonalization—"This isn't happening to me"—contains a denial, as does the underlying unconscious fantasy in derealization—"All of this isn't real. It is just a harmless dream, a make-believe" (Arlow 1966).

Negative Hallucination As a Mode of Interpersonal Perception

A frequently overlooked kind of negative hallucination is characterological defensive modes of interpersonal perception. In my clinical experience such characterological modes of inhibited perception are most common and prominent in more seriously ill patients. In Chapter 9, I describe a patient who ignored what the analyst said and who heard only those parts of interpretations that could be distorted or construed as directive. This patient had a narcissistic personality disorder manifested by his excessive concern with his own well-being and defensive need to ignore, to negatively hallucinate others and their communications.

Brodey (1965) describes the habitual and characterological use of negative hallucination in narcissistic parents who unconsciously refuse to perceive anything in their children or spouses that is discordant with the image they project onto them. For these parents, the primitive defense of externalization makes possible a way of life based on relationships with unseparated but distanced parts of the self. ("Projective identification" may be considered a synonym for externalization.) Externalization has the following characteristics: Projection is combined with the manipulation of reality selected for verifying the projection. The projector manipulates another person in such a way as to induce or compel the other person to conform with the projection. The reality that cannot be used to verify the projection is not perceived, and the projector negatively hallucinates anything about the object that does not fit in with his or her projections and expectations of the object. In Chapter 11, I describe the significance of shared denial and mutual projective identification in the kinds of narcissistic relationships studied by Brodey.

A physician with a compulsive character disorder had a considerably more limited and selective kind of inattention to the communications and behaviors of others than did the narcissistic patients mentioned earlier. Often he negatively hallucinated the emotional aspects of other individuals' communications. For example, he viewed analytic neutrality as being the total absence of feeling in the analyst's behavior or speech. In one sense of the word, he was affect-"deaf" and affect-"blind." His defensive inattention to others' emotional expression was traced in his analysis to an unconscious fear of identifying with his psychotic and paranoid father. He would not allow himself to perceive the emotions of others because he feared he would have to identify with their feelings and be as they were. This meant to him the loss of his identity and being "swallowed" by others. Although he was generally regarded as a sympathetic and conscientious physician, his emotional "deafness" to other persons often prevented him from being empathetic and understanding.

I disagree with the prevalent opinion that negative hallucination is always a primitive defense, because in this neurotic patient and others the negative hallucination does not involve any gross distortion of reality. Breznitz's (1983) concept of different degrees of denial applies also to negative hallucination.

Negative Hallucination in the Psychoses

An important aspect of the schizophrenic's withdrawal from reality is the negative hallucination of external sources of threatening stimulation. Mahler (1968) describes autism as a mechanism by which patients attempt to shut out, to negatively hallucinate potential sources of sensory perceptions, particularly those that demand affective response. Many clinicians have noted the chronic schizophrenic patient's amazing capacity for shutting out somatic and environmental stimuli. They may, for example, endure physically very painful experiences such as dissecting aneurysms or myocardial infarctions without a complaint or sign of any pain. Petrie (1967) presents experimental evidence indicating that the schizophrenic's negative hallucination of disturbing stimuli might also be associated with a reduction of sensory input from the body and the external environment.

Rubinfine (1962) explains how the negative hallucinations of psychotic patients serve as a defense against awareness of their objects and how negative hallucination is employed to conserve both the object and the self from aggression. He describes the analytic treatment of a psychotic young man who would become enraged when anything disrupted his symbiotic relation with his analyst. Then he would defend both the analyst and himself from his destructive rage by ignoring the analyst and turning his attention to daydreaming or physical objects. He avoided looking at or talking with the analyst, and by negatively hallucinating the analyst, he attempted to preserve his self-object relationship with the analyst from his destructive fury.

Scotomization and Negative Hallucination

Laforgue (1927) defines scotomization as "a process of psychic depreciation . . . by means of which the individual attempts to deny everything which conflicts with his ego" (p. 473). He describes a schizophrenic patient who, instead of hating his mother, became "blind" toward her. In order to shut out his mother, father, and the whole outside world, he shut himself up. Laforgue explains that the patient had not weaned himself from his mother and that he had unconsciously dealt with conflicts over his tie to his mother by behaving as if she did not exist. Normally the ego attempts to deal with conflict, but the schizophrenic avoids conflict by a process of scotomization in which he or she shuts out disturbing stimuli. This destroys the capacity for consciousness and the ability to create a clear field of consciousness. Actual life is replaced by dream life, and living facts by symbols.

My review of Laforgue's (1927) article did not reveal any difference between what he called scotomization and what others have called negative hallucination. With Bourguignon and Manus (1980), I consider scotomization to be identical with primitive kinds of negative hallucination and denial.

Negative Hallucination in a Borderline Patient

The following case vignette illustrates how and why a borderline individual who had not attained the stage of libidinal object constancy would negatively hallucinate (in her words, "blank you out") any threatening percepts or images of the analyst. Whenever she felt threatened by any sexual or aggressive feelings toward the analyst, she would typically inhibit her fantasy or her percept of the analyst by seeing him as "blank," "dead," or "unreal." Blanking out the analyst led to new anxieties over losing him. Early in her treatment she felt compelled to call him on weekends to see if he was still alive. The sound of his voice was sufficient to relieve her anxiety over object loss and to restore her capacity to form and remember an image of him. When she defensively blanked out the analyst, she could neither imagine nor perceive any actual or observable characteristics of him.

The patient had not attained the developmental stage of libidinal object constancy, as shown by her inability to sustain at times of frustration both negative and positive images and feelings for an object in its absence. Some Kleinian analysts might have described the defensive process in such cases as splitting. In my view, there was no active defensive process of splitting. (See Chapter 4 for a further discussion of splitting.) Rather, the patient would negatively hallucinate any threatening negative images of the analyst in order to maintain an idealized image of him. The so-called split between the patient's negative and positive images of the analyst was then a consequence of her denial defense.

Three Theoretical Investigations

Negative Hallucinations and Positive Hallucination

In what follows, I shall carry out a suggestion made by Freud (1917) in a brief footnote that any attempt to explain hallucination should be made from the starting point of negative hallucination rather than positive hallucination. The hypothesis presented here is that a negative hallucination is necessary for the formation of a positive hallucination. The loss of reality sense and reality testing brought about by negative hallucination is a necessary, if not a sufficient, condition for the subjective formation of the false reality contained in the positive hallucination. There are two perceptual distortions in positive hallucination: the false perception of what does not exist and the rejection by negative hallucination of that part of the perceptual field for which the positive hallucination has been substituted. Thus, any positive hallucination presupposes a negative hallucination (the non-perception of what is). Negative hallucination is the empty space, the blank screen, or the background against which the positive hallucination can take shape (Green 1977).

Positive hallucinations of the type observed in the psychoses serve a restitutive function in that they establish a new subjective relationship between the subject and hallucinatory objects to substitute for those aspects of the subject's self and his or her relations with the object world that have been subjectively lost through negative hallucination. The schizophrenic, for example, who complains that his or her perceptual world seems dead and unreal may recapture some sense (false, to be sure) of meaningful relationships with objects by means of positive hallucination.

This view of the central significance of negative hallucination and primitive kinds of denial in the psychoses is consistent with the classical view that the primary pathology in the psychoses is the psychic destruction of the patient's ties to reality and that symptoms such as hallucinations and delusions are secondary restitutive phenomena.

Positive hallucinations are probably the prototype for developmentally later kinds of screen behavior. There is a developmental continuum of screen behaviors ranging from the most primitive—that is, positive hallucination—to the most highly differentiated forms such as rationalization. The same line of reasoning used above to describe the relationship between positive and negative hallucinatory phenomena applies also to other kinds of screen behavior. For example, the false ideas contained in delusions screen the loss of reality brought about by denial. The screen behaviors discussed in Chapter 1 provide illusory, delusional, or even hallucinatory substitutes for whatever part of reality of whatever kind of object relations is subjectively destroyed by denial.

Evidence that the positive hallucination substitutes for the void created by the negative hallucination comes from hypnosis experiments cited by Stewart (1966). The setting of this experiment includes a hypnotist, his hypnotized subject, and another person, P, sitting in a chair. The hypnotist suggests to the subject that P is no longer in the room, and the hypnotized subject will agree that P is not present. When the subject is then asked to describe what he sees, he describes the chair, *including those parts of the chair that will be hidden from his view by P's sitting in the chair.* Stewart believes that the ego splits into three parts—one that registers the sensory perception, one that denies it, and one that hallucinatorily fills in the denial on a rationalizing basis. He discusses the subject's need for a rationalizing positive hallucination. Why not just have a blank space without filling it in with a positive hallucination? The answer, he suggests, is that normally one never sees nothing and that to see nothing would give rise to anxiety.

Developmental Levels of Negation

In Chapter 5, I presented arguments supporting the notion that the negative hallucination should be considered part of the primary process and that sensorimotor avoidance behaviors are the somatic precursors of negative hallucination. Though the primary process and negative hallucination do not contain any symbol of negation, a presymbolic kind of negation is contained in the negative hallucination. In this section, my purpose is to examine from a developmental point of view the property of negation, the unconscious "not this" idea contained in negative hallucination and other kinds of denial, and to show the developmental continuity between the unconscious negation in denial and its developmental antecedents and successors.

As Freud (1905, 1925a) indicates in several places, defenses are intermediary in their developmental position between reflex physiological activities and conscious acts of judgment or repudiation. Judgment, he claims, is formed out of the primitive defensive need of the infantile ego under the dominance of the pleasure principle to expel (or to spit out) anything unpleasurable (Freud 1925). Freud emphasizes the symbol of negation, the conscious "no," and conscious acts of judgment. He tells how psychoanalysis assists individuals in raising their psychic processes to a higher level where they can consciously judge or say no to whatever they had previously and unconsciously rejected in a defensive and automatic way.

In his "Negation" paper, Freud (1925a) is ambiguous in his use of the word negation (*Verneinen* in German). Sometimes he uses *Verneinen* in the logical and grammatical sense, and at other times he uses the same word to refer to a defense indistinguishable from denial. Freud is inconsistent in this regard, because in other papers he employs the term *Verleugnung* (translated as "denial" or "disavowal") to refer to the same defensive activity that he calls *Verneinen* in the "Negation" paper. To clarify matters, I propose that we should use negation in its logical and grammatical meanings, as I have done in this book, and not use it to designate a defense.

According to Freud, a negative judgment is the next highest developmental step beyond defense and is the intellectual substitute for defense. The view advanced here is somewhat different in that I conceive of verbal thought itself as the next developmental step beyond defense. The unconscious negation in negative hallucination and other forms of denial is transformed by developmental processes into verbal symbols that contain an implicit negation.

The theory proposed here envisions two major ontogenetic transformations of negation. First, the property of negation in the physiological precursors of denial—that is, the sensorimotor avoidance behaviors of infancy —is transformed and repeated at a higher level in the negative hallucination, in which the need to withdraw from painful stimulation attains psychic representation as the wish to avoid unpleasure. The final step in this developmental sequence is the gradual attainment of verbal thought, in which the property of negation is lifted to the symbolic level. This last phase is the neutralization of the aggression accompanying negation in the preceding defense and sensorimotor phases. Also, the aim of avoiding *thinking* about what is unpleasurable replaces the aim of avoiding whatever is unpleasurable.

Conditions are then established for the psyche to function in accord with the reality principle rather than the pleasure principle.

The sensorimotor avoidance and riddance reactions that are precursors to psychic defenses serve a biological protective function in the avoidance and/or riddance of noxious objects. Probably these avoidance and riddance activities are also some of the earliest manifestations of aggression in infants and may constitute the somatic precursors for the later ontogenesis of aggression. Hostile wishes in which concretely conceived painful objects are defecated, vomited, spit out, or in other ways attacked constitute the dynamic nucleus of unconscious fantasies (or attacks on linking) in denial reactions. In conversion and somatization reactions involving these sensorimotor avoidance and riddance reactions, the motor activities in the symptoms (e.g., hysterical vomiting) symbolize unconscious aggressive wishes. The so-called mysterious leap from the psyche to somatic innervation in conversion reactions is a regression from verbal thought to preverbal modes of expressing aggression. It appears likely that this regressive movement in conversion reactions returns, as it were, to the earliest modes of expressing aggression. These observations suggest that aggression may undergo the same or similar developmental transformations as does negation.

Negation is an essential and integral aspect of secondary process, verbal thought. Negation is contained not only in the content of thinking, in the capacity to say no to something or somebody, but more importantly in verbal thinking itself. Primary-process thinking is concrete, thinglike, and hallucinations and dreams are experienced as real. In contrast, secondary-process verbal thought is "no thing" (Langer 1967). A negation is contained in the implicit notation "not real" that accompanies all verbal thinking. Unlike signs and other primitive forms of thought and communication, verbal symbols are distinguished from their referents. This distinction breaks down in schizophrenia in which there is an impairment of abstraction capacity and words are treated concretely as if they were things.

A critical difference between verbal thought and primitive forms of ideation such as the positive hallucination is the implicit negation, the "not real" aspect of verbal thinking. The ability to tolerate and to symbolize a negative distinguishes verbal thought from primary-process thinking. In contrast, the negation in negative hallucination is presymbolic, preverbal, and unconscious.

Bion (1967) tells how the capability for developing thinking depends on the ability to withstand frustration. In the earliest oral terms, this means that the young child achieves a capacity for tolerating the "no breast" image. If the infant can tolerate frustrations and contain the no breast image, then an apparatus of thinking is developed. De Monchaux (1962) observes that the no breast idea is a more highly adaptive kind of mental work than the "good breast" image and that this must be stressed, even though the no breast thought depends in part on the earlier experience of a good internal breast imago.

The developmental significance of negation was examined by Spitz (1957), who writes about how the acquisition of the "no" in the young child is the indicator of a new level of autonomy, of the awareness of the "other" and awareness of the self. This permits a restructuralization of mentation on a higher level of complexity, and it initiates ego development in the framework of which the dominance of the reality principle becomes stronger.

In working psychoanalytically with defense, the therapeutic task is the same as the developmental task of lifting the mode of mentation from the unconscious and primary-process level to the level of verbal thought. Through interpretation, the patient is assisted in verbalizing whatever he or she has previously, by denying, avoided thinking and speaking about. For both insight and psychic development to take place, the patient must learn to tolerate psychic pain and frustration and to put into words whatever he or she has defensively avoided. This combined developmental and therapeutic step is prior to, and a necessary condition for, exercising the faculty of judgment that Freud (1925a) wrote about. Before one can decide yes or no about something, one must first be capable of tolerating the frustration of thinking about the issue requiring personal decision.

In this section we have traced the developmental transformations of negation through three levels. Negation is manifested somatically and at the biological level in the avoidance and riddance behaviors of infancy. At the next level—the level of negative hallucination and primary process—a pre-symbolic negation is expressed in the avoidance of painful percepts. At the final and symbolic level, negation becomes part of conscious verbal thinking. This development schema is, of course, an ideal one, and the other chapters of this book testify to how often humans fail to reach or to maintain the highest level in their psychic functioning.

The Role of Negative Hallucinations in the Development of the Secondary Process

This investigation expands on a suggestion made in the previous section that the unconscious and presymbolic negation in negative hallucination is transformed by developmental processes into verbal symbols that contain an implicit negation. In psychopathology, as in infancy, the processes underlying both positive and negative hallucination function separately. The hypothesis advanced here is that secondary-process, verbal thinking is developmentally and microgenetically derived in part from the synthesis of the positive hallucination and the negative hallucination. The word *micro-genetically* is included here because of the concept discussed in Chapter 1 that the microgenesis of thought recapitulates the ontogenesis of thought; in other words, I am suggesting that normally in thought formation, the negative hallucination mechanism is directed against the positive hallucination to form secondary-process thought.

Freud (1900, p. 691) emphasizes the central importance and role of inhibition of the primary process in the formation of the secondary process, and he describes the need for inhibition of both positive hallucination and of motor activity. The process that results from the inhibition imposed by the second system on the first (or primary) system he calls the secondary process. The negative hallucinatory mechanism fulfills the requirements of a system for inhibiting both perception and motor discharge. Evidence for the idea that the negative hallucination mechanism functions as an unconsciously motivated and regulatory control over involuntary motor and secretory reactions to external stimuli was presented in an earlier paper (Dorpat 1968).

As I previously stated, the negative hallucinatory mechanism is at first directed against disturbing external stimulation. Later, it is turned against internal stimuli, for example, positive hallucination, to form secondary-process thinking. The negation of negative hallucination is joined with the affirmation of positive hallucination to form thought.

Freud (1940) was the first to suggest that the stimulus barrier could be used against internal stimuli:

> A particular way is adapted for dealing with internal excitations which produce too great an increase of unpleasure; there is a tendency to treat them as though they were acting, not from the inside, but from the outside, so that it may be possible to bring the shield against stimuli into operation as a means of defense against them. This is the origin of projection which is destined to play such a large part in the causation of pathological processes. (p. 129)

The positive hallucination, according to Freud (1900) and others, is a basic precursor of mental imagery and fantasy. One may assume that the beginnings of unconscious fantasy occur when the individual becomes capable of differentiating the products of imagination from actual real percepts, that is, the development of reality testing. Hallucinations in a young child are not distinguishable from real sensory experiences. Such hallucinatory experiences possess psychic reality, for the ego has not yet acquired the capacity to *disbelieve*, to invest psychic contents with the knowledge of their unreality (Sandler and Nagera 1963). The subjective qualities of "unreal" and "real" are the indices or signs of the reality-testing function. The products of internal stimuli (e.g., memories, ideas, fantasies) are ascribed the quality of being unreal, and the products of perception are experienced as real.

The question arises, how does the reality-testing function develop, or how does the individual learn to distinguish internal from external stimuli? Garma (1946) argues that the reality-testing function depends on the greater facility with which the ego can bring to bear the negative hallucination mechanism against internal rather than external stimuli. A person's capacity for inhibiting external stimuli by the negative hallucination mechanism is limited; because such a stimuli, if sufficiently intense or prolonged, may break through the stimulus barrier (e.g., as in the traumatic neuroses). Garma's hypothesis is remarkably similar to the one proposed by Freud (1895) in the *Project:*

> It is accordingly *inhibition by the ego which makes possible a criterion for distinguishing between perception and memory.* Biological experience will then teach that discharge is not to be initiated until the *indication of reality* has arrived, and that with this in view, the cathexis of the desired memories is not to be carried beyond a certain amount. (p. 326; Freud's italics.)

Freud (1895, p. 327) also indicates that this inhibition by the ego brings about a moderated cathexis of the wished-for object, which allows it to be cognized as *not real.* These arguments suggest that individuals are able to test reality and designate internal stimuli as unreal because they can more readily negate internal stimuli than external stimuli by the negative hallucination mechanism.

In a formulation similar to the one proposed here, de Monchaux (1962) provides a thought-provoking explanatory hypothesis of the function of the negative hallucination in the inhibition of the positive hallucination and its role in the ontogenesis of symbolic thought and the secondary process:

> For it is acts of comparison and selection which mark the secondary process; the establishment of categories, of logical relations, of temporal order, and of negation. The fundamental feature of all these processes is the estimation of the relation between an image of a past stimulus and the nature of a present one. (p. 313)

For this act of comparison to be made, both positive and negative hallucination must be inhibited, because their "all or none" mode of functioning results in image representation split off from the stimulus impact. The inevitable discrepancy between need arousal and its gratification results in the hallucinatory image of the past gratifier (the breast) being linked with affective experiences of deprivation. The infant's frustrating experiences lead to the hallucinatory image of the breast's being experienced as painful. An attempt would then be made to deal with the unpleasure by negative hallucination, the primary-process mode of escape from noxious external stimulation.

Thus the positive hallucination is negatively hallucinated; in other words, it is inhibited. The primary (positive and negative) hallucinatory processes are mutually inhibited. This entails the diversion of negative hallucination from actual percepts of the external world to positive hallucinations. Inhibition of the positive hallucinations reduces its power, both as a substitute satisfier and as a persecutor. In this way, conditions are established for the system to function according to the secondary process.

Similar hypotheses of the role of negative hallucination in the formation of secondary-process thought have been advanced by Peto (1964) and Ninenger (1965). According to Peto, thought formation proceeds from positive hallucinations that are subjected to fragmentation. The fragments are then decathected by the negative hallucinatory mechanism to form thought. Ninenger suggests that individuals' conviction that their thinking takes place within the head is a form of denial initiated by the infant, because a painful prototype of thought must be denied. This is the hallucinatory image of the absent mother, evoked by hunger but ultimately rejected when memory demonstrates that it is associated with a persistence of hunger and tension. The unconscious fantasy is that the head is a container, filled with previous "things," yet not really existing. The complex origin of this container fantasy about the head is derived from the nursing situation in which the infant and mother are merged. The original container is the infant's mouth enclosing the nipple and milk, and simultaneously it is the enfolding mother who contains the infant.

The original infant-mother hallucination of nursing is denied and projected, only to be later reinternalized as a fantasy about the head being a container of thoughts.

Summary

We first examined the nature of negative hallucination and studies of negative hallucination in the neuroses, character disorders, and the psychoses. Negative hallucination is a denial of disturbing perceptual information, and it is defined as the unconscious and defensively motivated loss of a perceptual response to some stimulus. Clinical observations and hypnosis experiments demonstrate that negative hallucination does not prevent the registration and unconscious perception of the negatively hallucinated object.

Second, we made three brief theoretical investigations, and the conclusions reached in those investigations are as follows:

1. The negative hallucination is a necessary, but not a sufficient, condition for positive hallucination, and any positive hallucination presupposes a negative hallucination.

2. The developmental antecedents of the unconscious and presymbolic negation in negative hallucination are the sensorimotor avoidance behaviors of infancy, and the developmental successor is verbal thought.

3. Secondary-process, verbal thinking is developmentally and microgenetically derived in part from the synthesis of the positive and the negative hallucination.

8

Introjected Object Relations and Defense

My goal in this chapter is to use five case studies to illustrate and discuss the dynamic significance of introjected childhood object relations in defensive activity. A comprehensive and systematic theory on the relationships between object relations and defenses should include a person's current interpersonal relations and how they shape and maintain defenses. This interactional aspect of defensive activity is taken up in Chapters 11, 12, and 13.

Screen Behavior and Object Relations

The cognitive arrest theory includes an object relations perspective in its definition of screen behavior, given in Chapter 1, in which I defined screen behavior as the behaviors motivated by the need to fill in the gaps created by the cognitive arrest and to substitute a different object relation for the one subjectively lost because of the cognitive arrest. A common example is defensive idealization of an object, in which idealization is used to deny conflicts over aggression and threats of object loss. The defensive denigration of an unconsciously envied object is another example. An individual who finds his or her envy of an object to be intolerable may deny both the envy and whatever there is about the object eliciting it, by denigrating the object.

Object Relations in the Development of Defenses

Defenses are created, or at least strongly influenced, by parent-child interactions. The introjection of these interactions provides the unconscious and dynamic nucleus of defensive activity. According to child analysts such as

Spitz (1961), defense mechanisms are not innate; rather, they are formed out of parent-child relations. The infant uses various modes of sensorimotor avoidance or riddance reactions either actually or potentially available at birth, for defensive purposes. These sensorimotor modes provide the models available to the child in the first two years of life; the nature of parent-child relations determines the choice of a particular prototype suitable for a defense in a given situation.

Kernberg (1976) views defenses as the structuralized derivatives of *internalized object relations*, and he finds three components in these internalized object relations: an affective state, an object representation, and a self representation. According to him, the persistence in defensive splitting of nonmetabolized early introjections is the outcome of a pathological fixation of severely disturbed early object relations. My concept of the relationships between defense and internalized object relations is essentially the same as Kernberg's, except that I claim that denial, not splitting, defends against the awareness of pathological internalized object relations. In this book I have used the word *introjects* to mean the same as *internalized object relations*.

Introjects and Defense

Defenses are created and maintained to defend against unconscious pathological introjects. What is defended against are not objects but an interpersonal mode—a traumatically experienced relationship (G. Klein 1976). A pathological introject refers to a relationship linked with danger, anxiety, or fear and denotes an interactional or *relational* mode.

From the objective observer's perspective, an introject is a relational mode, but from the subject's conscious or unconscious point of view an introject is an alien presence. According to Schafer (1968a), an introject is an inner presence with which one feels a dynamic relationship. Introjects are experienced as part of the body or one's thought, but never as part of the self. For the subject, the introject is felt as powerfully influencing the self, but not as capable of being influenced by one's self. In order to study the significance of introjects in defensive activity, we first need to examine the nature and functions of both normal and pathological introjection.

Internalization Processes: Introjection and Identification

Introjection and identification are two sequential processes used to internalize object relations. Introjection precedes identification and provides the contents for identification (Dorpat 1979, 1981). Persons identify with their object representations of other people, not with actual individuals. Introjection first forms the introjects and object representations than can later be used for identifications and for the construction of the major psychic structures, that is, ego and superego.

Normal introjects, as I explained on a different occasion, become the psychic building blocks for identifications and ego and superego structure formation (Dorpat 1979). Pathological introjects, such as those associated with defensive activities, are "nonmetabolized" and unavailable for ego or superego formation. Pathological introjects are like foreign bodies: they cannot be integrated or assimilated into the person's self, and they cannot be destroyed or eliminated. G. Klein (1976) distinguishes between interpersonal schemata linked with defense and those associated with identifications. *Identifications* refer to an internalized relational mode that is brought into syntonicity with the self-schema, whereas pathological introjects, the introjected interpersonal schemata connected with defenses, are split off and dissociated from the self-schema. Introjects are experienced as distinct from the self, whereas identifications are viewed subjectively as parts of the self.

Introjection is the process whereby a subject transforms an interpersonal relation (i.e., interaction) into a psychic action and constructs representations of the self and the other person in the relation. A particular interpersonal interaction is consciously or unconsciously replicated and repeated in the subject's psyche. The product of this process I shall call an *introject*. An introject is an organized schema with three parts: a primary-process image of an object, an image of the self in interaction with the object, and an affect.

My view of introjects is similar to the concept of *internal object relations*, as formulated in various object relations theories. Ogden (1983) describes object relations theories as "fundamentally a theory of unconscious internal object relations in dynamic interplay with current interpersonal experience" (p. 227).

M. Klein (1955) and Schafer (1968a) limit the concept of introjects to primitive or primary-process representations of objects and leave the interaction linking representations of the self and objects. Klein and her colleagues (1955) consider each unconscious primary-process object representation as an unconscious introject. The reasons I reject their concept of introjects as incomplete are that first, object representations are not discrete, separable entities; they always occur associated with representations of the self and with the particular interaction involving both self and object. This is especially true at the primary-process level where self and object representations are undifferentiated. Second, from a developmental perspective, the relation (i.e., the specific mode of interpersonal interaction) is internalized long before the child is capable of representing and distinguishing between the self and object in the interaction. Childhood object relations become internalized in the unconscious, where they remain as the primary-process or concrete representations of interactions.

Martin Buber's (1970) statement "In the beginning is the relation" is true in the developmental sense because the internalization of the relation precedes the time when the young child can differentiate between the subject and the object in the relation. From the infant's point of view, the object is nothing but the prolongation of the infant's activity. Gradually, through a process of objectivation, the young child learns to distinguish between his or her activity and the object toward which this activity is directed (Fraiberg 1969, p. 87).

The Internalization of Relations

The essential and dynamic element internalized in the process of introjection is the relation between the subject and the object; what become internalized are not objects but interactions and relationships (Dorpat 1981, Loewald 1970).

Psychoanalytic theories of development have shifted from a predominantly biological orientation, which emphasized elements such as instincts and drives, to an orientation concerned with the role of the subject's interpersonal relationships in the formation and patterning of psychic structures. Personality development today is conceptualized as a result of the interaction and intermeshing of innate maturational givens with experiential elements derived principally from the subject's interactions with important persons, chiefly the parents. Psychoanalysis adheres to the epigenetic concept of development and views the formation of psychic structures as the products of successive transactions between the individual and his or her environment (Loewald 1978). Contemporary emphasis in psychoanalytic concepts of the psychic development is on the quality of parent-child transactions as determined by the parents' capacities to respond constructively and empathically to their children's changing needs.

Defense and Character

The psychiatric and psychoanalytic literature emphasizes the short-term and frequently reversible employment of denial and defense in traumatic situations and in the pathogenesis of symptoms. Less attention has been given to the defensive aspects of character formation, as manifested, in the ways in which persons related and communicate with others. In the following case studies, I shall focus on long-term or characterological denial reactions and discuss the role of disruptive parent-child interactions and pathological introjects in their formation. These deeply ingrained defensive modes of relating and communicating are central to psychoanalytic treatment, where they provide major and continuing sources of resistance and transference.

Case Studies

The Introject of an Unresponsive Mother

The analyst of a schizoid professor often felt "let down" and excluded in his interactions with the patient. He was able to discern two kinds of repetitive situations in the analysis in which he experienced these counter-transference responses. One was immediately after making an interpretation of the patient, who usually responded with a compliant agreement. Then he would switch to objective reality elements, claiming these also contributed to whatever content had been interpreted. His response to the interpretations was akin to what Abend (1975) calls the "Yes, but" response. His rationalizations and focus on reality concerns were used to deny the affective significance of the analyst's interpretation and to distance himself from the analyst.

The other situation evocative of the analyst's feeling "shut out" was when the analysand would shift from a personal and object-related mode of communication to a detached, highly abstract mode. In a detached manner, he typically would summarize in a few well-chosen abstract terms an interpretation about himself. Although these self-interpretations were often perceptive and accurate insights, the insights were used defensively. Insights communicated in an abstract, even impersonal manner were used to deny the affective significance of what was going on within himself and in his interactions with the analyst.

By speaking in a detached manner he distanced himself from his emotions and his interactions with the analyst. After several years of analysis, it became clear to both the analyst and the analysand that this subtle defensive strategy replicated his relationship with his deeply withdrawn and unresponsive mother. The patient could then remember how often he had felt left out and excluded by her impassive coldness.

The patient's defensive use of insight and abstraction was an unconscious replication of the relationship with his mother. He excluded both the analyst and the emotional part of himself by his excessive and defensive generalizing and abstracting in a way that was remarkably similar to the way in which he had been "shut out" by his mother.

The unconscious introject being defended against by these defensive maneuvers was the concrete image of a cold, withdrawn, and unresponsive mother. He defended against his anger toward his mother by identifying with her cold detachment, and under stress he treated himself and others in a distancing way similar to the way she had treated him. (The defensive and temporary identifications with pathological introjects, such as shown by this patient, should be distinguished from the more lasting kinds of identifications, mentioned earlier, used for ego and superego formation.)

I would like to emphasize the initial unconscious nature of this patient's introject. For this patient, and for others to be described later, months and even years of analysis were required before both the analyst and the analysand could understand the nature of these introjects, their developmental origins, and the relationships between the introjects and the patient's defenses and resistances. Awareness of the introjects was defended against by denial and repression. Most aspects of the introjects had never been conscious before their analysis, though in some instances a few aspects of the introjects stemmed from repressed contents and memories, ideas that had once been conscious. Oftentimes, as in the case example, the first clues as to the nature of unconscious introjects are the therapist's affective responses to the patient's communications.

The Introject of the Ignoring Mother

A 36-year-old businessman in analysis negatively hallucinated almost anything that his analyst said or did, and he ignored any communications discordant with his wishes for an idealized self object. (Other aspects of this case are presented in Chapter 9.) His negative hallucination for the analyst's communications was not a total one: if the analyst said anything that the patient could construe as some kind of directive, he would use the analyst's communication as a guide for how he should behave. In negatively hallucinating many of the analyst's communications, he was denying the analyst's separateness and personhood. For him, the analyst was simply a need-fulfilling person, and any of his communications that did not conform with his needs he did not attend to. His characterological defensive style developed early from his relationship with his borderline mother. The patient ignored others as his mother had ignored him in his childhood. Ignoring others served to deny his needs for others and protected both himself and others from his frustration and rage.

Midway through his analysis, he spent much time trying to reconstruct his early childhood and infancy by talking with his relatives. His investigation gave credibility and credence to the new ideas developed in his analysis of his defenses and early object relations as manifested in his transference to the analyst.

His historical method of understanding his past dovetailed with the psychoanalytic depth-psychology approach to reconstruction. In home movies taken when he was a young child, he would observe his mother's ignoring him in much the same manner as he had ignored the analyst. A compassionate aunt revealed to him how she had rescued him when he was age two from a railroad switching yard. His mother was either indifferent or oblivious to the obvious danger to the patient and had allowed him to play alone on the railroad tracks.

The Defense of "Extinguishing" the Self

For a long period, the major resistance in the analysis of a young professional woman was silence. Sometimes this was abrupt: she would be talking normally and then suddenly stop herself. At other times the silence had a more quiet, prolonged quality. Often the analyst sensed that the silences served to break off any contact with him.

Over time, the analyst and the patient were able to discern the meaning and function of these long silent periods. They protected her from disturbing positive feelings, especially sexual wishes, for the analyst. The prohibition against sexual desires for the analyst was transferred from repressed and forbidden sexual wishes for her father. Both denial and repression were contained in what she came to call "extinguishing" the self.

During her silences, she would stop all feeling and thinking and, in her words, go "blank." At such times she feared she would faint, as she had done numerous times during adolescence. In order to avoid anxiety she unconsciously obliterated any ideas or emotions regarding the analyst. The entire object relation, including her representations of herself, the analyst, and the emotions linked with feared and wished-for interaction with the analyst was subjectively destroyed and barred from consciousness.

She came to the realization that this was a defense she had developed for extinguishing or hiding her "real self." The patient compared the extinguishing of herself in analysis with her adolescent years when she had "bottled up" and contained herself so completely that she had been unaware of any sexual feelings. Her unconscious defense of extinguishing herself, in addition to being a defense against forbidden sexual strivings, was also an aspect of her character and style of relating to others. She was shy and self-effacing; she tended to conceal her real self from others and from herself.

The patient's mother was a vindictive woman prone to dramatic suicide attempts and violent tantrums. During childhood, the patient— regarded as the black sheep of the family—had introjected her mother's projections of blame and hatred.

Two events occurring a few days apart led to her insight into how her extinguishing herself repeated what her mother had done to her. First, the analyst interpreted her defensive blanking out of sexual feelings as stemming from her fear of the analyst's blaming her as her mother had done. The second experience was a long and disruptive telephone conversation with her mother, when her mother again attempted to coerce the patient into feeling guilty over the mother's misfortunes. Her mother screamed at her for being "selfish."

The patient realized that her mother failed to validate or acknowledge what the patient had told her on the telephone; instead, the mother had treated the patient as the hated and despised parts of herself. What she feared from the analyst and what she actually did to herself (i.e., extinguishing her self) was a replication of what her mother had done to her from early childhood on. The patient defended against the introjected image of her mother's hating and blaming her.

Defensive Helplessness: The "I Can't" Attitude

In the following case study, my aim is to show how a patient's defensive attitude of helplessness—his "I can't" attitude—was used to deny his competency and his separateness from his mother and others. Also, I shall trace the development of his defensive helplessness to its childhood origins in the patient's relationship with his mother.

The patient was a 33-year-old attorney who started analysis with symptoms of depression and work inhibition. He came to one analytic hour in a state of anxiety over his new wife's possible pregnancy: she had missed a menstrual period. In an obsessive and guilty manner, he considered different options, including abortion, of dealing with the unwanted pregnancy. His anxiety stemmed from mainly unconscious conflicts over being angry at his wife for risking pregnancy by failing to take her birth control pills regularly. Although troubled, he was able to examine rationally both his mental state and his external reality situation. With a tone of helpless resignation he exclaimed, "*I can't* think objectively about my wife and this pregnancy!" He sighed, and some of the tension left his voice. Then he became depressed. After saying "I can't" he carried out his self-diagnosis of helplessness and stopped attempting to think through the problem. Affects of guilt, worthlessness, and helplessness seemed to overwhelm him, and he began to berate himself unreasonably for his failure to check on his wife's taking her pills.

In this instance, as in many others, his "I can't" expression functioned as a signal for the suspension of certain ego functions needed for realistic thinking, including judgment, planning, and decision making. In suspending these functions, he assuaged his anxiety but initiated a sequence of psychic events that led to his becoming depressed and relatively ineffective. The patient's denial of his psychic abilities was an important precipitating cause of his depressions. In Chapter 9, I discuss various consequences of denial and show how denial leads to cognitive and affective dyscontrol and symptom formation.

This patient unconsciously pretended to be helpless when he really was not. This was not a conscious pretense; rather, his "I can't" attitude was an unconscious denial of his capabilities for rational thought and action. He habitually and defensively underestimated and denigrated his abilities. Sometimes the "I can't" attitude was a denial of, as well as a substitute for, "I won't" or "I don't want to" or some other unacceptable idea. Often he unconsciously used "I can't" communications as a way of seducing others to provide attention, help, and other narcissistic supplies. During childhood, he did this mainly because of his mother's unconscious need to keep him dependent on and attached to her. In his childhood (from age two to six), his father was absent from the home while serving in the army. His mother projected onto him her own unconscious and unresolved dependency needs and treated him in an overly solicitous and protective way.

Even after he graduated from law school and began a successful law practice, his mother continued to shower him with unwanted and unneeded gifts of things and attention. She reinforced his dependency on her and supported his withdrawal from painful situations. His denial of his own competence derived from the introjection of his mother's unconscious communications of his helplessness and needfulness. The exaggerated and defensive attitude of helplessness was unconsciously used to maintain his symbiotic tie to his mother and thus to deny his separation from her.

The "I can't" attitude had its beginnings in conflicts stemming from both oedipal and preoedipal periods. He unconsciously feigned helplessness and incompetence in order to reduce his anxieties over forbidden sexual strivings and to disarm actual or potential rivals. Conflicts and fixations related to the separation-individuation phase of development also contributed to his defensive attitude of helplessness. Unconsciously, the idea of being a competent and independent person had the meaning of disappointing and abandoning his mother. He felt as if he could not say "no" to his mother's insistent offers of help and care, because he believed she needed him to be her grateful and "needy" little boy. His movements toward separation and independence from her evoked intense and painful emotions of separation guilt.

This patient's defensive helplessness defended against the unconscious introject of his mother's smothering and engulfing him. His "I can't" attitude both warded off forbidden sexual and aggressive impulses toward his mother and, at the same time, unconsciously gratified those impulses. These gratifications were not entirely made up of fantasies, because his "I can't" communications often led his mother and surrogates for her to do things for the patient.

Whining as a Defense Against the Introject of an Abandoning Mother

A young woman began analysis with complaints of depression and marital conflict. One behavior that posed an obdurate resistance was her repetitive and nearly lifelong whining. Sometimes her whining had an accusatory, blaming quality; at other times it communicated a plaintive, pathetic quality. Whining was often associated with whimpering or crying, and when she cried, others were more impressed by the manipulative, dramatic quality of her crying than by any genuine expression of sadness. By her whining, she unconsciously attempted to evoke in others (including her analyst) various affects, attitudes, and functions that she could not tolerate containing within herself. Whining was the vehicle for her projective identification and for initiating with others pathological sado-masochistic interactions.

Whining denied her rage and her wishes to control, castrate, and torture others at the same time that it unconsciously gratified those wishes. Anxieties over wished-for oedipal victories were denied by maintaining an image of herself as a helpless and abused little girl. By acting and dramatizing the role of the helpless victim-child, she denied her hostile rivalry with her mother. Whining denied who she was, a grown woman.

Associated with whining behaviors, there was a regression to an early childhood dependent state that included a denial and suspension of her own ego functions of verbal thought and self-regulation. She suspended these functions and attempted to project them onto the analyst or others.

The patient's whining defended against the introject of an abandoning mother. Her mother frequently rejected and neglected the patient as a child, often leaving her in the care of servants. One of the few times the patient could depend on her mother's attention, if not affection, was when she cried and whined. Although whining during childhood had adaptive value in maintaining a bond with her mother, in adult life, whining had the opposite and destructive effect of alienating herself from others.

In all five cases discussed in this chapter, the behaviors described as defensive had an adaptive value during early childhood. These defensive attitudes had been the best means available to these patients as children for protecting themselves against disturbing parent-child interactions and at the same time maintaining a relationship with their parents.

Discussion

The return of the denied relational mode appears in the defense against the introject. In other words, elements of the unconscious and internalized interaction being defended against often emerge unconsciously expressed in the defense itself.

The whining of the patient described earlier defended against awareness of the image of an internalized abandoning mother and at the same time expressed how she felt about being abandoned. The defensive actions of the woman who extinguished herself replicated both the internalized relational mode and the original relationship with her mother. The lawyer with the "I can't" attitude viewed himself as helpless and incompetent in a manner similar to the way that his mother had treated him.

Transferences of Pathological Introjects

Any part of the introject, including the affect, the specific interaction, and either the subject (self) pole or the object pole, may be projected onto the individual's representations of others. For example, the schizoid professor described earlier projected the subject pole and, by his detached, impersonal mode of relating, severed emotional contact with other persons, including his analyst. In contrast, the whining patient projected the object pole of her introject, and she often related to others as if they were abandoning her.

According to Ogden (1983), projective identification is a universal feature of the externalization or transference of internal object relations. Internal object relations may be reexternalized by means of projective identification in an interpersonal setting, thus generating the transference and counter-transference phenomena of analysis and other interpersonal transactions.

Painful Affects and Introjects

In Chapter 1, I explained how unpleasurable affects trigger the cognitive arrest in denial reactions. Painful affects are the preconscious tip of the iceberg, with the principal part of the complex psychic constellation of disruptive introjects being below the surface of consciousness. All affects have objects. Persons are afraid *of* someone, guilty *about* something, angry *at* others. The painful affects that evoke defensive activity are associated with unconscious pathological introjects. A person's current interpersonal interactions with others may be disturbing because of the similarity between the current interaction and the person's unconscious disruptive introjects.

Unconscious Content of Introjects—Unconscious Fantasy, Memory, and Perception

According to George Klein (1976), the cognitive activity of an introject is an unconscious fantasy. The term *unconscious fantasy* refers to the activity of internalized relationships that have the status of schemata dissociated from the self. Introjection of a disruptive interpersonal schema results in a schema that replicates the dilemmas, conflicts, and wishes of that relationship. The behavior-inducing activity of an unconscious fantasy is very potent; it has far-reaching effects in structuring the individual's view of reality and influencing his or her interpersonal relations.

Klein views the activity of the unconscious introjected relational mode as an unconscious fantasy, and he, like classical and Kleinian analysts, claims that the dynamic core of defensive functioning is unconscious fantasy. In Chapters 10, 11, 12, and 13, I criticize this incomplete and misleading conception and argue for expanding the concept of unconscious content in all kinds of psychic activity to include unconscious memory and perception as well as fantasy. The concept of unconscious fantasy implies an endogenous kind of wish-fulfilling activity wholly created from sources within the subject. Klein's valid idea about introjected relational modes in defenses replicating actual interpersonal interactions attests to the significance of unconscious enactive memories of actual interpersonal experiences.

Unconscious psychic activity is like conscious fantasy, inasmuch as some (but not all) unconscious dynamisms are initiated and regulated by wishes. According to Freud, the most characteristic unconscious activity is that of wishing, and he stated that the nucleus of the unconscious consists of wishful impulses (1915c, p. 186). This concept does not preclude the possibility of unconscious activities other than wishing, and in Freud's (1920) later writings on the repetition compulsion, he noted that some unconscious activities were "beyond the pleasure principle" and therefore not a form of wishing. The similarity between the wishful-thinking property of conscious fantasy and the wishing property of *some* unconscious activity had led psychoanalysts to the mistaken view that unconscious activity is a kind of fantasy that is not conscious. So-called unconscious fantasy is not equivalent to fantasies that are not conscious (Rubenstein 1976).

Empirical evidence for the enactive memory content of pathological introjects comes from the case histories and reconstructions of childhood object relations of the five patients described earlier. In each case, there was abundant evidence supporting the hypothesis that the patient's pathological introjects developed out of actual preoedipal parent-child interactions. The introject is shaped by the nature of the original parent-child interaction, even though it does not bear a one-to-one correspondence to the original object relation.

Fates of Pathological Introjects and Psychoanalysis

Despite what patients and others wish, pathological introjects cannot be eliminated or exorcized; once formed, psychic structures cannot be dissolved. The recognition and acceptance of these disruptive relational modes are necessary for working through the patient's denials of the psychic existence and power of introjected relations.

Psychoanalytic treatment cannot abolish pathological introjects, but it does provide a new relationship that patients may use to create new and normal introjects needed for the inhibition and regulation of the older, pathological introjects. Interpretations ascribe words to the different parts of the introject (i.e., interaction, affect, representations of self and object) and thus raise the patient's mentation regarding the introject to a higher, secondary-process level. This transformation from predominantly primary-process to secondary-process, verbal thought is associated with improvements in reality testing, judgment, and other higher-level regulatory functions.

Interpretations of introjects and the transference manifestations of introjects do not yield simply insight. Interpretations give the patient the words and psychic tools needed both to alter the defenses against the introject and to devise better means of modifying and regulating introject activity. The gradual uncovering and elucidation of pathological introjects and defenses against them are a process leading to both insight and structural change.

Summary

Five case studies were used to illustrate and discuss the significance in defensive activity of introjects internalized during childhood. Introjects are shaped by actual parent-child interactions, and defenses are constructed and maintained to defend against pathological introjects. An introject is an organized schema with three major parts: a primary-process image of an object, an image of the self in interaction with the object, and an affect. Pathological introjects and the defenses against them play important roles in character development and provide major sources of transference and resistance in psychoanalysis.

Patients may transfer onto their representations of others either the subject (self) pole or the object pole of the introject. Often the return of the denied interaction appears in the defense against the introject; elements of the internalized interactions being defended against are unconsciously expressed in the patient's defensive activity. Psychoanalysis does not abolish pathological introjects, but it does offer new object relations that patients may use to form more normal introjects and identification needed for the inhibition and regulation of older, pathological introjects.

9

Defects, Dyscontrol, and Symptom Formation

The purpose of this chapter is to demonstrate and explain how denial contributes to psychic defects, dyscontrol, and symptom formation. Case studies will be used to illustrate the relationships among denial reactions, defects, and symptom formation. As used here, the term *defect* refers to the results of the failure to symbolize—to put into words—whatever is defended against. One such defect is *dyscontrol*, a term I am using to mark the loss of direct, conscious control over what is denied.

The Constructive, Integrating, and Regulatory Functions of Consciousness

In Chapter 1, I proposed that the cognitive arrest in denial leads to the suspension of the ego's constructive, integrating, and regulatory functions over what is denied and that this suspension, in addition to unconscious dynamics (e.g., the "return of the denied") explains such consequences of denial as the splitting of the ego, developmental defects, and enactive memory.

The classical psychoanalytic view as advanced by Freud (1905) proposes that the only thing that is psychically effective is what is unconscious. Freudian metapsychology has resulted in a devaluation of conscious experience and overlooks or minimizes the dynamisms of consciousness. Much attention in psychoanalysis has been given to the unconscious conflicts expressed in symptoms, but there has been little study of the defects in consciousness that contribute to symptom formation.

To explain the consequences of denial reactions (which, by definition, are states in which the denier is *unconscious* of something), I shall briefly outline the functional values and uses of consciousness.

The recent revolution in psychology has readmitted cognition and consciousness as legitimate areas of scientific investigation. Psychology, like psychoanalysis, until recently has either minimized consciousness or dismissed it as a mere epiphenomenon (G. Klein 1976, Mandler 1975). George Klein (1976) holds that an appropriate role of conscious experience can be restored to psychoanalysis in the context of the contemporary concept of feedback.

According to Klein (1976), the core principle of defense is an unconsciously active idea that is dissociated from a person's self-experience. Defense inhibits comprehension of an enacted idea, but this inhibition does not prevent substitute gratification. It is not *thought* that is unconscious but a *person* who is unconscious of a thought product. In defense, a dynamically unconscious idea is denied the attributes of self-relatedness, and it is excluded from the self as agent, self as object, and self as place. The disavowal of some action means that the impulse in question is never experienced as self-initiated or self-connected. An idea defended against is not exposed to the organizing activity of conscious experiencing. An important aspect of the noncomprehensiveness (or unconsciousness) in defensive actions is its unresponsiveness to feedback influence. A train of thought or orientation that is disavowed is impervious to change by feedback from action. This lack of feedback regulation leads to what I shall later call *dyscontrol*. According to Klein, what is lacking in defensive activity is self-relatedness, ownership, and responsiveness to feedback that would lead to experiencing a disavowed meaning of the behavior.

Fingarette (1969) describes how the self-deceiver's failure to avow and to spell out particular engagements causes important defects in personal integrity. Instead of assuming responsibility for the avowed actions, the denier disclaims responsibility for whatever is denied. In place of an *integration* of what is avowed into the personal self, there is an isolation of whatever is denied. The loss in denial reactions of the feedback regulatory control over thought and overt action brings about what Fingarette called a certain *irrational persistence* in the pursuit of the disavowed actions and what could also be called *repetition compulsion functioning*. (See Chapter 6 for a discussion of repetition compulsion functioning.)

New psychological concepts of the regulatory feedback function of consciousness are consistent with the conclusions of recent neurophysiological investigations (Popper and Eccles 1977, Sperry 1982). According to Sperry (1982), one of the more important results of split-brain investigations is a revised conception of consciousness and its fundamental relation to information processing in the brain. Recent studies show that the mental forces of the conscious mind are restored to the brain of objective science from which they had long been excluded on materialist-behaviorist principles. The key development in these neurophysiological studies is a switch from an earlier, noncausal view of consciousness to a new causal or "interactionist" concept that ascribes to consciousness an integral, causal, and regulatory role in brain function and behavior.

According to Eccles, consciousness integrates and unifies the brain's activities (Popper and Eccles 1977). The self-conscious mind exercises a superior interpretive and regulatory influence on neural events, including feedback control over lower centers. An individual's mind is not just engaged passively in reading out operations of neural events. Eccles describes the biopsychological functions of consciousness as including activities of choice, searching, discovering, and integrating. Consciousness should not be viewed as a passive spectator or a "mind's eye"; rather, it has an active and dynamic function in regulating brain activity and behavior.

Denial or Defect in Object Relations?

The following sections use case vignettes to examine the defects that result from the cognitive arrest in denial reaction; I shall later argue that dyscontrol is the immediate cause of psychiatric symptoms.

The clinical significance of the psychic defects resulting from the cognitive arrest in denial is illustrated by the following account of an analysand who suffered from a narcissistic personality disorder. What follows summarizes a discussion of the analysis in a case seminar. The analyst reported that he had become increasingly frustrated by the patient's unconscious need to ignore him and to "blank out" many of his interventions. Because of his unconscious wish to merge himself with an idealized and omnipotent selfobject, the patient often misinterpreted the analyst's interventions as some kind of directive. For many months he was unable to comprehend the analyst's communications as interpretations, as efforts to help the patient make sense of his experience. The analyst frequently had the impression that the patient had not paid any attention to his verbal interventions.

A debate ensued among the seminar participants, with one group favoring the view that the patient's blanking out the analyst stemmed from a developmental defect in his object relationships and another group hypothesizing that this behavior was the manifestation of denial. Considerable clinical evidence was presented in favor of each of the seemingly different and conflicting ideas about the patient's psychopathology. Actually, both were right. Denial implies defect; stating that the patient was egocentric in many of his relationships and that he defensively denied the interpretive meaning of the analyst's communications was to present two different perspectives on the same phenomenon.

This patient's trait of ignoring others typified many of his object relations from early childhood. In part, this trait represented a defensive identification with his borderline mother, who had ignored many of his needs. The patient's object relations were characterized by what Brodey (1965) calls *externalization*. He unconsciously manipulated others in order that they would comply with his wishes for them, and he ignored communications from others that were discrepant with his wishes.

Ignoring the analyst and others was both a characterological mode of relating to others and a defensive denial in which he shut out of his conscious awareness anything that did not conform to his wishes for an idealized self object. His denial of the analyst's separateness was unconsciously carried out to maintain a self-object merger and to defend himself against anxieties over the sense of separateness. He viewed the analyst as an embodiment of his wishes for an idealized self object, an unconscious projection of his undeveloped superego. Communications from the analyst that differed from his needful preconception of the analyst were denied. Modell (1961) also describes a patient who used denial to avoid separateness from his need-fulfilling object.

The cognitive arrest theory provides a partial explanation of the patient's object relations defect. Clinical data from his analysis supported the conclusion that the denial and the associated defect in his object relations had their origins early in life, probably in the separation-individuation phase of development. Anxieties over achieving psychological separateness from his mother and others led him to use denial. We may reasonably assume that the repeated employment of defensive denial in his relations with others had, from early childhood on, prevented him from representing himself and others as separate persons. The working through of his denial reactions, especially in regard to his self-object transferences to the analyst, was then interrelated with his gradual formation of developmentally higher-level representations of himself and others and with an improved capacity for differentiating self and object representations.

Reconstructive interpretations of his early relations with his mother focused on transference and resistances to transferences. His defensive need to ignore and to blank out the analyst was interpreted as stemming from an unconscious hostile identification with his mother's attitude toward him. By this reversal of role he became the active agent in ignoring others rather than its helpless victim.

The Fallacy of Unconscious Knowledge in Denial Reactions

It would not be accurate to say that the patient denied the analyst's separateness and at the same time had an unconscious knowledge of the analyst's separateness. Clinical findings from his analysis indicated that in important sectors of his object relationships, he had never formed representations of other persons as psychologically separate from himself. Psychoanalytic and psychiatric writings on denial and philosophical works on the related concept of self-deception frequently commit the fallacy of ascribing to the denier an unconscious knowledge of what he or she has denied. Many psychoanalytic formulations of denial, including some made by Freud, are paradoxical insofar as they claim that the denier both knows something and at the same time does not know it. The seminar members who claimed that the analytic patient had an unconscious knowledge of the analyst's separateness made this kind of mistake. The fact that a person denies something does not require that the person has previously defined and represented in words what he or she has denied. Clinical and experimental evidence presented in Chapters 1, 7, and 10 supports the idea that the denying individual has not formed a mental representation of what he has denied. The denier does have, as I explain in Chapters 7 and 10, an unconscious perception of whatever has been denied, and he or she may have a sufficient and rudimentary awareness of some potentially painful object to initiate his or her denial response. But this prereflective and preverbal awareness is not sufficient for the denier to have a full conceptual knowledge of the painful object or his or her relation to it.

As demonstrated in Chapters 1 and 10, perception is arrested after there has been registration and processing by the primary process of the disturbing stimulus object but before there has been formed a conceptual (verbal) conscious awareness of the object. In the case of the patient discussed earlier, the available evidence supports the conclusion that as soon as he registered the fact that the analyst's interventions did not coincide with his self-object transference wishes, he would stop "listening" to the analyst. He "heard" only what he wished to hear, and like the other patients described in Chapter 7, he negatively hallucinated what he did not wish to hear.

In his discussion of several patients who denied the death of their fathers, Freud (1927a) committed the fallacy of ascribing to them an unconscious knowledge of what they had denied. He said that there was only one current of their mental life that had not acknowledged their father's death and that another part of their psyche "took full account" (p. 156) of the parental loss. Findings by Altschul (1968), Dorpat (1972), and others of analytic patients who had denied the death of a parent show that Freud was incorrect when he said that there was an unconscious current of their mental life that "took full account" of the parental death. The patients in these studies were not fully aware of the facts and meanings of the parental death until their denial defense was worked through and there was some significant resolution of their pathological mourning reactions.

A 27-year-old analytic patient whose mother had died when the patient was 15 had denied various meanings of her mother's death. She never spoke of her mother as "dead." After some months of painful working through of the denial, she finally was able to say with appropriate feelings of sadness, "My mother is dead." Her newly acquired capacity to say the word dead in connection with the loss of her mother made a decisive breakthrough in her analysis. For the first time she could begin to affirm and accept the *final irrevocable* quality of the loss of her mother. The cognitive arrest of denial had previously prevented her from understanding, accepting, and verbalizing various meanings of her mother's death, including its irrevocable nature.

Similar findings are reported in the other psychoanalytic studies cited above of patients who had denied various meanings of their parents' death. It was not true that these patients were unconsciously aware of these meanings. The previously denied personal meanings of their parents' death were ones that they gradually and painfully constructed during their analyses. Although these patients did not have an unconscious knowledge of these meanings, they did possess the psychic resources, such as conscious and unconscious memories of their relations with the lost parent, which they could use with the assistance of the analysis to form and accept the new meanings. The analysis of denial defenses, the reconstruction of new meanings about the parental death, and the working through of arrested and unresolved mourning reactions were interrelated.

Denial and Repression

Those who have mistakenly ascribed to the denier an unconscious conceptual knowledge of what he or she has denied have probably confused denial with repression. In the case of repression, the subject does have an unconscious knowledge of what he or she has repressed. One may, for example, for defensive reasons be unable to recall the name of something and still have an unconscious knowledge of the name. The cognitive arrest in denial reactions prevents the subject from fully and accurately symbolizing in words whatever it is that he or she has defensively negated. Denial prevents the formation of secondary-process products, verbal representations. Repression blocks the recovery of these products; that is, the one who represses cannot recall what he or she once consciously knew. (See Chapters 14 and 15 for more discussion of the differences between denial and repression.)

Denial and Defect

As mentioned earlier, the term *defect* refers to the consequences and complications resulting from the denier's failure to symbolize consciously whatever he or she is defending against. Psychoanalytic concepts of defensive activity and the effects of such actions on symptom formation and psychic development have emphasized the unconscious vicissitudes of what happens to whatever is defended against. For example, repressed or disavowed contents may "return" as symptoms or appear in encoded forms in dreams or speech. What has been overlooked are both the short-term and the long-term consequences of the failure to make conscious whatever is defended against. The two factors are of course interrelated, and a comprehensive explanation of defensive activity should take into account both whatever occurs unconsciously with the warded-off content and an assessment of the consequences of the failure to become conscious of something.

Because the unconscious vicissitudes of whatever contents have been defended against are well known, this chapter will focus on the defects that are formed and maintained by the cognitive arrest in denial. It is a clinical commonplace that denial reactions tend to be repetitive: what the individual denies in childhood, he or she continues to deny in adult life. When we speak, then, of the psychic defects associated with denial, we are referring to developmental defects, to the long-term consequences of repeated denial reactions for psychic development and structure. My almost exclusive attention to the causal significance of denial reactions in the formation of psychic defects should not be misunderstood to mean that other factors such as the nature and quality of the child's object relationships, trauma, and developmental fixations do not also play significant contributory roles. In the following section I aim to show how the suspension of self-reflection in denial reactions results in psychic defects.

The Suspension of Self-Reflection in Denial

In denying, the subject arrests his or her cognitive activities concerning something psychically painful at a primary-process, or prereflective, level. A crucial aspect of this arrest is the suspension of self-reflection about whatever is painful; the subject stops reflecting on his or her thoughts and emotions regarding whatever is painful and his or her relation to it. Many of the psychopathological consequences of denial reactions—such as symptoms, acting out, and character malformations—can be explained by the suspension of self-reflection.

In what follows I propose to examine the concept of self-reflection and to review the consequences and complications that arise from the suspension of self-reflection. The word *self-reflection* refers to those psychic processes and actions that persons carry out in making something explicitly conscious. Self-reflection has a meaning similar to what Fingarette (1969) calls "spelling out," to what Rapaport (1951) calls "reflective awareness," and to what Schafer (1968a) describes as the "reflective self-representation."

Self-reflection is the ego function essential to normal consciousness and the regulatory control over unconscious conflicts and processes (Habermas 1971). The normal awake state of consciousness is characterized by self-reflection; that is, by having psychic contents and being capable of awareness of having them. All of the ego functions require self-reflection to operate at a reality-appropriate and secondary-process level. For example, the subject's reflective awareness of personal psychic activity implies, in the case of memory activity, the notation "this is my memory." Without this self-reflective notation, the experience would be hallucinatory.

Self-reflection requires the subject's conscious representation that what he or she is doing is thinking. Reality testing, the capacity for differentiating between thought and reality, also requires self-reflection. The presence of self-reflection distinguishes objective secondary-process ideation from primary-process ideation. It is the hallmark of primary-process ideation to consider what is thought as a reality. In primary-process ideation the subject's self-reflection is suspended or impaired, and there is no recognition that he or she is the thinker of the thought. The essential mechanism of the turning away from reality in primary-process ideation is the suspension of self-reflection. This occurs in such states as denial, dreaming, daydreaming, and the distortions of the neuroses and psychoses.

In daydreaming the subject partially suspends self-reflection pertaining to the act of daydreaming (Schafer 1968a). This suspension permits the daydreamer to treat the daydream as if it were real. The suspension of self-reflection means that the subject has inhibited himself or herself from reflecting on and representing what he or she is doing, for example, daydreaming.

Self-reflection is not a passive, mirrorlike perceptual process. As Freud (1915c) suggested, becoming conscious of something or other is not merely a perceptual process. According to him, the existence of the censorship between the *Pcs.* and *Cs.* indicates that becoming conscious means a hypercathexis, a further advance in the mental organization. In my view, the experiential referent of the word *hypercathexis* is the complex action of self-reflection.

According to Loewald (1978), reflection is a *con-scire*, a knowing together. Self-reflection stems from the internalization of the mirroring interplay originally occurring between the infant and mother. For the infant the mother functions as a living mirror in which the infant gradually begins to recognize, to know himself or herself, by being recognized by the mother. Loewald (1978) held that conscious reflection is needed for the development of the ego, which he defined as the condition of higher organization of psychic processes. Unconscious forms of mentation become integrated into a higher mental organization or organized in a hierarchy of differentiated levels of mentation through conscious reflection.

Becoming fully and explicitly conscious of something requires *avowing* what one is thinking and doing. Avowal is an active process, as is its opposite, disavowal, and avowal is an important aspect of self-reflection. To avow is to define one's personal identity for oneself. Some forms of self-reflection are in their implications a person's clear affirmations of his or her personal identity.

As Fingarette (1969) points out, "In speaking of avowal we are concerned with the acceptance by the person which is constitutive, which is *de jure* in its force, which establishes something *as for him*" (p. 71). The structure of the self may be viewed as a product and synthesis of acts of avowal. Denial aborts this constructive and synthesizing process of self-reflection and leads to psychic deficit states. Failures in synthesis bring about what Freud called splits in the ego.

An important consequence of denial and the suspension of self-reflection is the avoidance of responsibility and the surrender of authority or "ownership" over what is denied. This attention to the moral aspects of self-reflection should not be taken to imply moral condemnation of the denier. The one who denies is not irresponsible; he or she is *aresponsible* (the prefix has the same force as does the *a* in words like *amoral*). Denial is marked by an unconscious rejection of personal responsibility for some action, rather than a conscious shirking of responsibility. The denier does not act in an immoral or irresponsible way but, rather, cuts short the self-reflection regarding his or her actions before even knowing what he or she is doing.

The theory of denial and dyscontrol presented here is similar to Basch's (1981), who explains that the blocking of inner speech by disavowal means the loss of the self-regulatory function of speech over what is disavowed. The disavowal content is not subjected to the corrective action that the feedback system called consciousness initiates.

The denier's failure to avow and to assume responsibility over what he or she has denied leads to the loss of direct, conscious control over what was denied. This dyscontrol is a consequence of denial and one of the defects related to denial. The relationships between denial and dyscontrol are illustrated in the following sections, in which the denials of accident-prone and suicidal patients are investigated. These vignettes will demonstrate how denial and dyscontrol result in acting-out symptoms.

Denial of Danger, Dyscontrol, and Accident Proneness

A previous publication (Dorpat 1978) examined psychological aspects of accidents in three analytic patients and concluded that their denial of danger played a causal role in their repetitive accidents. The three patients typically denied the danger in some dangerous situations and consequently failed to take precautionary steps to protect themselves and prevent accidents. The following case study will show that one patient's denial of danger contributed to dyscontrol and to accidents and that reconstructions of his relations with his father led to insight into his accident proneness.

The patient was a 30-year-old lawyer who came to analysis with complaints of depression and marital conflict. Before age six the patient had had a close relationship with his father. Thereafter, the relationship had become strained, partly because his father, a salesman, was frequently away from home. The patient had two different and discordant sets of representations of his father. One set of images was associated with memories before he was six and depicted his father as strong, masculine, and generous to his sons. The memories after age six were connected with images of his father as weak and depreciated.

The patient had a lifelong history of athletic, vehicular, and other kinds of accidents. His mother had told him that even as a toddler he had had many accidents, such as climbing on furniture and falling. Once he sustained a wrist fracture in a fall from a tree. During the early phases of his analysis he had several automobile accidents. The psychological aspects of all of his accidents were unexplained, and he had the recurring, worrisome thought that he had unconsciously caused his accidents in order to punish himself.

The patient's depressive symptoms were characterized by feelings of fatigue, self-contempt, and a loss of direction and purpose in his life. In the transference situation, depressed episodes occurred during weekend and vacation separations from the analyst. Only when he felt accepted and approved of by an idealized male, such as the analyst, could he maintain a sense of well-being and self-cohesion.

In the twentieth month of the analysis he came to his Monday hour in a state of alarm and anxiety. On the day before he had capsized his sailboat during a race. Soon after the race had started, a storm had developed, and most of the other sailboats dropped out of the race and headed for port. The few remaining boats trimmed their sails in order to avoid capsizing in the turbulent seas. Although he was aware of the storm and the desirability of taking precautionary measures, the patient made no changes in handling his craft. As a result, his sailboat capsized, and he nearly drowned before he was able to right the boat and climb back aboard.

Other participants in the race were puzzled and surprised by his apparent recklessness, and when they met him at the dock, they asked why he had not prevented his sailboat from capsizing. Confronted with his irrational behavior, he had felt deeply ashamed and unable to account for his poor judgment. While talking with them he began to tremble and feel frightened, and this condition continued until he came to his analytic session. To the analyst he emphasized that he had not felt any fear or anxiety until he had talked with the other contestants. The accident, like other accidents in his adult life, occurred in a situation in which the signs of danger were readily apparent to the subject and to others. His failure to slow his sailboat and to trim its sails was not due to either ignorance or a lack of skill.

During the succeeding analytic sessions we were able to discern a pattern to his accidents. All of them were characterized by the following features: (1) the inappropriate absence of conscious fear or alarm at the time of the dangerous situation and at the time of the accident; (2) his failure to take precautionary and self-protective measures to avert the accident; and (3) a state of anxiety, even panic at times, *after* the accident, when he began to acknowledge his peril and how close he had come to injury or death. After many hours of analysis it became clear to the patient that his irrational attitude in dangerous situations stemmed from his unconscious need to deny danger. The patient's insight into his denial of danger came about mainly through the analysis of his idealizing transference.

The Idealizing Transference

Several days after the accident, he reported feeling depressed over his failure to receive an expected promotion. He had just been told by his employer that because of his irritability and provocativeness to other employees, he would not be promoted. This news shocked and disappointed him, because he had assumed that his special relationship with his superior would ensure his success.

Previously the patient had idealized his employer, but now the relationship became full of strife and conflict. He vilified and denigrated the man he had formerly "put on a pedestal." Several days later he related a dream in which a famous attorney was giving a lecture using slides; in the dream the patient operated the slide projector. His associations to the dream were about experiences in which he attempted to ingratiate himself with his superiors by performing menial services for them. With intense emotion he spoke of how he had always felt like the "right-hand man" for some admired person. He told of memories of this "right-hand man" relation with a series of idealized men, beginning with his father, later with an older brother, teachers, military officers, his employers, and the analyst.

The transference elements in the dream were apparent to the patient as he talked of wishing to perform some service for the analyst in order to regain the feeling of safety he had had before the boating accident and his failure to obtain a promotion. In the "right-hand man" relation he felt safe and worthwhile through a silent merger with the strength and protectiveness of an idealized figure. His experience with these idealized persons followed a characteristic pattern. First he would feel secure and free of anxiety through his "right-hand man" relationship. Later, when the idealized object disappointed him, he reacted with anger and feelings of helplessness. Disruptions of the idealizing transferences, such as the analyst's empathic failures and weekend separations, evoked such reactions. In other situations, disappointments in his idealized relationships led to rage reactions, denigration of the formerly idealized object, and dissolution of the relationship.

The gradual working through of his idealizing transference and his denial enabled him to repair the split in his ego and to integrate those aspects of his personality that had formerly been discordant. Over time he learned to evaluate dangerous situations realistically, to experience appropriate fear, and to prevent accidents by taking adequate actions to protect himself.

Kohut (1971) discusses the maintenance of the idealized parent imago within the realm of the ego by means of a vertical split in the ego. The organization of mental processes, motives, and representations connected with the idealized parent imago is kept inaccessible to the influences of the reality ego through the defense of disavowal, which in Kohut's formulation imposes the vertical barrier between the reality ego and the split-off sector.

In this patient and in many other patients with narcissistic personality disorders, the analytic task and process centers on bringing to consciousness the dynamic and developmental roots of their idealizing transferences and in working through the denial created and maintained to keep separate the discordant and unintegrated aspects of their ego splits.

The interpretations that led to the patient's understanding of the psychological causes of his accident proneness were predominantly reconstructions. Both sides of the vertical split were analyzed and interpreted in terms of their transference manifestations. Occasions in which the patient was disappointed or angry with the analyst were used to reconstruct his relations with his disparaged father. Similarly, idealizations of the analyst provided material to reconstruct the early idealized father-son relationship.

These reconstructions facilitated the gradual working through of his denial defense, which was operative in both his "right-hand man" relations and his accidents. The patient learned that his attitude of illusory safety and invulnerability experienced in his idealized relationships was the same attitude he had in dangerous situations just before his numerous accidents. The genetic roots of his denials and his alternate idealizations and denigrations of other men were traced back to traumatic disappointments in his relationship with his father, whom, as I noted earlier, he had at first idealized and later depreciated.

In this patient and in the two other accident-prone patients there was a partial failure in the development of their self-preservative function. Psychoanalytic treatment assisted all three of the patients in completing the development of the self-preservative function. As Frankel (1963) explains, the function of self-preservation develops in the preoedipal and oedipal phases as functioning according to the pleasure principle, then is gradually replaced by the reality principle, and finally the child takes over the self-protective function from his or her parents.

Denial and Dyscontrol

How do we account for the subjects' absence of fear and failure to take self-protective measures in dangerous situations? Clinical evidence and reconstructions of their accidents indicated that they used fantasies of invulnerability to deny that they could be injured or killed. Because they felt invulnerable, they did not take precautions to prevent the accident. A normal reaction to dangerous situations contains the following: the recognition and appraisal of the signs of danger, an affective fear response, and finally the mobilization of adaptive responses designed to minimize the danger and protect the subject.

Unconscious fantasies that some omnipotent self object was taking care of them were used to deny danger and to maintain an illusory sense of safety. Their denial of danger was associated with dyscontrol, and their failure to protect themselves was the immediate psychological cause of their accidents.

Denial, Dyscontrol, and Suicidal Acting Out

This author's previous studies on the subject are among the few investigations concerned with the psychic functions that involve the control or failure to control (dyscontrol) the individual's acting out of suicidal wishes and fantasies (Dorpat 1975). Previous studies on attempted and completed suicide have emphasized the psychodynamics of unconscious suicidal wishes and fantasies. Meerloo (1962), for example, discusses 52 different conscious and unconscious motives for suicide.

Suicide and attempted suicide are acting-out symptoms of unconscious conflicts, and acting out may be considered the nonverbal translation of unconscious conflict (Litman 1970). But unconscious conflicts are present in everyone and are seldom expressed in symptoms or acting out. Most people have at one time or another self-destructive wishes that are not acted out in suicidal behavior (Williams 1957). The important questions about suicide acting out are: "Why do they *do* it?" (not "Why do they *think* it?"); "What are the dynamics and conditions that push the patient from thought to self-destructive actions?"; and "What brings about the failure of the controls that normally inhibit the acting out of suicidal wishes?"

Case Study

The following vignette regarding a borderline suicidal woman illustrates some of the relationships between denial and suicidal dyscontrol. The patient was a 42-year-old married woman with a childlike demeanor that made her appear younger than she really was. A birth injury had left her with a moderate weakness on the left side of her body. In part because of her physical handicap, she was closely attached to and dependent on her mother. One day while stepping off a street corner she and her mother were suddenly struck by an automobile. The mother died. The patient, then over 40 years old, was inconsolable, and she developed severe depressive and phobic symptoms, including the fear of crossing the street alone. Her insomnia was especially distressing. She often told others of her wish to die and her longing for her mother. One year after her mother's death she attempted suicide by ingesting over 20 barbiturate sleeping pills. Her husband, a seaman, unexpectedly returned from a voyage and found her comatose. He took her to the hospital and she survived but remained depressed and suicidal. She told the interviewer that if she found herself on a street with a car bearing down on her, she would not move. Her fondest desire was for death and reunion with her mother "in heaven." She said of her symbiotic tie to her mother, "We were never separated; we were like one person."

As a member of a fundamentalist religion, the patient considered "deliberate" suicide sinful and a sure way of going to hell. Here, then, was her dilemma. Only in death could she rejoin her mother, but to die by a deliberate act of suicide meant eternal damnation and continued separation from her mother in heaven.

Immediately after describing her wish to die and telling the author that she had taken the sleeping pills, she said, "I *can't* think I deliberately did it." Her statement of explicit denial reveals that she was able to make the suicide attempt and still avoid feeling guilty. She could do it because she denied doing it "deliberately." The denial of the intentionality of the act, as shown by her use of the word *can't*, was done to avoid the fear of punishment for attempting suicide.

The patient was aware of suicidal wishes before, during, and after her attempt. The act was planned, intentional, and voluntary. Still, she denied that she had tried to kill herself. The denial was not a conscious lie, for she was a rigidly truthful person. Nor was it a conscious effort to conceal from others the nature of her act. Rather, it was a denial unconsciously determined by her fear of punishment for attempting suicide.

The patient's explicit denial, coupled with defensive isolation, brought about a split in her ego, with part of herself actively seeking to kill herself, while at the same time another part of her denied that she had intended to take her own life. Through denial she had sought to die by means of the sleeping pills and at the same time to avoid eternal punishment and separation from her mother.

She had isolated the wish to commit suicide from the execution of the wish in her suicide attempt. These unconscious defensive maneuvers allowed her to avoid responsibility for her act and relieved her anxiety over being punished for carrying out the suicidal wish. Her statement that she would not move if a car were bearing down on her describes her continuing desire to die passively without responsibility for her own death. The wish to be struck down by a car also expressed her identification with her mother's mode of dying.

In all her behavior her sense of active intention, deliberateness, and planning for the future was markedly impaired. This mode of experience formed the basis of her defensive operations, which meant an externalization of responsibility for the decisions and conduct of her life. Related to this were the prominent qualities of impulsivity and passive-dependence on others, chiefly her mother.

Her extensive denial of suicide intention led to the loss of control over her suicidal impulses. The split in the ego between the part that wishes and plans suicide and the part that denies the intentional nature of the suicidal act is aptly illustrated in Eugene O'Neill's play *Long Day's Journey into Night* (1956). Mary, the depressed and addicted heroine, says, "I hope, sometime without meaning it, I will take an overdosage. I never could do it deliberately. The Blessed Virgin would neer forgive me, then."

Denial of Death in Suicidal Patients

Many individuals who attempt or commit suicide deny some aspect of their self-destructive actions and/or their lethal consequences. Modell (1961) describes a patient who made a serious suicide attempt but who denied any suicide intention or wish to kill himself at the time of the act. The patient

> made a serious but entirely unconscious, suicidal attempt. He overingested sleeping medication, conscious only of a powerful desire to sleep, there was no thought of suicide and it was only upon his subsequent recovery that he recognized with horror the danger of self-destruction which had been denied. (p. 539)

Denial reactions take different forms in different suicidal persons. Some, like Modell's patient and the patient described above, deny that their self-destructive actions were intentionally suicidal. Nearly all suicidal persons deny the meaning of death as a final loss and an irrevocable separation. Rather, they represent death as a continued existence superior to the baneful life they want to leave. For most people, death means the end of life and separation from loved and needed objects. Those who are suicidal reverse these usual meanings of life and death. For them, continued living in this world means death, but dying is a gateway to a better life. The denial of death as the end of life is implicit in their frequent conscious and unconscious suicidal fantasies of rebirth or reunion with lost loved ones. Such wishful and pleasant fantasies are used to disavow the painful meaning and fear of death. Shneidman and Farberow (1957) make a similar observation that suicidal persons think of a continued existence of their experiencing self after their suicidal death. Hendin (1964) warns that the eroticization of death, as exemplified in fantasies of suicide involving a sexual reunion with a lost object, is an ominous sign presaging suicidal dyscontrol. The suicidal person may deny one or more of the following: the meaning of death as loss of life, the fear of death, the guilt over killing oneself, the wish to kill oneself, and the intentionality or the fact of suicidal actions.

In the symbols for death there is an ever-present ambivalence and ambiguity. Death can mean loss, separation, and the end of life. On the other hand, it can have a pleasurable or even erotic meaning when it is equated with a peaceful sleep, immortality, and union with the "good" mother of one's infancy or with lost loved ones. Suicidal persons deny the former meanings of death and cling to its pleasurable meanings.

How do these denials bring about suicidal dyscontrol? Ordinarily a suicidal impulse will elicit danger signals, such as anxiety over dying and death or guilt over the anticipated destructiveness. The ego normally responds to these danger signals by initiating defensive actions, such as repression, in order to control the suicidal impulse itself. Denial acts against the anxiety or other danger signal but does not act against the suicidal impulse itself. Under these conditions, suicidal wishes may enter consciousness and be carried out in action unopposed by defenses or other conscious or unconscious ego controls. Here the ego reacts to the danger signal—for example, the anxiety over death—by an immediate attempt to ignore the anxiety. It is this immediate, initial denial of anxiety or guilt that prevents the ego from instituting controls over the impulse and the execution of the impulse.

The hypothesis that the denial of death and the anxiety over death and dying are powerful causal factors in suicidal dyscontrol is consistent with the results of controlled psychological studies. Lester (1967) finds that suicidal subjects fear death less than nonsuicidal subjects do. Studies by Keith-Spiegal and Spiegal (1967) and Spiegal and Neuringer (1963) demonstrate that individuals just before committing suicide had a reduced level of dysphoric affects. According to these investigators, the diminished dread of death in these patients led to the acting out of their suicidal wishes.

The Self-Protective Function of Painful Affects

Unless they are overwhelming in intensity, painful affects of anxiety, shame, guilt, and helplessness may have a self-preserving and self-protective function. The individual's expectations of certain painful events such as death, injury, or loss of needed objects evoke one or more disturbing affects that then initiate defensive and adaptive maneuvers designed to avoid or minimize the painful event. Freud (1926) first described the mental mechanisms wherein the expectation of danger evoked signal anxiety, which in turn elicited defensive and adaptive operations. His formulation may be generalized to other kinds of painful affects such as guilt and shame (Brenner 1975, Dorpat 1977). The self-preserving function of painful affects is dissolved when the formation of these painful affects is blocked by the denial of actual or threatened danger. This prevents the denying individual from taking effective action to preserve and protect his or her emotional and bodily integrity. As we noted in a previous section, this kind of denial plays a causal role in the pathogenesis of some accidents. The studies reviewed in this section indicate that the denial of painful affects often may also play a critical role in suicidal dyscontrol.

Anxiety, dread, and guilt over the anticipated consequences of suicidal actions on the subject and others serve as powerful controls over the acting out of self-destructive fantasies and impulses. The subject's denial of the consequences of suicidal acting out eliminates these controls and therefore often leads to the acting out of suicidal wishes.

The Dyscontrol Hypothesis of Symptom Formation

Thus far we have seen that the cognitive arrest in denial results in psychic defects, with undeveloped and infantile patterns of psychic functioning. Also, we have examined the role of denial and its consequence, dyscontrol, in the pathogenesis of some accidents and suicide behavior. In this section my aim is to sketch the broad outlines of a hypothesis on dyscontrol as the immediate or proximal cause of psychiatric symptoms, including those of the neuroses, the psychoses, and the organic brain diseases. Though the suspension of self-reflection in denial is, in my opinion, the most common cause of dyscontrol, there are undoubtedly other psychic, interpersonal, and somatic influences that may contribute to dyscontrol. In Chapter 13, interactional aspects of denial and dyscontrol are discussed.

What follows is a summary of the dyscontrol hypothesis: The impairment of higher-level psychic functions compromises their regulatory action and control over lower-level functions, with the consequence that the contents and products of the lower-level functions emerge as symptoms. Or to put it another way: Defective secondary-process functioning brings about the loss of its regulatory control on the primary process and the emergence of primary-process products as symptoms.

Dyscontrol is manifested by impaired functioning of the higher-level psychic functions, for example, rational thinking, reality testing, judgment, and capacity for abstraction. The quality and nature of consciousness are affected by dyscontrol, and dyscontrol is associated with pathological and altered states of consciousness. Although dyscontrol is often linked with symptoms and frequently occurs simultaneously with symptoms, it is possible to distinguish between dyscontrol and symptoms as separable, albeit related phenomena. Dyscontrol precedes symptoms and may occur without them. Subjective indications of dyscontrol include the subject's feeling of being out of control, the subject's sense of loss of self-cohesion, and a variety of other complaints having the common property of the subject's sense of not being in command or control of his or her ego functions.

Psychoanalytic concepts of the derivatives of unconscious conflict help explain the unconscious *meanings* of symptoms, but not the causes of symptoms or how the symptoms are formed. The dyscontrol hypothesis is a causal hypothesis inasmuch as it explains the proximal causes for psychological symptoms. It does not, of course, cover the more distal and predisposing causes of symptom formation.

Some neurological symptoms that stem from disorders of the central nervous system are conceptualized as the products of release phenomena in which lesions of the higher neural centers release their inhibitory control over the functioning of lower centers. Psychological symptoms also may be viewed as a kind of release phenomenon in which the impairment of higher-level functions results in the disinhibition of lower-level functions and the emergence of symptoms.

The dyscontrol hypothesis of symptom formation is congruent with Freud's later theories of defense, the primary and secondary process, and the regulation of the unconscious mind. Freud (1940) held that the unconscious mind is not regulated only by indications of pleasure and pain. Parts of the unconscious ego, including defensive operations, may be regulated by assessments of danger and safety. Unlike regulation by the pleasure principle, this latter regulation is not automatic. It is carried out by the employment of higher mental functions, perceptions, anticipations, and judgments.

In the *Outline*, Freud (1940) shows that unconscious processes are regulated by higher-level mental functions and their appraisals of safety and danger. The constructive function of the ego consists in interpolating between the demand made by an instinct and the action that satisfies it, the activity of thought that calculates the consequences of the proposed action. Secondary-process cognition encompasses what Rapaport (1960) calls a structuralized delay between impulse and overt action.

The dyscontrol hypothesis is consistent with Freud's (1900) concepts of the development and dynamic relationships between the primary and secondary processes. According to him, the primary processes are present from the beginning, whereas the secondary processes develop during the course of life, regulating the primary processes and inhibiting the discharge of excitation. Only in the prime of life do the secondary processes gain complete control over the primary processes.

Psychoanalytic writings on symptom formation have stressed the importance of compromise formations and unconscious conflict. There has been a striking absence of clinical studies or research on the causal role of dyscontrol, of defective ego functioning, and of altered states of consciousness on symptom formation. Fenichel (1941) briefly notes that neurotic phenomena are based on insufficiencies of the control apparatus. Some of the phenomena and processes subsumed under the rubric of dyscontrol have in the past been explained by theories of topographic or ego regression (Gill 1963, Rangell 1959, Schur 1955). In his study on somatization, Schur (1955) stresses the role of ego regression in the emergence of somatic phenomena. He holds the ego regression, specifically the prevalence of the primary process, results in the failure to neutralize aggression and the resomatization of responses. Although ego regression does occur in symptom formation, I think that the theory of ego regression does not account for all of the clinical phenomena as well as does the dyscontrol hypothesis.

The hypothesis that symptom formation is caused by the impairment, developmental failure, or temporary suspension of higher-level mental processes is compatible with theories of psychic functioning of other investigations in diverse fields, which have it that the higher-level structures develop later and regulate the functions of lower-level structures. Under the influence of Darwin, many prominent authors (Goldstein 1939, Jackson 1932, Piaget 1929, Werner 1957) have advocated a developmental hierarchical structure of the psyche.

Although Kohut (1971, 1977) does not use the concept of dyscontrol, his description of the precipitating factors in symptom formation and his attention to the context in which symptoms occur indicate his awareness of the developmental failures associated with dyscontrol. He outlines the emergence of symptoms when the self-object transference is disrupted by weekend separations and the analyst's empathic failures. In Kohut's (1971) discussion of premature ejaculation as it occurs in the narcissistic personality disorders, he holds that the symptom is due to a defect in the psyche's basic, drive-controlling structures. Kohut's (1971, 1977) view of symptoms in the narcissistic personality disorders as being breakdown or disintegration products can validly be extended and generalized to the symptoms of other disorders, even the neuroses.

The dyscontrol hypothesis is supported by Rubinfine's (1973) studies of the role of altered states of consciousness in the psychogenesis of symptoms. He maintains that psychic conflicts alone do not cause psychiatric symptoms. Unconscious conflicts are not ubiquitous; what brings such conflicts to the fore and expressed in symptoms is altered states of consciousness (hereinafter abbreviated as ASC). He provides evidence for the proposition that impairments and defects in consciousness are one of the necessary conditions for symptom formation. My clinical observations are in accord with those of

Rubinfine (1973), who shows the ASC of neurotic patients at the time that they report transient conversion symptoms during their analytic hours.

Rubinfine describes the pathological deployment of attention in hysteric patients as resembling the process of falling asleep or that during the induction phase of hypnosis. His description is reminiscent of what Breuer and Freud (1893–1895) called the "hypnoid state" in hysteric patients. Breuer thought the hypnoid state was a cause and a necessary condition for the hysterias. Freud, after initially agreeing with Breuer on the importance of the hypnoid state as a factor in the production of hysterical symptoms, later rejected the notion in favor of his defense theory. Loewald (1980), however, contends that both repression and the hypnoid state (defined as an early ego state) are essential elements of hysterical mechanisms.

According to Rubinfine (1973), ASC play a decisive role in symptom formation in the neuroses, the psychoses, and organic brain syndromes: "Given a radical disturbance of consciousness due to any cause (toxic or organic states, extreme fatigue, panic, etc.), all of the other ego functions, thought, judgment, memory, reality-testing, and self-observation are disrupted" (p. 392). Instead of investigating the nature of unconscious conflict and taking for granted its effect on consciousness, Rubinfine recommends that we investigate consciousness and explore its effects on conflict. He traces the impairments of consciousness to defects in the development of the ego apparatus. Among the causes of such developmental defects are the psychic effects of trauma in childhood. Both Stein (1965) and Rubinfine (1973) adduce evidence for the hypothesis that psychically caused ASC in adults are replications of childhood ASC induced by trauma.

In a panel discussion reported by Atkins (1970), Stein and Monroe present evidence that ASC play an important causal role in various kinds of acting out. Frosch (1970) writes of the bizarre acting out of psychotic characters during ASC. Stein (1965) studies the relationship between alterations in states of consciousness and a history of specific traumatic experiences such as physical illnesses in early childhood. He argues that severe childhood traumas are connected with a response consisting of a modification of awareness in the direction of dreams and sleep. These childhood modifications of awareness act as a prototype for later changes in ego states that will tend to recur under the impact of stress and trauma.

My emphasis on psychological defects, dyscontrol, and altered states of consciousness should not be construed to imply any downgrading of the importance of unconscious conflict in symptom formation. There has been a tendency in the recent literature to make a false dichotomy between psychopathology based on conflict and psychopathology based on defects and deficits. As I explained on a previous occasion, psychic conflict occurs at all levels of development, and the manifestations of such conflicts may be discerned in the latent content of symptoms in disorders ranging from the neuroses through the psychoses (Dorpat 1976). Patients suffering from disorders of the self have psychic conflicts as well as psychological defects, though their conflicts are at a different developmental level than are the conflicts found in the neuroses. Similarly, psychic defects appear in the neuroses as well as in the more severe disorders. Psychic defects and unconscious conflicts are omnipresent, essential elements of all psychopathology. (For a similar point of view, see Wallerstein 1981.)

Summary

Psychoanalysis and psychology have long ignored the regulatory, constructive, and integrating functions of consciousness of an individual's behavior. Both the short-term and long-term consequences of denial come about because of the suspension or impairment of these functions. The denier's failure to conceptualize what is defended against results in psychic defects, and the suspension of self-reflection in denial is associated with the denier's dyscontrol over what has been denied.

Case vignettes of an accident-prone individual and a suicidal patient were used to illustrate the role of denial and dyscontrol in accidents and suicidal behavior. Dyscontrol is the immediate cause of psychiatric symptoms. The dyscontrol hypothesis of symptom formation is summarized in this way: The impairment of higher-level psychic functions compromises their regulatory action and control over lower-level functions, with the consequence that the contents and products of the lower-level functions emerge as symptoms.

10

Unconscious Perception and Denial

The goal of this chapter is to examine clinical and theoretical studies of the relationships among denial, unconscious perception, and conscious perception. The clinical description of unconscious perception by Searles (1979) and Langs (1975, 1980, 1981, 1982a, 1982b, 1983) is an important discovery with far-reaching implications for psychoanalytic theory and technique.

A review of Searles's and Langs's writings on unconscious perception will be followed by a discussion of a case vignette. Concepts derived from investigations of perceptual defense, negative hallucination, and subliminal perception will be used to construct a psychoanalytic theory of the relationships between denial and unconscious perception that is congruent with contemporary concepts of perceptual processes.

Cognitive psychology investigations reveal two stages of perception, with the first stage being prereflective and preattentive and the second stage including focal attention and conscious awareness of the perceived object (Neisser 1967). A major hypothesis presented in this chapter is that denial arrests the second stage of perception with the result that the denier does not form a conscious percept of the denied object. Because denial does not block the first stage of perception, the denier may continue to perceive unconsciously and to respond unconsciously to those unconscious perceptions.

Clinical Studies of Unconscious Perception— Harold Searles

Searles (1979) was probably the first to describe unconscious perception in the clinical situation. He writes that a patient's unconscious perceptions of her analyst's (Searles) personality, actions, and interventions were woven into her symptoms, especially some of her delusions. Searles emphasizes the extent to which her experienced world, so remarkably delusional, was based on the analyst's reality components—no matter how greatly distorted her experiencing of these by reason of such processes as transference, ego dedifferentiation, and psychotic defenses.

For example, when in one analytic session Searles shifted into conventional psychiatric jargon, the schizophrenic patient responded with, "When you talk like that, I feel as though we've been riding in an airplane together and I've suddenly been dropped into the bottom of the ocean." The patient then confirmed Searles's hunch that she felt that way whenever he talked like a psychiatrist. According to Searles, he had unconsciously used the psychiatric jargon to flee from what he and the patient had been experiencing. The patient had unconsciously perceived his distancing and defensive maneuver and symbolized it in the image of being dropped into the bottom of the ocean.

Langs's Views of Unconscious Perception

Langs (1982a, p. 103) holds that the key to neurosis lies with disruptive unconscious fantasies and perceptions. These perceptions occur unconsciously and are communicated, in turn, in encoded form outside the receiver's awareness. These two unconscious elements (i.e., fantasies and perceptions) are central to the understanding of seemingly irrational and unrealistic symptoms. Langs notes that the role of actual and valid unconscious perceptions of highly disruptive inputs from other individuals in the etiology of emotional disturbances has been neglected. Both unconscious fantasies and perceptions are processes that require derivative communication, disguised expressions that are always present in some form in the manifest content of verbal communications. He defines unconscious perception as "a term used to describe evidence of valid perceptiveness of another person's (an object's) communications and cues of which the subject is unaware" (Langs 1979, p. 557).

Langs (1980, 1981) indicates that the majority of unconscious perceptions have important valid dimensions, although sometimes there are misperceptions. Despite the predominance of irrational mechanisms, derivative communication includes functions that are often highly sensitive and perceptive and in touch with reality. Because of the threat in perceiving traumatic qualities in the therapist, patients often register and express these realizations indirectly and through derivatives. In the clinical examples provided by Langs (1975, 1979, 1980, 1981, 1982a, 1982b), the products of unconscious memories, fantasies, and perceptions are fused. Because unconscious perceptions are processed in accord with the patient's own unconscious conflicts and needs, accurate unconscious perceptions are mixed with distortions and fantasy elements.

Case Vignette

Langs (1982a, pp. 198–215) tells of a patient who reported a dream in which a man was chasing her. The man cornered her in a motel room and wanted to rape her. Langs traces this element of the dream back to the therapist's extension of the patient's previous therapy hour by ten minutes. The dream of being chased and cornered was a valid unconscious perception of one implication of the therapist's error. He had indeed attempted to entrap the patient, even if momentarily and unconsciously. The dream of being chased also symbolized the patient's own involvement in self-punitive rape fantasies that she tended to act out on some level in her daily relationships. The patient's unconscious perceptions may be utilized by the therapist as a means of checking out his or her own contributions to the patient's experience and detecting his or her countertransference-based communications (Langs 1982a, 1982b). Unconscious perceptions are the core of nontransference and noncountertransference functioning and form a vital basis for the nondistorted components of the bipersonal field. Psychotherapists should continually evaluate the unconscious communications from patients for their veridical elements, as this is the only means through which distinctions between transference and nontransference, reality and fantasy, accurate perceptiveness and distortion can be made. Because many analysts have neglected this component of unconscious communication, they have interpreted certain communications and perceptions of the patient as transference distortions when actually they represent accurate unconscious perceptions of the analyst and the analytic interaction.

Case Vignette

The following vignette taken from the supervision of an analytic candidate illustrates the remarkable acuity of unconscious perception. In the session to be discussed, the analysand was troubled about her two-year-old daughter's toilet training. In the previous analytic hours the psychoanalytic frame had been disrupted by the analyst's inappropriate interventions, including changing some analytic hours and making educational and supportive comments. The patient pressed the analyst for answers about how she should "train" her daughter. "Isn't it really hard to teach and train a two-year-old?" she asked. The analyst responded, "Yes, it is very difficult" and then proceeded with a lengthy educational intervention describing the typical struggles of the two-year-old with habit training, autonomy, and the like. In reply, the patient said:

> Well, I wouldn't want to be like some of the mothers
> I hear about. My friend Lorraine told me about one
> mother who would sit on the bathtub while her two-
> year-old child was on the pot. Then the mother would
> wait and read to the child until the child would eliminate.
> My husband told me that analysis wasn't like education
> or like going to school. It's supposed to have more
> to do with a person's inner thoughts and feelings.

What follows is an examination of both the candidate's and the patient's conscious and unconscious communications, in order to detect and analyze derivatives of the patient's unconscious perceptions of the candidate. The patient's first comment (i.e., "Isn't it really hard to teach and train a two-year-old?") probably contains derivatives of the patient's unconscious perceptions of the candidate's previous noninterpretive interventions. Some of the important adaptive contexts for these derivatives were the analyst's educational remarks made in previous sessions and his granting the patient's request for a change in the times of several analytic hours. The patient's term two-year-old could refer to aspects of both the candidate's and the patient's behaviors. The candidate's failure to maintain the boundaries of the analytic frame and his inability to cope with the patient's manipulations were like the actions of a two-year-old child. Contained in the patient's question was a disguised commentary on and confrontation-interpretation of the candidate's antianalytic and uncontrolled interventions and his educational interventions. The "two-year-old" image also probably refers to the patient, whose demands for inappropriate gratification were similar to the behaviors of a two-year-old. The patient's question about training two-year-old children was a test unconsciously designed in such a way that the patient could not lose. If the analyst maintained the frame and responded to the question in an analytic way, the patient would stand to gain by a restoration of the frame and the therapeutic alliance. If, on the other hand, the candidate acceded to her request for an educational reply to her question, then the patient would gain an inappropriate and pathologically symbiotic kind of gratification. Unfortunately, the candidate did not stand the test: he abandoned the psychoanalytic frame by answering the question and proceeding to make another educational intervention regarding the typical conflicts of two-year-old children.

A word of caution is needed before examining the communications of the analysand following the analyst's lengthy educational remarks. Speculative hypotheses about the unconscious meanings of a patient's derivatives should be validated by analyzing further derivatives. This I did with sufficiently numerous similar derivatives to validate the following hypotheses about the unconscious meanings of the patient's comments.

The patient's first comment about the mother who sat on the tub while the child sat on the toilet was derived from unconscious perceptions of the analyst's inappropriate educational intervention. Unconsciously the patient's image of the two-year-old child sitting on the toilet represents herself, and the "educational" mother who sits on the bathtub and reads to her child symbolizes the implications of the candidate's overly solicitous and defensively indulgent educative remarks to the patient. Her second comment (i.e., "analysis wasn't like education or going to school") may also be viewed as a derivative of her unconscious and valid perception of the analyst's failure to maintain a psychoanalytic stance. Almost all of what the patient said after the analyst's answer to her question was derived from her unconscious perceptions and introjections, stimulated by the candidate's countertransference-based educative interventions. There are elements of an unconscious confrontation-interpretation in the patient's remarks. Unconsciously she was communicating to the analyst something like "Stick to your job as an analyst and help me understand my thoughts and feelings. Your educational technique is disruptive and infantilizing."

The patient unconsciously perceived the inappropriate and disruptive nature of the candidate's interventions. Because these realizations would be disturbing to her, she denied their meaning. Another unconscious motive for denying the meanings of her unconscious perceptions was to protect the candidate and to safeguard her relationship with him. She probably unconsciously recognized that the candidate would have become anxious about a revelation of his mistakes. These unconscious perceptions were disguised by the patient's defenses and displaced onto extraanalytic presentations in which the manifest content concerned the training of two-year-old children.

Clinical studies presented earlier in this chapter and in Chapters 11, 12, and 13 support the conclusion that denial of threatening information prevents conscious perception and leads to delayed manifestations of unconscious perceptions in verbal communications, dreams, and symptoms. The same defensive process that inhibits the formation of conscious perception also produces delayed effects on behavior so that the information that is registered but not consciously perceived may appear later in derivative forms in speech, dreams, and symptoms.

An Alternative Hypothesis Involving Repression

What was unconscious: the patient's *perception* of the overly indulgent analyst, or the *repressed memory* of what was once a conscious perception? A skeptical reader could argue, "It was not the perception but the memory of what was once a conscious perception that was unconscious. The patient consciously perceived the errors of the analyst, and then repressed those perceptions. Later, she displaced these unconscious memories of the analyst onto her ideas about the mother sitting on the bathtub and the two-year-old child." This alternative hypothesis is somewhat plausible in instances in which an appreciable amount of time has elapsed between some event and an individual's unconscious communications about the event. In such instances it is probably not possible to rule out this alternative explanation based on Freud's concept of repression and the return of the repressed. However, in the case vignette just presented, the patient's communication about the mother who sat on the bathtub came immediately after the analyst's educative intervention. Therefore, it is highly improbable that the patient ever *consciously* perceived that the candidate was being overly indulgent and infantilizing toward herself, the patient.

Because the patient's perceptions of the analyst's interactions with her had never been conscious, it would not be correct to say that the analyst's percept had been repressed. Rather, the findings from the above vignette and other studies of unconscious perception support the hypothesis that the perceptual process was aborted by the patient's denial. The cognitive arrest in denial prevented the transformation of the primary-process elements of the patient's perception into secondary-process (verbal) conscious perceptions.

Freud's Concepts of the Relationship Between Disavowal and Perception

In his writings on disavowal and the consequences of disavowal (e.g., the splitting of the ego) Freud (1927, 1938a, 1940) erroneously assumed that the denier first forms an accurate and conscious perception and then disavows the normal perception. Freud's view differs from the cognitive arrest theory, which postulates that disavowal prevents a normal, conscious perception of a threatening stimulus object. Freud's belief that the denier first forms a normal, conscious perception followed by a disavowing distortion of the percept was based on his mistaken concept of perception's being identical with consciousness. (This error is also discussed in Chapter 2.) Because of Freud's incorrect idea, he was unaware of unconscious perception. In his view, disavowal brings about a splitting of the ego in which two psychical attitudes are formed: a normal attitude that takes full account of reality and an abnormal, distorted attitude (Freud 1938a, 1940). In some instances (e.g., fetishism) the normal attitude is conscious, and in other instances (e.g., psychoses) the normal attitude is unconscious.

In sum, according to Freud, an individual who is threatened by a conscious perception may defend himself or herself by disavowing the normal perception and substituting a distorted idea for the disavowed normal percept. Finally, either the normal idea or the distorted idea is repressed but remains dynamically active in the unconscious.

Clinical and experimental evidence presented in this and other chapters disputes Freud's idea that the denier first forms a normal, conscious percept and later disavows and distorts the percept. Denial arrests perception of a threatening object and thus prevents the construction of a normal, conscious percept of the denied object. Denial affects the perceptual process *after* the threatening object has been registered but *before* the perceiver constructs a conscious percept of the object. A distorted screen percept fills the gap created by the cognitive arrest. The disavowed contents of the aborted perception remain active in the unconscious and are called *unconscious perception*.

Experimental Studies of Subliminal Perception

Experiments on subliminal perception support the concept of unconscious perception. Fisher (1954) and others stimulated by Fisher's work demonstrated that stimuli exposed tachistoscopically at a speed so great that nothing more than a flicker of light could be consciously perceived would nevertheless register in the brain and affect behavior. For example, when subjects were asked to free associate or to draw whatever came to their minds immediately after such subliminal exposures, aspects of derivatives of the stimulus would frequently appear in their productions. Later Silverman (1967) discovered that if the stimulus had "psychodynamic content" (i.e., content related to unconscious wishes and conflicts) in addition to the content's becoming retrievable, the person's level of psychopathology would be affected. The subliminal input would silently evoke psychodynamic motives congruent with the particular stimulus, and symptoms rooted in those motives would appear or become intensified. Silverman's and his associates' (1967, 1976) studies on the role of subliminal perception in the genesis of symptoms support Langs's (1982a, 1982b) contention that unconscious perceptions may contribute to symptom formation. Further clinical studies on the role of unconscious perception in the formation of symptoms may be found in Chapter 13.

Subliminal Perception and Perceptual Defense

Spence (1967) reports on two perceptual phenomena: subliminal perception and perceptual defense. The first refers to the registration of faint stimuli outside awareness, and the second refers to the nonrecognition of threatening stimuli. He argues persuasively that both are parts of a single continuum and should be studied together. The same process that raises recognition thresholds—perceptual defense—also produces delayed effects on behavior—subliminal effects. Spence's thesis can be rephrased in this way, using the clinical language of psychoanalysis: the same process (i.e., denial) that prevents conscious perception brings about unconscious perception and the delayed effects of unconscious perception.

Unconscious Perception in Hysterical Blindness

In "The Psychoanalytic View of Psychogenic Disturbances of Vision" Freud (1910) indicates that experiments show that patients who are hysterically blind do nevertheless see in some sense, though not in the "full sense."

In the following sections I shall discuss the two kinds of "seeing" described by Freud to explain the differences between the restricted kind of unconscious seeing of hysterically blind patients and normal, conscious perception (or perception in the full sense). The reception and registration of sensory stimuli are not impaired in cases of hysterical blindness. Furthermore, as Freud (1910) noted, visual stimulation of the hysterically blind eye may have certain psychical consequences, such as the formation of affects, even though the patients may not be conscious of the stimuli or their reaction to them. Patients with hysterical blindness do retain unconscious perceptual functions, even though they have defensively inhibited conscious perception. The failure to construct an accurate, verbal representation of the stimulus object in cases of hysterical blindness is similar to what occurs in subjects with negative hallucinations and in the neurological disorder, *visual agnosia*.

The Loss of Verbal Representations in Visual Agnosia

The distinction between a purely sensory awareness of an object and its conceptual identification has been made by neurologists for over a century (Brown 1972, p. 201). Visual agnosia of the associative type (a symptom of damage to specific areas of the brain) is viewed as a kind of "psychic blindness" in which there is a retention of vision with a loss of the signs and symbols through which conceptual identification takes place. When confronted with a physical object such as a cup, patients with visual agnosia are able to make a reasonably accurate drawing of the cup, but they are not able to make a conceptual identification of the object by saying "cup." Often they confabulate incorrect words for the perceived object, and Chapter 16 includes a discussion of agnosia patients' denials. Registration of the visual object is not impaired in visual agnosia, and the defect in that disorder is in the final and linguistic phase of the perceptual process (Brown 1972). The functional defect in visual agnosia is similar to the defect in denial reactions, inasmuch as both fail to complete the last stage of the perceptual process of the conceptual (verbal) identification of the stimulus object.

Contemporary investigators of perception agree that perception is an *active* investigatory activity and not merely the passive reception of information from the outside world or from the body. The object of perception does not come to us as a sensory given; rather, it must be actively sought and constructed through cognitive processes (Brown 1972, p. 8). Perception is the construction of meanings, and these meanings are constructed from the senses' physical input, memories of past experience, and motivations and expectations.

Two Stages of Perception

Between the reception of a sensory stimulus and the subject's conscious awareness of the perceived object, there is a complicated information processing of the received signal. Brown (1972), Neisser (1967), and others have offered convincing evidence for the hypothesis that the flow of information has two consecutive stages.

In the first or preattentive stage, features of the stimulus object are unconsciously detected, analyzed, and registered. This very brief automatic process is followed by a second stage in which the object receives the subject's focal attention. The second stage of perception is linguistic processing and an act of construction in which the perceiver conceptually identifies the object and forms the perceptual object. These sequential stages can be arrested at any subphase; hence, not all information that is processed by the first stage will be processed by the second stage.

The first stage of perception and cognition follows the laws of the primary process and produces an array of crudely defined concrete objects. Then, in waking individuals, the secondary process of conscious—directed thought—selects among these objects and develops them further into conscious perceptions. Rational secondary-process cognition and perception are secondary in the sense that the secondary process works with concrete objects already formed by a primary process.

Negative Hallucination Experiments

Neisser (1967) uses the concept of two stages of perception to explain what happens to the perceptual process in cases of negative hallucination. Under hypnosis, it is possible to induce a negative hallucination in which the subject is told not to see something, such as a chair, which is actually present.

Neisser suggests that the success of such hypnotic suggestions can be understood in light of the processes of focal attention. In the negative hallucination experiments, the subject withdraws his or her attention from the critical part of his or her visual field and excludes the object (e.g., a chair) from focal attention. Because of this the subject does not conceptually identify the object in question, has no detail vision of its parts, and can truthfully say that he or she does not see it. Nevertheless, the preattentive mechanisms (i.e., the mechanisms of the first stage of perception) continue to function, and because of this the subject does not bump into the negatively hallucinated object (e.g., a chair). In other words, subjects in negative hallucination experiments do maintain the capacity for unconscious perception even while inhibiting their conscious perception of some object.

Observations of subjects in perceptual defense experiments, of subjects with negative hallucination, and of patients with hysterical blindness indicate that they have retained the same kinds of unconscious perceptual capabilities as have the patients discussed earlier in this chapter. These clinical and experimental observations lead to the conclusion that these various phenomena (e.g., perceptual defense, hysterical blindness, and negative hallucination) have a common explanation. In all of them, denial has arrested the perceptual process after the first stage of perception.

Denial arrests the second stage of perception, thus preventing the denier from forming a conscious and veridical conceptual identification of the perceived object. Because denial does not block the first stage of perception, the denier may continue to perceive unconsciously and to respond unconsciously to those unconscious perceptions.

The Hierarchical Relationships Between Conscious and Unconscious Perception

The two *stages* of perception just described correspond to the two different *modes* of perception, conscious perception and unconscious perception. Unconscious perception is perception that has not progressed beyond the first stage of perception. These two modes of perception are hierarchically organized, with the unconscious mode coming, both developmentally and microgenetically, before conscious perception. Unconscious perception is automatic, preattentive, and prereflective and follows the laws of the primary process. Conscious perception involves focal attention and self-reflection, and it is formed and regulated by the secondary process.

The failure to become fully conscious of some stimulus object is not always due to the individual's unconscious wish to deny some part of reality. Rather, denial employs the normal inhibitory and screening (stimulus barrier) functions that organisms require to select out of the superabundance of incoming stimuli those items to which they give their focal attention. Out of the innumerable stimuli in our perceptual world we choose to attend to only a few of them in a consciously intentional (focal attention) manner.

In everyday life much of our perceptual activity is preattentive and automatic. Many habitual motor responses—such as walking, driving, and visual tracking—are regulated by unconscious perception. Both the speed and the direction of vehicle driving are ordinarily governed in this way. According to Neisser (1967), this automatic mode of perception uses the preattention mechanisms of the previously described first stage of perception.

Summary

Clinical and experimental studies of unconscious perception, hysterical blindness, negative hallucination, visual agnosia, perceptual defense, and subliminal perception were reviewed and compared in order to devise a theory of the effects of denial on perception.

Unconscious perception is a long-neglected aspect of unconscious psychic activity described first by Searles and later by Langs. Clinical studies of unconscious perception indicate that patients often unconsciously perceive aspects of their therapist's behaviors and represent these perceptions in derivative form. When denial prevents patients from becoming conscious of their perceptions of the analyst, then the percept remains unconscious and emerges in derivative form, frequently through indirect allusions to the analyst but also sometimes in symptoms.

Contemporary studies of perception describe two stages, with the first stage being prereflective and preattentive and the second stage reaching focal attention and conscious awareness of the perceived object. Unconscious perception is perception that has not progressed beyond the first stage of perception. Conscious perception is regulated by the secondary process, and unconscious perception follows the laws of the primary process. Denial arrests the second stage of perception, with the result that the subject does not form a conscious percept of the denied object. Because denial does not block the first stage of perception, the denying subject may continue to perceive unconsciously and to respond unconsciously to those unconscious perceptions.

11

Interactional Perspectives of
Denial and Defense

Psychiatrists and psychoanalysts often speak or write about defense mechanisms as if they were independent mental operations dissociated from the ebb and flow of interpersonal events. This review will show that in fact defense is an important aspect of how individuals communicate with and relate to one another. Until recent times the classical psychoanalytic literature contained few studies of the influence of interpersonal relations on the formation or maintenance of defensive operations. The investigations summarized in this chapter reveal how both the form and the content of a person's denials and defensive functioning are throughout life influenced and even partly shaped by predominantly unconscious interactions with other individuals.

Studies of Denial in Disabled and Seriously Ill Patients

Several investigations of seriously ill and/or disabled patients have revealed that interactional factors profoundly influence patients' denials of their illnesses. Weinstein and Kahn (1955) observe that denial is by no means restricted to the patient and that many relatives, nurses, and physicians showed varying degrees of denial of the hospitalized patients' illness or disability. In nurses, for instance, denial occurred in the forms of ignoring, minimizing, or excusing behavior changes. Weinstein (1980) underscores the importance of interpersonal factors in the denials of brain-damaged persons, and he indicates that the denial syndromes served an adaptation function in dyadic interactions and would not exist if not created or solicited by the hospital situation.

In his study of denial reactions of seriously ill and terminal patients, Weisman (1972) notes that a common threatened danger that evokes denial is a jeopardized relationship with a key person. He (1972) writes, "The distinctive quality of denying and denial is that it occurs only in relation to certain people, not to all, and has the primary purpose of protecting a significant relationship" (pp. 75–76). This explains why patients tend to deny more to certain people than to others. Weisman tells of a patient with an inoperable carcinoma who showed considerable denial of her impending death with various hospital personnel, including physicians, nurses, and social workers. Only with the consulting psychiatrist was the patient able to speak openly and frankly of her illness and death. Many severely ill patients, according to Weisman, have an overriding need to preserve contact and stabilize their relationships with someone essential to their well-being. They deny their illness to these particular persons because an admission of their illness, they assume, would jeopardize their relationship with them.

Weisman (1972) observes that seriously ill patients can venture to speak with individuals who do not have authority over them because with such individuals they do not risk the rupture of a significant relationship. Weisman's conclusion about the role of denial in interpersonal relations is similar to Rubinfine's (1962) formulation that denial in young children is needed to preserve object relations when aggression threatens object loss.

According to Weisman (1972), clinicians tend to ignore the significance of the external observer or participant in making the diagnosis of denial. Equivocation on the part of physicians produces uncertainty in patients, which creates an excess of denial. Patients in the studies by Weisman (1972) and Kübler-Ross (1969) used denial when the doctor or family member expected denial.

Kübler-Ross (1969) investigated the psychological reactions to impending death among 200 hospitalized patients who had terminal illnesses. She notes that doctors who needed denial themselves also found it in their patients. Those physicians who could talk with their patients about their terminal illness created the conditions for their patients also to talk about their concerns about death and dying. The patient's need for denial, she concludes, was in direct proportion to the doctor's need for denial.

Studies by Rothenberg (1961) and Waxenberg (1966) show that physicians commonly facilitate denial in cancer patients by their tendency to discourage such patients' communication about themselves, their illness, and its consequences. They found that many doctors, when dealing with cancer patients, tend to support denial by encouraging social isolation and underestimating their patients' capacities for understanding. Communication under these circumstances is always discouraged, and as a result little information is sought or exchanged.

The above-cited investigators and others who have studied denial reactions in seriously ill and terminally ill patients agree that both the quality and the quantity of such patients' denying are strongly affected by the attitudes and communications of their physicians and other medical personnel. All of these studies emphasize the importance of free and open communication on the part of medical personnel in minimizing pathological denial reactions in patients.

Denial of Parental Suicide

A number of studies of the traumatic effects of parental suicide on the surviving children reveal that the child's denial of the parental suicide is facilitated and supported by similar denials and evasions used by the adult surviving relatives to hide from themselves and others both the facts and the affective significance of the suicide (Cain 1972, Dorpat 1972, Rosen 1955, Wallerstein 1967). Not being able to talk with others about the parental suicide deprives the surviving children of opportunities for appropriate mourning and for testing and comparing the reality of the traumatic events with their fantasy distortions and fabrications about the suicide (Dorpat 1972). Cain (1972) notes that surviving parents, to an extent difficult to imagine, avoid directly communicating with their children about the suicide. Distortions of communication among surviving parents and children are even more profound.

Rosen (1955) describes an analytic patient with severe disturbances in reality testing and derealization symptoms whose ego struggled since childhood to carry out the command of his father (and later his superego) to deny his mother's suicide attempt, which he had witnessed when he was three-and-a-half years old. His father had denied the traumatic episode and had treated any mention of the event by the patient as something he had imagined or a "bad dream." The patient's derealization symptom could be traced back to the trauma of witnessing his mother hanging, and his use of denial was supported and sustained by his father's deceptions and denials of the mother's suicide attempt.

These investigations of suicide survivors revealed that the patients' denial of the parental suicide was a prominent and long-lasting defense associated with arrested mourning reactions and developmental fixations. Clinical studies of these survivors, including the psychoanalysis of some of them, agree on the importance of interactional factors in the formation and sustenance of the patients' denials. The evasions and distorted communications of the surviving parents regarding the parental suicide played a critical role in causing, supporting, and perpetuating the surviving children's denial of the parental suicide.

Theories of Interactional Defenses: Transactional Defense Mechanisms

Räkkölainer and Alanen (1982) propose that defensive processes that cannot be properly understood outside their current interpersonal context should be called "transactional defense mechanisms." The authors comment on the contradiction between the strict intrapsychicity of the basic theory of psychoanalysis and the interactional nature of the psychoanalytic situation itself. They accurately observe that most definitions of defensive functions limit the scope of inquiry to the individual's intrapsychic world. Their paper deals with "transactionality," that is, the intertwining of defensive functions in lasting and intimate—though conflictual—dyads, groups, and families. From the individual point of view, the transactionality defense concept refers to the use of those defensive functions through which the person tries to protect himself or herself against anxiety by drawing on other persons and/or fantasies about them.

The authors describe families who remained in a lasting mutual state of projective identification, a concept that simultaneously conveys the complementary as well as the transactional nature of the phenomenon. This author's studies in Chapters 12 and 13 about the interactional aspects of denial reactions are in accord with their conclusion that some element of transactionality is found in most, if not all, defensive activities.

Transpersonal Defenses

Laing (1967) introduces the term *transpersonal defenses* in a paper entitled "Family and Individual Structure." He notes that the defenses described in psychoanalysis are intrapsychic defenses and pertain to what a person does to his or her own experience. In actual families and in real life generally, people attempt to act on the experiences of other people in order to preserve their own inner worlds. Laing emphasizes the need for a systematic psychoanalytic theory of the nature of transpersonal defenses, wherein one person attempts to regulate the inner world of the other in order to preserve the integrity of his or her own inner world.

According to Muir (1982), the so-called primitive defenses (e.g., denial, splitting, projective identification) are in fact the transpersonal defenses that Laing (1967) speaks about. Because these defenses require the active participation of other individuals for their successful operation, they may also be called shared or group defenses. The studies reviewed in this chapter and the investigations reported in Chapters 12 and 13 agree with Muir's (1982) conclusion that the environment must go along with, if not actually share in, certain defensive processes if these defenses are to be sustained.

Langs's View of Interactional Defenses

Langs (1981, p. 467) criticizes the classical conception of defenses because it has ignored the interactional aspects of defensive functioning. The classical theory of defenses is essentially an intrapsychic conception, with an overriding emphasis on the individual's use of a variety of inner protective mechanisms that are mobilized to defend against instinctual drive wishes. The classical line of thought and its concentration on issues of intrapsychic conflict and unconscious fantasy-memory formations have been challenged by Kleinian analysts and others who have written from an object relations point of view. Writings on object relations present persuasive arguments for a conception of defense that would take into account both intrapsychic and interactional factors and processes. Langs argues for a revised theory of defenses that would recognize the role played by object relations in the development, sustenance, and internalization of defenses. This approach would expand the classical conception of defenses, which is so exclusively intrapsychic at the present time, to include interactional defenses such as projective identification.

Langs (1982b) defines interactional defenses as

> intrapsychic protective mechanisms that are formed through vectors from both patient and therapist. This type of defense may exist in either participant to the therapeutic dyad, and has both intrapsychic and interpersonal (external) sources. (p. 729)

Communicative Modes and Defense

Langs (1978) names three communicative modes and types of bipersonal field (Types A, B, and C) that are related to specific kinds of defensive interactions. The Type A mode, characterized by a predominance of symbolic imagery, communicates the most meaning and is geared toward insight. It is the optimal and constructive mode for both therapist and patient. In the Type A mode, defensive activity can be inferred from the manifest and latent content of the patient's verbal communications. This is not true of Type B and Type C communicative modes, in which the patient's defensive activity is expressed mainly in the communicative mode itself rather than in the content. Defense in the Types B and C modes is expressed much more in *how* the individuals communicate than in *what* is communicated. The Type B communicative mode is one characterized by major efforts at projective identification and action discharge. This mode is basically designed not for insight but instead to facilitate the riddance of unconscious conflicted and unpleasurable contents.

In the Type B field, either the patient or the therapist, or both, extensively employ projective identification and use the other member of the dyad as a container for disruptive projective identifications. Langs's (1976a, 1978, 1979b, 1980, 1981) psychotherapy seminars for psychiatric residents clearly demonstrate that major contributions to the development of a Type B field often come from *both* the therapist and the patient. My supervisory work with psychotherapy trainees and analytic candidates indicates that a Type B field is a common one in both psychiatric and psychoanalytic practice and that often therapists and analysts unconsciously either initiate or sustain this pathologically symbiotic mode of communication and relatedness.

A primitive kind of denial is often operative in the Type C model, in which spoken language is used to erect barriers against the emergence of disturbing affects and ideas. In the Type C mode and field, the essential links between the patient and the therapist are broken, and verbal communications are designed to destroy meaning and relatedness. Communications destroying meaning and relatedness are called "attacks on linking" by Bion (1959a). (See also Chapters 1 and 4 for a discussion of primitive kinds of denial and attacks on linking.) Some of the narcissistic patients described by Kohut (1971, 1977) and Kernberg (1976) communicate by treating the analyst as nonexistent and often evoking intense feelings of boredom and deadness in the listener.

Projective Identification

The most intensely studied kind of explicitly interactional defensive activity is projective identification. It was first described by Melanie Klein (1946), and Grotstein (1981) provides a comprehensive review and discussion of the subject. Langs (1976) holds that projective identification and introjective identification are the primary interactional mechanisms in the bipersonal field. Bion (1959b) views projective identification as the single most important form of interaction between patient and therapist, as well as in groups of all kinds.

Projective identification has been investigated in family relationships, in groups, and in individual and group psychotherapy sessions, and it has been described by diverse investigators with disparate theoretical perspectives. The following include some of the various labels attached to the different variants of a broadly defined concept of projective identification: "merging"

(Boszormenyi-Nagy 1967), "trading of dissociations" (Wynne 1965), "irrational role assignments" (Framo 1970), "symbiotic" (Mahler 1952), "evocation of a proxy" (Wangh 1962), "externalization" (Brodey 1965), "scapegoating" (Vogel and Bell 1960), "actualization of wished-for object relations" (Sandler 1976), and "dumping" (Langs 1982a).

Ogden (1982) sees projective identification as a psychological process that is simultaneously a type of defense, a mode of communication, and a primitive form of object relationship. He has made an important contribution by integrating object relations, defense, and communicative approaches. For him, projective identification is a type of defense in which one can distance oneself from an unwanted or endangered part of the self while in unconscious fantasy keeping that aspect of oneself "alive" in another. As a mode of communication, projective identification is one in which the subject makes himself or herself understood by exerting pressure on another person to experience a set of feelings similar to his or her own. Projective identification is a primitive kind of object relatedness in which the subject experiences the object of the projection as separate enough to serve as a receptacle for parts of the self, but sufficiently undifferentiated to maintain the illusion that one is literally sharing a given feeling with another person.

Sandler (1976) identifies one kind of transference reaction in which the patient unconsciously manipulates the therapist in order to actualize some wished-for relationship. Sandler reinforces the link between transference and countertransference from the standpoint of seeing transference as the patient's attempt to manipulate the analyst into reactions that represent to the patient a concealed repetition of old object relations. Countertransference is viewed as a compromise between the analyst's own tendencies and his or her response to the role that the patient attempts to force upon him or her. The relationship between transference and countertransference is conceptualized as a specific instance of the general phenomenon of *actualization*.

In psychotherapy and in everyday life, individuals attempt to actualize the particular object relationships inherent in their dominant unconscious wishes and fantasies. This striving toward actualization, J. and A. M. Sandler (1978) explain, is part of the wish-fulfilling aspect of all object relationships.

Evocation of a Proxy

Wangh (1962) discusses the manner in which individuals, for unconscious defensive motives, attempt to mobilize in other persons their own forbidden instinctual drive needs and a variety of ego experiences and functions. In these persons, there is an unresolved symbiotic tie to the mother that produces a deficit in the sense of identity and an inability to control their impulses. With them there is a special sensitivity to separation from any object that has served as a narcissistic extension of the self (a self object). The *evocation of a proxy* utilizes the symbiotic mode of relatedness for defensive purposes, in which another person is mobilized to function as an alter ego.

Selected unconscious contents and functions are not only assigned to the partner but also evoked in him or her instead of in oneself. Wangh emphasizes that there is something more than projection here. The subject's aim is to mobilize and activate the object's feelings and reactions, and it is therefore a manipulation by proxy evocation. This evocation has the purpose of preserving a good relationship with a narcissistically cathected object (a self-object). Wangh underscores the importance of both denial and projection in the evocation of a proxy. Individuals use their perception of the activated emotional and instinctual manifestations in the proxy object to deny those impulses and contents in themselves. In an article on Shakespeare's *Othello*, Wangh (1950) underlines the point that Iago needs to rid himself of an intolerable jealousy and succeeds in doing so by arousing the same emotion in Othello.

Anna Freud (1936) describes a form of projection, "altruistic surrender," in which an individual evades the pressures of his superego by participating, through unconscious identification, in the instinctual gratifications of another person. Anna Freud's patient found some proxy in the outside world to serve as a repository for her forbidden, unconscious impulses. Greene (1958, 1959) found such proxy mechanisms in the context of vicarious object functioning. He explicates the need for the existence of the vicariously functioning object and observes that some patients become physically ill when the proxy mechanisms are no longer feasible. In a panel discussion reported by Kanzer (1957), Adelaide Johnson reviews her studies on the pathogenesis of acting out. She notes that ostensibly forbidden impulses in children are unwittingly sanctioned and induced by their parents, who then derive a vicarious gratification of their own unconscious impulses through their children's behaviors.

Projective Identification in the Families of Disturbed Adolescents

Zinner and Shapiro (1972) report on 45 emotionally disturbed adolescents and their families at the Clinical Center of the National Institute of Health. Their observations focus on parental perceptions of and behavior toward their children, and they refer to the parents' acts and statements that communicate to the adolescents the parents' image of them as *delineations*. Among parental delineations are those determined more by their service in behalf of parental defensive needs than by their capacity for appraising the adolescents' actual attributes. Defensive delineations are the expression at an individual level of family group behavior that is determined more by shared unconscious fantasies than by reality considerations. Family group behavior and subjective experience both are determined to varying degrees by shared unconscious fantasies and assumptions. Role allocations for the collusive living out of these unconscious fantasies and assumptions are communicated and evoked in family members by the mechanism of projective identification.

For projective identification to function effectively as a defense, the actual nature of the relationship between the self and its projected part in the object must remain unconscious, although the subject may feel an ill-defined bond or kinship with the recipient of his or her projections (Zinner and Shapiro 1972). The disavowal of the projected part of the self is not so complete that the subject loses the capacity to experience the feelings that the subject has evoked in the object. These vicarious experiences may contain features of punishment, rejection, and deprivation as well as those of gratification.

Denial and Projective Identification

An implicit denial is an essential component of projective identification, and it profoundly affects the subject's self and object representations in the projective identification. What the subject denies as some part of the self he or she projects onto the object. Also, in projective identification the subject most often denies the meaning of any communication or behavior of the object that is not congruent with his or her projections onto the object. A further discussion of the relationship between denial and projective identification may be found following a case study in Chapter 14.

What are the denied parts of the self that are projected in projective identification? Clinical reports in the literature reveal that a wide range of unconscious contents, conflicts, and affects may be denied and then projected. When the object is idealized, the "good" parts of the self are projected, and when the object is denigrated, it "receives," as it were, the "bad" parts of the self. Thus whole objects, part objects, self objects, introjects, conflicts, affects, functioning, ego ideal, superego elements, drive representations, and many other contents have been identified as the projected elements of the personality. Often projection is used as a means of distancing conflicting parts of the self. For example, an individual may marry a person with the ego-dystonic aspects of the individual's unconscious psychic conflicts.

In projective identification the object is perceived and related to as a distanced but not separate part of the self, and any behavior of the object that does not fit the subject's projection is frequently ignored or discounted.

The reality of the object that cannot be used to verify the projection is not consciously perceived, and according to Brodey (1965), the subject has a negative hallucination for whatever it is about the object that is discordant with his or her expectations and wishes.

Stages of Projective Identification

The common threads that have been noted in the various studies may be summarized as three stages of projective identification. Stage 1: The subject perceives the object as if the object contained elements of the subject's self. This is usually explained on the basis of an unconscious fantasy in which the subject projects parts of the self onto an object. Most investigators of projective identification have given too much weight to the causal significance of unconscious fantasy and too little to that of unconscious interactional dynamics. As an interactional process, projective identification is unconsciously activated and sustained by the projector's communicative interactions with others. As I shall argue in a later section, unconscious processes of perception, memory, and introjection, as well as fantasy, often play important roles in projective identification.

Stage 2: Through any one or more of a wide variety of pressures (e.g., manipulation, persuasion, coercion, intimidation, idealization, and so on), the subject elicits or provokes conflicts and affects in the object that conform with the subject's unconscious projection. Through these pressures the subject seeks to control the object's responses and to actualize an unconsciously wished-for kind of symbiotic relationship. These pressures are transmitted by both conscious communications and, more often, unconscious verbal and nonverbal communications.

Stage 3: The object of the projective identification receives the subject's conscious and unconscious communications and responds to their pressures. There is a wide range of both normal and pathological sorts of reactions to projective identification. When the object of a projective identification "contains" (Bion 1967) and "processes" (Langs 1978) the induced thoughts and feelings in a more mature way than did the projector, the recipient's methods of handling the projected thoughts and feelings become available for therapeutic internalization by the projector via introjection and/or identification. If, however, the recipient expels the induced feelings, the projector's introjection of the recipient's rejecting and defensive attitude will lead to augmentation of the projector's pathology.

The individual who receives the projective identification may identify with what has been attributed to him or her. This reaction is called *projective counteridentification* by Grindberg (1962), and depending on how much and how long the individual has identified with what has been projected onto him or her, it could have pathological effects.

Mutual Projective Identification

The object of projective identification may respond by communicating with another projective identification. In so doing, he or she will be participating in what Langs (1978) calls a Type B communicative field and in what may also be called *mutual projective identification*. Relationships in which there is a mutual projective identification enact pathological symbiotic (or self-object) modes of relatedness and communication. In such interactions each party unconsciously colludes with the other in verifying and validating the other's projections.

In mutual projective identification, both parties unconsciously support and sustain the denials and other defensive activity of each other. How do we account for the fact that the object of projective identification may collude in this defensive activity, with the result that the subject's defensive projections become a self-fulfilling prophecy? There is a consensus in the literature that one of the most powerful unconscious motives for sustaining these shared denial systems and symbiotic patterns of relatedness is the participants' anxieties and fears over object loss.

Brodey (1965) notes that the terror of abandonment perpetuates these kinds of relationships. Adolescents studied by Zinner and Shapiro (1972) feared that object loss would ensue if they did not verify their parents' defensive projections. These adolescents were afraid not to collude, not to comply, and not to identify with what their parents had projected onto them. Räkkölainer and Alanen (1982) found that the primary target of trans-actional defense mechanisms was separation anxiety. According to Wangh (1962), separation from objects experienced as part of the self was an important factor in both initiating and maintaining relationships based on the "evocation of a proxy."

Unconscious Communications and Processes in Mutual Projective Identification

As I noted earlier, most investigators on this subject give exclusive attention to the importance of unconscious fantasy, and they conceptualize projective identification as the enactment of an unconscious fantasy. Their view excludes the crucial role of unconscious perception, unconscious memory, and unconscious introjection. As it is commonly used, the concept of unconscious fantasy implies that the origins of the fantasy are wholly endogenous and isolated from the subject's current interactions with others. This exclusive focus on unconscious fantasy excludes the powerful effects and meanings of the subject's conscious and unconscious communication with other individuals in both the formation and the maintenance of projective identification.

In interactions marked by mutual projective identification, there exist complementary modes of communicating in which the subject's mode of communicating evokes a complementary communication in the object. Compliant communications, for example, tend to elicit directive communications from the object. Similarly, in other interpersonal situations, masochistic and passive-dependent modes are apt to evoke, respectively, sadistic and active-independent modes of response.

In pathological symbiotic relations, such complementary modes are used not only for their defensive and adaptive function but also for the sense of wholeness and integrity they offer to both partners of the relationship. According to the dictionary, the word *complementary* means "to make whole or perfect."

In order to demonstrate the significance of unconscious communications and processes in mutual projective identification, I shall present a schematized and sequential account of the interactional dynamics in a sadomasochistic type of interaction. For the purposes of this exposition the terms *sadistic* and *masochistic* are used in a general sense to refer to a variety of related behaviors, affects, and ideas. Though this outline is about a hypothetical interaction, it is derived and abstracted from my psychoanalytic and supervisory experience, and it is consistent with reports in the literature on mutual projective identification.

What follows is a schematic and condensed outline of the important and typical interactions in the sadomasochistic type of mutual projective identification. The sadist unconsciously denies the masochistic part of himself or herself, projects the rejected part onto an object (hereinafter called the *masochist*), and by means of his or her sadistic mode of communicating manipulates the masochist to behave masochistically. Then the masochist introjects what has been projected onto him or her and acts out the masochistic role (e.g., behaves or communicates in a weak, demeaned, submissive, or punished manner). At the same time, the masochist denies the sadistic part of himself or herself, projects it onto the representation of the object, and by the masochistic mode of communicating provokes the sadist to behave sadistically. By responding sadistically, the sadist completes and renews the vicious cycle of spiraling communication in mutual projective identification in which the communication of each party acts as a signal and a provocation for the complementary behavior of the other party.

Now we are in a position to outline the role of unconscious processes of perception, introjection, memory, and fantasy in the masochist's unconscious motives for projective identification. One motive is defensive: by behaving masochistically the masochist can deny his or her sadism and attempt to actualize the wish to be rid of sadistic feelings by projecting the sadism onto the sadist. Other important unconscious motives are associated with the introjection of the sadist's projected masochism and the unconscious perceptions of the sadist's communications. He or she may for various reasons feel compelled to comply with the masochistic role ascribed to him or her, to introject and to identify with what has been projected onto him or her, and to gratify the sadist by behaving masochistically. The masochist's interactions with the sadist may activate the masochist's unconscious childhood memories that are then acted out in his or her masochistic behavior.

The masochist may unconsciously perceive, for example, that the sadist is attempting to intimidate and control him or her. By behaving masochistically, the masochist also attempts to control and shape the sadist's actions. Often the masochist unconsciously perceives the sadist's underlying vulnerability and defensiveness, and by behaving masochistically, he may be attempting unconsciously to support the sadist's denial and projection by acting out in his or her own behavior the rejected vulnerable part of the sadist's personality.

An additional powerful unconscious motive for the projective identifications of both participants is their wish to maintain the relationship and to avoid a rupture in their symbiotic bond. They unconsciously seek to carry out these aims by unconsciously supporting the defenses of the other. For example, by behaving masochistically, the masochist verifies and confirms the sadist's denial and projection. The foregoing are only a few of the many possible unconscious motives for projective identification that are triggered and energized by the subject's communicative interactions with another individual.

To sum up: in mutual projective identification, unconscious wishful fantasies are only one aspect of a complex matrix of unconscious aims associated with the subject's unconscious introjection of what has been projected onto him or her, with unconscious perceptions of the object, and with the activation of unconscious memories. These unconscious processes (i.e., projection, perception, memory, fantasy, and introjection) are strongly affected by the individual's conscious and unconscious communications with others. Unconscious wishes for maintaining symbiotic bonds, for supporting the defenses in the object that safeguard these bonds, are often potent underlying motives for both initiating and sustaining states of mutual projective identification.

Shared Denial

In the hypothetical sadomasochistic interaction just described, *both* the masochist and the sadist deny aspects of the masochist's unconscious sadism and the sadist's unconscious masochism. Through their unconscious communications, each of the parties reinforces and contributes to the denials of the other party.

Both parties to mutual projective identification unconsciously participate in denying important aspects of their interactions, and they unconsciously support each other's defensive oeprations. For mutual projective identification to function effectively for both individuals, the actual nature of their communicative interaction must remain unconscious. An unconsciously collusive or shared denial is an integral element in mutual projective identification. Through the shared denial, both parties can disavow the dystonic aspects of their own unconscious conflicts and project them onto the other party. Their shared denial is the binding force that protects their symbiotic mode of relating and gives both individuals a sense of illusory wholeness and freedom from anxieties over separation and object loss.

Although it is a common phenomenon, there are few reports in the literature on shared denial. The *folie à deux* syndrome is based on a shared denial of psychotic proportions in which a more disturbed and psychotic individual induces a less disturbed person to join him or her in believing some delusion. Silverblatt (1981) reports six cases of denial of pregnancy in which there was an unconscious collusion with the patient by others, including physicians, to deny any awareness of the pregnancy. In a previous publication, I wrote about the relatives and physician of a young suicidal woman who unconsciously joined her in denying the seriousness and lethal meanings of her suicidal behaviors (Dorpat 1974). Their shared denial kept them from taking the kinds of preventive and therapeutic actions that might have prevented her eventual suicide.

Concluding Remarks

An individual's defensive functioning is influenced by many causes, including the status of one's ego and superego development, unconscious conflicts, and the psychic consequences of trauma and developmental deficits. The psychoanalytic literature has emphasized preexisting structural and developmental elements, but until recently it has paid scant attention to adaptive and interactional processes that affect how a person defends himself or herself, why he or she defends, and what he or she defends.

The different investigators agree that anxiety over object loss, broadly defined, is the most important and powerful of the motives for denying in interpersonal situations. Under the category of anxiety over object loss, I would include the following specific unpleasurable contents: separation anxiety, separation guilt, fear of rejection, fear of abandonment, and anxieties over loss of love and narcissistic supplies. In short, individuals in interpersonal situations will deny something in order to maintain their relationship with the other person and to avoid disrupting their relationship.

How people deny and what they deny is strongly influenced by the conscious and, more significantly, the unconscious communications of others. In the studies of seriously ill and disabled hospitalized patients there was abundant evidence that the patients' denials of death and disability were profoundly affected by how the hospital staff communicated with them. The patients' denials were sharply reduced when staff members invited and participated in open, free communication. All of the studies reviewed of a child's denial reactions to the suicidal death of a parent revealed that these denials were shaped and maintained by the evasions, denials, and lack of open communication with the surviving adult relatives.

The behavior and communications of groups of all kinds, including family groups and the therapist-patient dyad, are determined to varying degrees by shared unconscious fantasies and unconscious assumptions. Role allocations for the collusive enactment of these unconscious fantasies are communicated and evoked by the mechanism of projective identification. In such groups, individuals often unconsciously collude with one another in establishing and maintaining their mutual projective identifications. In mutual projective identification there is a shared denial concerning the actualities of their interaction, and each participant's communications validate and verify the other's projections. The important unconscious processes in mutual projective identification are those of projection, introjection, memory, perception, and fantasy.

Defensive operations affect the mode of communication as well as the content. Denial may be an aspect of *what* one communicates and *how* one communicates. In the Type B and C communicative modes, denial occurs in how one communicates. Projection of a denied part of the self is the central feature of projective identification and the Type B mode, and a primitive kind of denial of meaning and relatedness is an essential element of the Type C mode.

Several studies reviewed earlier testify to the inadequacy of the classical concept of defenses as isolated events occurring in a closed "intrapsychic" system. These investigators recommend establishing a revised theory that would conceptualize defensive operations as an aspect of how individuals relate and communicate with one another, a comprehensive theory that would account for the role of unconscious communications in initiating and sustaining defensive actions in individuals, dyads, and groups. Some analysts propose a special class of defenses for the individual's interactions with others, and they label this category "transpersonal" (Laing 1967), "interactional" (Langs 1982b), and "transactional" (Räkkölainen and Alanen 1982). Though I agree with the criticisms made by the above authors about the lack of attention to the interactional aspects of defenses in the psychoanalytic literature, I do not agree with their proposals for establishing two different categories of defensive activity, with one category concerning the intrapsychic or inner world and the other concerning the outer or interpersonal world.

As I argued in a previous paper, there is a fallacy in the concept of a dichotomy of "intrapsychic or intrapersonal (or interactional)" (Dorpat 1981). The word *intrapsychic* is a spatial metaphor that is commonly and incorrectly interpreted in a lateral sense to mean inside the psyche or mind. Using the word in this way, the subject commits the error of reification, because he or she speaks of the mind as if it were a space. It does not make sense to speak of defenses or any other kind of human activity as taking place in two different worlds, an inner or intrapsychic world and an external physical or interpersonal world. Only in fantasy and not in actuality do humans exist in two worlds.

This is not to say that individuals defend themselves only in interpersonal situations, as one may defend in one's thinking and imagination. Denial and defense are just as much a part of how individuals communicate with and relate to one another as it is an aspect of how and what they think to themselves. A valid and meaningful distinction can be made between carrying out defensive activity *privately* and defending oneself *publicly* in one's transactions with others. The word *private*, as Schafer (1976, p. 160) usefully explains, is not just another word for *inner*, because it expresses an entirely different way of conceptualizing psychic actions.

Even those defenses carried out privately do contain conscious or unconscious fantasies and memories of a person's feared or wished-for relationships with objects. Also, as I explained in Chapter 8, defensive activity is developed from the individual's relations with others. What is internalized and ultimately transformed into defenses and other psychic structures is interactions with objects (Loewald 1970). Therefore, an object relations element is essential to all defensive activity, whether that defensive activity is carried out privately in one's thinking and imagination or publicly in one's interactions with others. There is no need for a new and different category for interactional, transactional, or transpersonal defenses. What is needed is an expanded awareness of the interactional aspects of defensive activity and clinical research and developmental studies of the role of object relations in the development, maintenance, and internalization of defenses.

It is not possible to describe or explain completely an individual's defensive actions without taking into account interactional dynamics, the mainly unconscious ways in which persons influence and contribute to both the conscious experience and the unconscious psychic functioning of other persons. The interactional point of view should be part of any systematic theory of defense. The studies reviewed in this chapter demonstrate that why people defend, how they defend, and what they defend are strongly influenced by their communicative interactions with other individuals.

12

Shared Denial in
the Psychoanalytic Situation

Studies of the interactional aspects of denial and defense reviewed in the previous chapter were derived from a variety of sources, including family and group therapy, individual psychotherapy, and observations of hospitalized medical patients. To the best of my knowledge, there are no reports on the interactional aspects of defensive operations in the analytic situation. In this chapter, the interactional aspects of denial reactions in a psychoanalytic situation are investigated by means of a systematic examination of all of the process notes of an analysis recorded by Dewald (1972).

The communicative method used in this investigation is adapted from the one developed by Langs (1981, 1982b), and it is the systematic study of the communications, functions, and meanings of analyst-analysand interactions. Each intervention by the analyst was taken as an adaptive context, and the patient's responses to it were analyzed in terms of derivatives and as conscious and unconscious communications. This is the method that analysts use in forming and testing hypotheses about the conscious and unconscious meanings of their patients' communications.

The analyst's interventions evoke unconscious as well as conscious perceptions and responses in the patient, and the parts of the analyst's communication that are processed unconsciously lead to the formation of unconscious perceptions, introjects, and fantasies. The patient's communications are "derived" from these unconscious contents, and so they are called *derivatives*. Derivatives are the products of the ego's defensive and adaptive revisions of unconscious contents, and verbal derivatives can be analyzed in much the same way as symptoms and dreams can.

Dewald wrote virtually verbatim process notes of the analytic process as it occurred during alternate months of his two-year analysis of a patient. He also includes discussions and critiques of the individual sessions and a general theoretical discussion of the psychoanalytic process. Dewald's book is perhaps the most comprehensive record of an analysis, and it provides a unique opportunity for testing different hypotheses regarding the psychoanalytic process and technique.

A systematic study of the process notes of the analysis showed that the analyst denied certain directive and controlling interventions. In this study I shall describe the unconscious ways in which the analyst induced the patient also to deny the meaning of the analyst's controlling communications and their effects on the patient. Clinical evidence will be provided by demonstrating the nature and content of the unconscious communications related to the denied interaction. In short, I aim to show how the analyst and the patient developed a shared denial of particular interactions.

Because it would take several volumes to cover the entire book, I shall limit most of my report to an examination of the first four sessions. The data from these four sessions affords sufficient empirical evidence to support the hypotheses being presented. The basic pattern of their shared denial had its beginnings in the first hour and endured throughout the entire analysis.

The patient was a 26-year-old married, white housewife with two children. The diagnosis made before the analysis was "mixed psychoneurosis with phobic, conversion, and depressive symptoms and free-floating anxiety" (p. 15).

Session 1

The analysis began with the patient's question, "What will I do if I'm pregnant?" In response, the analyst told the patient of the need "to try to understand what's behind the question and see if it has other meanings than the question itself." After the initial transaction in which the analyst replied to the patient's question, there followed a series of interactions in which the analyst responded to the patient's communications by questions such as "What comes to your mind?" and "What's the detail?" Although questions of this type made up the majority of his interventions, he sometimes used suggestions, confrontations, and other interventions in order to pressure the patient into talking and free associating. For example, his fourth intervention in Session 1 was "Rather than jump to conclusions as to whether or not there is a reason, let's just look and see what comes to your mind." Several interventions in the initial hours were attempts to educate her on how to free associate and associate to dreams. Throughout Session 1 the analyst maintained his active role of questioning and exerting pressures on the patient to talk and free associate. As he indicates in his discussion of this hour, his explicit policy was to interrupt the patient's silences with questions in order to get her to speak.

Early in this session the patient explained that she was frightened about her feelings toward the analyst and that she hoped she "had found someone who cared and that somehow I would get a relationship here even though I know that that's ridiculous and I'm just a patient." After a minute's pause, Dewald intervened with another directive: "Try to pursue what comes to your mind about this." Then the patient was silent for two minutes before she said, "I have the feeling that you'll be mad at me if I don't say something, and so I just can't say anything. But the longer the silence lasts the worse it gets." This is the first of many communications in which the patient described her reaction to the pressures brought to bear on her by the analyst. The majority of her communications about the analyst's pressures were unconscious, although sometimes in the early sessions, as in this example, she made explicit and conscious reference to the analyst's directiveness.

After the patient told about her fear that the analyst would "be mad" at her if she didn't say something, the analyst asked her, "What comes to your mind about the idea that I would be mad at you?" The patient replied, "I think of the way Mr. Harris [her former therapist] used to react if I didn't say anything. It also makes me think of my father and the way he would say "jump" and I'd have to jump or else he would call me stupid." The patient's association to the analyst's question vividly described the dilemma she faced in her interactions with the analyst. She intensely disliked being pressured by the analyst, but if she did not do what he wanted, she would risk being criticized.

Her statements about Mr. Harris and her father were disguised commentaries on the analyst's need to direct and to control the patient's thinking and speaking. The patient's reference to the way her father would say "jump" to her or call her "stupid" unconsciously refers to pressures placed on her by the analyst and to his critical remark, "Let's not jump to conclusions. . . ." Her remarks about her father and Mr. Harris can also be viewed as derivatives of unconscious perceptions of the analyst and of introjections of his demeaning attitudes toward her. Her responses strongly suggest that she unconsciously perceived and reacted to his need to control her communications.

Undoubtedly there were significant unconscious transference elements to her responses, but the most relevant meanings for the purposes of this study were the veridical aspects of the patient's indirect references and allusions to the analyst's efforts to control her through questions and other interventions.

Her anxious and repeated comments about feeling controlled can also be understood as unconsciously motivated to rectify the situation and the relationship, to induce the analyst to ease off, and to relinquish his need to control her. Her unconscious need to remedy the situation and her frustration about what has transpired thus far in this hour are unconsciously expressed in the following remarks that, on the manifest level, are about her history of dating men. She said, "I would immediately start with someone new but it always made me so tired. Every time I grasp hold of somebody he slips away from me." Her statement, "he slips away from me," is probably a derivative of her unconscious perception of Dewald's denial of his controlling and directive actions toward her.

The analyst continued to question and to pressure her to speak. Toward the end of the hour the patient became more frightened and submissive, and said, "I'm completely placing myself in your hands. . . . I feel as if I'm in a vise and that I'm caught. . . . I'm so easily suggested to. . . . I just have no mind of my own."

Evidences of the Analyst's Denial

Evidences that the analyst denied the controlling quality of many of his interventions come not only from his process notes but also from his discussions of the individual sessions. At no time in Session 1 or in the discussion of Session 1 does the analyst acknowledge that he had been directive with the patient.

The process notes of each session are followed by a one- or two-page discussion of the session. These discussions indicate that Dewald was unaware of the controlling quality of his interventions and their effects on the patient. The realistic or valid nontransference aspects of her reactions to him and to his questions are not mentioned, and he tends to ascribe her reactions to "transference." In his discussion of Session 1 he gives the following reason for his interventions:

> Because she is anxious over the prospect of beginning the analysis,
> I chose not to permit any lengthy silences. The same is true in
> regard to my requests for detail, and for further information, as
> well as my statement regarding jumping to conclusions.

He indicates in his discussion of Session 2 that his requests for the details of information and of feelings were to help the patient learn how to work in an analysis, and in the discussion of Session 3, he notes that many of his interventions, such as his questions, were ways he used to get the patient to follow the analytic rule.

The Technique of Questioning

Throughout this first session and for the remainder of the analysis, the analyst maintained a steady pressure on the patient by his repetitive questioning. In Session 1, 13 out of 18 interventions were questions. As the process notes for Session 1 demonstrate, the analyst's questions had a directive and controlling quality. Although the analyst's conscious intention in asking questions was the laudable one of opening up free association and therapeutic communication, there is abundant evidence from this study and from previous investigations by Dorpat (1984) and Langs (1976a, 1978, 1979a, 1979b, 1980) that questioning tends to shift communication away from derivative communication toward communication that is matter-of-fact and superficial. Questions often are used to create or maintain pathological symbiotic relations and interactions in which the analyst carries out a directive position in relation to the analysand.

In order to determine the relative frequency of questions compared with other kinds of interventions used in this case, I counted all interventions and all questions in 30 analytic sessions. All interventions except the opening greeting and the ending statement ("We'll stop here for today") were counted for the first ten sessions, for ten sessions taken from the middle of the analysis, and from the final ten sessions of the analysis. Two hundred and sixty (or 70.5 percent) of the 369 interventions made in these 30 sessions were questions. The average number of interventions per session for the entire 30 sessions studied was 12.3, and the average number of questions asked per session was 8.7. The total number of interventions dropped from 198 in the first ten sessions to 132 interventions in the middle ten sessions and to 39 interventions in the last ten sessions. The percentage of interventions that were questions was 76.3 percent in the beginning ten sessions, 63.7 percent in the middle ten sessions, and 64.1 percent in the final ten sessions. These data show that the analyst's most frequent kind of intervention was questions and that the ratio of questions to the total number of all interventions remained fairly stable throughout the analysis.

Session 2

The analyst maintained his pressure on the patient to free associate and to speak, and 17 of the analyst's interventions in Session 2 were directive questions. Her communications in the early part of this session make sense and pertain to what was probably the most important adaptive context—the analyst's directive comments and questions in the previous session. A major manifest theme in the first part of the hour was that of feeling helpless and dependent on her parents. She spoke of feeling "as if I'm tied to them with strings." Her statement may be viewed as an allusion to what was going on in the analysis: she felt tied to the analyst with strings.

> She described her anger toward her mother, saying,
> I feel like killing her sometimes . . . but I do blame all
> of my problems on my mother. I wonder why. I think it
> has something to do with my father because she caused
> him to do what he did and so it all hurt me.

According to the traumas she had suffered in her relationships with her parents (revealed in later sections of this book), the above statement of the patient's was a partially correct, though distorted and incomplete, interpretation of her emotional difficulties and their history. Therefore, it is difficult to understand and find a rational reason for the analyst's need to interrupt and interfere with her attempts to understand herself with his admonition that the patient should not jump to conclusions.

Analyst: Let's not jump to conclusions about why you feel that way. What are your associations to the thought of her causing him to do the things he did?

Patient: Somehow I feel as if my father's fate was inevitable. (Elaborates.) She kept him a child. I don't blame my father for his affairs. He couldn't help it. But I do blame my mother for her problems. She's been thirty years trying to get my father under her thumb.

Analyst: What's the detail?

Patient: If she says, "jump," he does. He's not having any more affairs now. She mammas him in order to control him. (Elaborates.) He's not even a man anymore – – –*. It would be much better for me now to run away from them and have no communication with them. Why do I hate my mother? – – –

Analyst: Let's go back to your fear of exploding if you ever let go of your feelings. What comes to your mind?

Patient: My hands feel paralyzed right now. I wonder if I want to kill her? I know that I do want to get back at her. I'd like to stand and scream. I did once, but she just sat there and looked at me. Something is holding me back.

The patient's statement, "Somehow I feel as if my father's fate was inevitable" is a derivative that describes her unconscious reactions to the analyst's directiveness. She unconsciously perceives that the analyst is trying to get her under his "thumb." Her unconscious responses to the analyst's controlling interventions are displaced onto memories of power conflicts between her parents.

In our discussion of Session 1 we observed that the patient unconsciously responded with pain and indignation to the analyst's critical remarks about her jumping to conclusions. A similar interactional sequence is repeated in this second hour when the analyst again chides her about jumping to conclusions. She has unconsciously introjected the analyst's deprecatory remarks about her and displaced these ideas onto the relationship between her parents. Clearly, the patient's description of the sadomasochistic relationship between her parents unconsciously describes the controlling aspect of the analyst's unconscious communications to her. Her father unconsciously represents herself and her mother

*Each dash (–) represents a 30-second period of silence.

represents the analyst, whose unconscious communications are controlling and demeaning.

After stating that her mother controlled her father and that she would be better off if she had run away from them, she asked, "Why do I hate my mother?" The analyst responded, "Let's go back to your fear of exploding if you ever let go of your feelings. What comes to your mind?" To this question she replied, "My hands feel paralyzed right now." She went on in an anguished way, ventilating her anger toward her mother. The analyst's response—"Let's go back to your fear of exploding"—was even more disruptive and directive than many of his other interventions. At the very moment that the patient was telling him about her rage at her mother (and unconsciously at the analyst) for the mother's contemptuous attitude toward the father and toward herself, he interrupted by asking her to go back and discuss issues she had talked about earlier in the hour.

The analyst's interventions functioned as a projective identification, an unconscious effort to project his conflicts onto the patient. In projective identification the subject unconsciously attempts to manipulate another person so that the other person will experience the kinds of affects and conflicts that the subject has denied having within himself or herself. The specific kind of manipulation the analyst used was to interrupt the patient's flow of associations by asking her to go back and talk about an earlier theme, her fear of exploding. His abrupt changing of the subject at the time that she was already emotionally distraught was disruptive to her psychic disequilibrium, and it contributed to the patient's dyscontrol and symptom formation. The unexpected switching from one conversational topic to another in analysis or in everyday life can have a significantly disintegrating effect on the other person's psychological functioning.

Contradictory Communications in Questions

Dewald's intervention, "Let's go back to your fear. . . . What comes to your mind?" was probably based on his defensive need to deflect the patient from expressing her anger. It is likely that he unconsciously perceived that she was talking about him as well as about her mother. Questions, like other interventions, always carry unconscious meaning and messages in addition to the manifest content (Dorpat 1984). Often the unconscious communication contradicts the consciously intended communication. The analyst's conscious message in the above intervention (i.e., "What comes to your mind?") is contradicted by the unconscious communication, "Don't express your rage, because I can't tolerate it."

Uncontrolled affects of anxiety and rage toward her mother (and unconsciously toward the analyst), coupled with the analyst's defensive avoidance of dealing with the disruptive actualities of his interactions with the patient, led to pathological regression and symptom formation in the patient.

In reaction to the contradictory communications contained in the analyst's question and to the psychically disruptive nature of his intervention, the patient developed a conversion symptom (the feeling that her hands were paralyzed).

Throughout the next six brief interchanges she showed mounting anxiety as she talked (while sobbing) about fantasies of standing over her helpless mother. Then after the analyst accurately suggested to her that she was reversing the situation and that she was the one who was feeling helpless, she began to speak of her own helplessness. During these interchanges she continued her unconscious commentaries on her interaction with the analyst. While telling of how she feared losing control over her rage, she said, "It is much easier to be controlled and to be told what to do." Later she unconsciously commented on her inability to speak directly of her anger to the analyst with the statement, "I wish I could put my aggression onto the person that I feel it's for, but somehow I can't."

Interactional Symptoms

While telling of her anger and temper toward her mother, she gradually began to regress and to shift from murderous rage to childlike helplessness. She said, "I feel helpless now and I couldn't fight back and I feel so sorry for this little girl who is so helpless [90-second pause]." The analyst commented, "There seem to be some gaps in your associations. It's as if you're afraid to talk without editing here."

Here the analyst again made an implied criticism and directive, which probably repeated the kind of traumatic relationships the patient had had in the past. One might anticipate that this could trigger further dyscontrol and another release of symptomatic behavior, as occurred earlier after the analyst intervened with "Let's go back to your fear of exploding." Then the patient replied,

> Sometime I'll get back at her. I'm just waiting for the chance. . . .
> This frightens me . . . I feel as if it's crazy. I can't . . . when I
> get mad like this I get a sexual feeling. I've got one now. It
> happens whenever I get anxious like this. It's as if I'm masturbating.

The sexual feeling she experienced in a context of rageful and helpless feelings and following the critical, directive intervention was what Langs (1981) calls an interactional symptom. That is, the analyst as well as the patient contributed to the formation of the symptom. The analyst's comment about gaps in her associations was prompted by his countertransference, and it was an attempt to project his own impatience and probably other unconscious contents onto the patient. This particular symptom complex recurred many times in the analysis under similar circumstances, and Chapter 13 will provide additional data and discussion on the significance of interactional factors in the formation of symptoms experienced by this patient during the analytic hours.

In later occurrences of this symptom, the patient described the sexual feeling as consisting of genital (clitoral and/or vaginal) sensations. As she explicitly stated, her sexual sensations came when she felt anxious. This is the first of many instances in the analysis when the patient attempted to defend herself by the sexualization of anxiety. This symptom complex occurred when she had unconsciously introjected the analyst's projective identifications and when there was a consequent dyscontrol or temporary breakdown in her higher-level ego functions. One evidence of her dyscontrol was her statement "I feel as if it's crazy," which was expressed just before she admitted having the "sexual feeling."

In his discussion of this hour Dewald is aware that he had brought undue pressure on her, saying,

> Toward the end of the session my comment about the gaps in her associations and her continuing fear of talking without editing is inappropriate and unnecessary, since it puts the patient under too much pressure at the moment to follow the basic rule. It represents a countertransference demand that she immediately behave the way that I want her to. . . .

The Pattern of Shared Denial

In the second hour we can see a continuation of the pattern noted in the first session in which the analyst brushed aside the patient's conscious and unconscious communications regarding his efforts to direct and control her communication. She complied with the analyst and defensively displaced her concerns about his controlling communications onto extraanalytic relationships. The emerging pattern of the mutual or shared denial of analyst-analysand interactions became more structuralized.

Out of her fears that she would lose the relationship with the analyst, she gradually began to comply with his pressures on her. She unconsciously perceived his need to deny his directiveness and aggression toward her, and in order to preserve the relationship with him, she adapted to the situation by also denying emotionally charged aspects of their interaction. With few exceptions, such as vacations and canceled appointments, both the patient and the analyst unconsciously colluded in avoiding talking about or analyzing the nontransference aspects of their relationship. On the patient's part, this was a partially adaptive defense, as her efforts in the early sessions of the analysis to communicate her concerns about being controlled were rejected or went unrecognized. These observations indicate that denial behaviors are not solely or simply motivated by defensive wishes; they also spring from basic needs for adapting and relating to significant others.

Session 3

The important adaptive contexts for Session 3 were the analyst's pressures on the patient to perform and his demeaning criticisms when she did not perform up to his expectations. The patient's conscious and unconscious communications in Session 3 show a marked reaction to and commentary on these adaptive contexts. She arrived five minutes late, and the analyst began the first of his 17 questions in this session with the inquiry, "What comes to your mind about the trouble getting started today?" To this question the patient responded by telling him that she felt hostile toward him. He rejoined with, "What's the detail?" She continued to protest, saying that he was the coldest man she had ever met. She complained that she could not get anything out of him and that she felt like a child. After another question from the analyst she said, "You just sit and you judge me and you expect me to be perfect and to get right into this and not to have any hesitations." Her reference to his not permitting any hesitations refers to his policy (explicitly formulated in his discussions of individual sessions) of not tolerating silences and interrupting silences with questions. Again, as she did briefly in the first interview, she correctly described the analyst's impatience and directiveness. Several more brief exchanges follow, each one involving a directive type of question. She paused a minute after the analyst's question, "What are your associations?" and then said,

> I think of the time that my father was teaching me how to drive the car. He told me to put on the brake and somehow I couldn't do it. He got furious and screamed at me, "Get out of my car." (Elaborates.) I have such hostility, but I've never shown it. I think about my terrible temper when I was little. Mother had such pride that she was able to squelch it.

The patient's memories about her father's rejection of her while teaching her how to drive may be viewed as derivatives that contain incisive commentaries on the analyst's educative interventions and impatience. Her comments about her father's rejecting attitude and her mother's squelching of the patient's anger provide further clues to why the patient had not more directly and consciously expressed her anger toward the analyst and why she was unable to confront the analyst with his directiveness. In order to maintain her relationship with him and not be "squelched" or rejected, she unconsciously colluded with him in denying his directiveness and its effects on her.

Gaslighting Interventions

The analyst responded,

> So we can see how hard it is for you to accept this basic idea of
> analysis. You expect me to react either as your father did and tell
> you to get out, or else as your mother did and try to squelch you if
> you show your feelings.

In this intervention the analyst is unconsciously engaging in what Calef and
Weinshel (1981) call a "gaslighting" manipulation. Gaslighting is a form of
behavior in which an individual attempts to influence the judgment of a
second individual by causing the latter to doubt the validity of his or her own
judgment. Gaslighting generally involves one person, the victimizer, who
tries to impose his or her judgment on a second person, the victim. This
imposition is based on the "transfer," via projective identification, of painful
unconscious mental conflicts from the victimizer to the victim.

In the above situation, the analyst's intervention functioned to deny the
valid aspects of the patient's complaints about the analyst's directive behaviors. Through this and later similar gaslighting interventions, the analyst
unconsciously attempted to intimidate her and to enlist her as an ally in his
denials rather than have to face her confrontations and protests about his
aggressive and directive actions toward her.

After four minutes of silence the patient replied, "I really think that you
do feel this way. I think that it's in your tone of voice. It's as if you're saying,
'Be perfect or else forget it.'" In this spirited response to the analyst's
gaslighting intervention, the patient showed considerable ego strength in
being able to maintain her perception of what was transpiring between
herself and the analyst in the face of his pressures on her to relinquish her
perception.

The analyst responded, "Your feeling is that I expect you to be perfect
here. What comes to your mind?" Following a minute's pause the patient
replied, "You expect me to be perfect and I'm not. I never will be. (Elaborates.) You can't control my mind and I want to express myself. It's just
your tough luck."

Again in the following intervention the analyst used a gaslighting technique to reassert his control over the analysand and to displace her protests
away from himself. He interpreted, "I wonder if this thought doesn't really
reflect your own fear about your feeling and your thoughts and your ideas
and your fear of the whole process of analysis?" The patient maintained her
conscious defense of her judgments and perceptions by stating, "What
happens if I can't accept my imperfections? I could do that if my parents only
had. I feel as if you are detouring me and you are making me direct my
hostility against myself." Note how accurate and perceptive was the patient's

interpretation of the analyst's behavior. His interventions were clearly unconsciously aimed at getting the patient to displace (or "detour") to others her concerns about the analyst-analysand interactions. Also, as she observed, he was probably attempting to get her to direct her hostility against herself and away from him.

Unconscious Communications in Gaslighting Interventions

Let us examine the meaning and function of the unconscious communications contained in the analyst's two gaslighting interventions. A basic unconscious motive for them was a defensive one in which the analyst implicitly denied that he had been controlling toward the patient and that there were valid aspects of her perceptions of him. By attempting to induce the patient to doubt the validity of her judgments, he denied and discounted her perceptions of him and her protests. His gaslighting interventions contained several emotionally charged unconscious communications, including a prohibition, "Do not tell me about my being controlling." The evocation of emotional distress and confusion in the patient through the gaslighting manipulation had the function of reinforcing the prohibition. These intimidating gaslighting interventions contained a warning similar to the following: "I'll make you feel confused and crazy if you continue to point out things about me that I don't like to hear."

In his discussion of Session 3, Dewald mentions that he became aware of the countertransference pressures that he was exerting on the patient when she said that he was making her direct her hostility against herself. His awareness of the countertransference did not, however, lead to any lasting changes in his technique, as the process notes of the remaining analytic sessions show his continued use of gaslighting manipulations and directive questions.

After the analyst became aware of his countertransference pressure, he temporarily modified his approach by saying, "You feel as if I'm blaming you and as if something is your fault. What's the detail there?" Here he made some attempt to rectify the interpersonal conflict and derailed psychoanalytic frame. This point marks a change also in the affective tenor and manifest content of the patient's communications. From here to the end of the hour she no longer consciously protested about the analyst. Instead she told of how helpless and rebellious she felt in the face of what she perceived to be her parents' coercive control over her. Although her conscious protests and confrontations with the analyst recede, one can interpret her anguished expressions about her power struggles with her parents as unconscious commentaries on her transactions with the analyst.

Unconscious Communication and Shared Denial

Why did the patient switch from conscious confrontations and complaints about the analyst in the first part of the hour to unconscious commentaries and perceptions of the analyst's directiveness in the second part of the hour? The same or similar conflicts and themes concerning helplessness, aggression, and rebellion against control are found in both parts of the hour. A partial explanation comes from studying the impact of the analyst's unconscious communications on the patient's communications and on her defensive functioning.

She unconsciously perceived the unconscious communications contained in his directive questions and in his gaslighting interventions, and she responded to them by switching the manifest focus of her concerns about aggression and control from the analyst to her parents. In other words, one unconscious reason that the patient stopped communicating directly and explicitly regarding the analyst's controlling actions was because the analyst had unconsciously communicated to her his strong wish that she should stop talking to him about them. The analyst's transference interpretation in which he stated that the patient expected him to behave like her parents offered to both the analyst and the patient a mutually gratifying channel for denying the here-and-now meanings underlying the patient's angry and helpless feelings and for displacing them onto the patient's parents.

Session 4

In Session 4 the analyst continued the same kind of directive questions, and according to his discussion, he did this because he did not want there to be long silences and because he was concerned with "teaching her to associate more freely and to suspend her critical judgment." In the first four interchanges of this hour the patient described the differences between her experiences with her former therapist and with Dr. Dewald. She seemed to feel confused and she complained that she did not "understand what I'm supposed to do." An important unconscious source of her misunderstanding and confusion was her unconscious reaction to the confusing and contradictory messages from the analyst. In our study of Session 3 we explained that gaslighting techniques are unconsciously designed to evoke psychic confusion and disruption in the recipient's mind. The patient's confusion and misunderstanding resulted from the analyst's gaslighting manipulations in the previous session and by the contradictory communications conveyed in his questions.

Analyst: What comes to your mind about wanting to hide here?
Patient: I could make Mr. Harris like me but I can't do that with
          you. So I'm not even going to try. I know that I can't. I feel

	very hostile towards you and I don't understand what I'm supposed to do.
Analyst:	I think that really you do understand what you're supposed to do here in analysis, but you can't believe it.
Patient:	I don't really understand this. Somehow we don't seem to be discussing things and it seems as I'm doing all of the talking. − − − I think of Mr. Harris and the way he used to support me. But somehow we never really talked about me. − − I've felt anxious all day. [Elaborates symptoms.] I don't know why.
Analyst:	Let's see what your associations are without jumping to conclusions about it.
Patient:	I feel as if someone is trying to overpower me. As if they are trying to . . ."
Analyst:	What is it that you're afraid to say?
Patient:	As if you are trying to sit on me and squash me.

Immediately after the patient said that she did not understand what she was supposed to do, the analyst countered with a confrontation that had pronounced gaslighting qualities: "I think that really you do understand what you're supposed to do here in analysis, but you can't believe it." Actually, he was the one who either could not or would not believe what she had said. He denied his disbelief and projected it onto the patient by saying she was the one who "can't believe it." She replied, "I don't really understand this" and then went on to admit feeling anxious and having symptoms before the analytic hour.

What is striking about her reply is to what extent it follows both in form and in some of its content the analyst's previous utterance. She contradicted him, as he had just done previously with her, and she used the word *really* just as he had done. The point here is that patients tend unconsciously to adopt more or less temporarily the same communicative mode as that used by the analyst. Langs (1980) shows that patients tend to use the same communicative mode (Type A, B, or C) as used by their their therapists. A careful study of Dewald's book reveals that frequently the patient switched from a predominantly Type A mode to a Type B mode under the influence of the analyst's frequent use of interventions (questions, confrontations, gaslighting interventions, and some interpretations) that had Type B qualities.

Apparently in another effort to assert his control over the patient, himself, and the analytic situation, the analyst then again criticized her with "Let's see what your associations are without jumping to any conclusions about it." Again, as in so many of his interventions, the analyst had not acknowledged to the patient that what she has complained about may have had some measure of validity. He continued to direct her to talk, while at the same time implicitly negating the significance of what she had said. She responded anxiously with "I feel as if someone is trying to overpower me. As if they are trying . . ." She hesitated and the analyst

asked, "What is it that you're afraid to say?" She answered, "As if you
are trying to sit on me and squash me."

The patient's fantasy of being physically squashed was a concrete
metaphor that described in visual imagery actual aspects of her interactions
with the analyst. Her image of being squashed was derived from unconscious introjects and perceptions of the analyst stimulated by his
controlling interventions. In response, the analyst interpreted, "I think
this is one of your fears about starting analysis. It's as if you fantasize
that you're going to end up in my power and that you're going to be
helpless." By interpreting her image of being squashed as a transference
fantasy, he implicitly denied that the fantasy had anything to do with their
ongoing interactions. Dewald's transference interpretation employed a
gaslighting manipulation in that it repudiated the patient's perception of
what was occurring in their relationship. His tactic of negating her
perceptions and attempting to manipulate her to accept his judgments
instead of her own is one of the methods Searles (1959) mentioned for
driving another person crazy. Dewald's transference interpretations denied
the actuality of his controlling techniques and their oppressive effects
on the patient. Both his interpretations and his discussion of this hour
ascribed her mounting anxieties over being controlled to the emergence of
transference fears and fantasies.

In the next four brief interchanges she became increasingly anxious,
and she described in various ways her fears of being overpowered and
controlled by the analyst. In these interchanges the analyst continued to
apply pressures on her by his directive questions. He responded to her
anxiety by a lengthy intervention that was a mixture of a generalized
interpretation, reassurance, and education. In his discussion of this hour and
of what he called his "lengthy generalized interpretation about her fear of
such transference phenomena," he indicates that he had intervened at this
point to reduce the patient's anxiety about her transference feelings. He
began with, "I think at the moment that you're frightened by a number
of feelings that you're having toward me. Some of these are sexual and
some of these are involved with your hostility." He went on to explain to
her the basic rule of free association and the requirement that she was
supposed to express her feelings, even though she was afraid of them.

Here and elsewhere in the analysis the analyst used the transference
concept in a defensive way to deny his contributions to the patient's
experiences. The analyst's remarks in this session, as well as in the discussion of the session, may be interpreted as a disavowal that his controlling
interventions had caused the patient to feel overpowered and helpless.
In his generalized interpretations about her sexual feelings, he offered her
an interactional resistance, a shared defense in which both of them would
later collude in ascribing her anxieties to endogenous sources disconnected
from analyst-analysand interactions. Dewald's intervention unconsciously
supported what was called earlier the patient's defensive sexualization of
anxiety and the later development of a defensive eroticized transference.
Dewald is not alone in his defensive use of the transference idea, for as

Langs (1982a) shows, many psychoanalysts, beginning with Freud, have unconsciously used the transference concept defensively to disavow their contributions to their patients' experiences. In this way many analysts have discounted the nontransference and valid aspects of their patients' conscious and unconscious perceptions of their analysts.

Relief of Anxiety Through Type C Communication

In his discussion of Session 4, Dewald states that he thought his generalized interpretation was ineffective and that the patient's response was to plunge into "intellectualized material about penises, masturbation, womanhood, pregnancy, etc." An examination of the remaining material in Session 4 confirms Dewald's conclusion that what the patient said had a high resistance quality with much intellectualization and a compliant need to please the analyst. Although his generalized interpretation was ineffective in leading to interpretable derivatives, it did, in my opinion, reduce her intense anxiety.

In order to demonstrate just how his intervention reduced her anxiety, let us examine first the interpersonal context of her intellectualized and compliant response to his intervention. First of all, one notes the similarity in communication style of the analyst's intervention and the patient's response. Both were intellectualized, and both had a considerable degree of what Langs (1978) calls the Type C communicative mode. As we noted in the discussion of the early part of this session, the patient often followed the lead of the analyst not only in what she communicated but also in how she communicated. Now we can see why and how Dewald's intervention helped reduce her anxiety. In the first part of the hour they were locked in a power struggle that caused mounting anxiety in the patient. Dewald's "generalized interpretation" rescued both participants from their interpersonal conflict, and it relieved their anxieties about a disruption in their relationship by affording both of them the comparative comfort of a Type C mode of communication in which they could distance themselves from each other and deny the meaning of the emotionally charged events in the early parts of this session. Dewald's intervention solicited and gained the patient's participation in an interactional resistance that reduced her fears about the analyst's pressures on her and gave her a means of adapting to those pressures.

Through communicating in an impersonal and intellectualized mode, both the analyst and the patient gained some relief from their intense conflicts with each other and from their own psychic conflicts. However, they paid a high price for this emotional relief because their shared denial of what was occurring in their interaction and their Type C communication temporarily blocked derivative communication and the attainment of insight.

Discussion

What Was Denied?

A recurrent interaction that was denied first by the analyst and later by the patient was the analyst's controlling and directive behavior toward the patient. He attempted to control and to direct the patient's experience and expression by his active questioning and sometimes by other interventions, including confrontations, explicit directives, educative comments, and interpretations. The patient responded to the analyst's repetitive controlling pressures by both conscious and unconscious protests, perceptions, commentaries on his directiveness, and largely unconscious communications regarding her reactions of anger and helplessness.

In response to the patient's communications regarding his controlling actions, the analyst denied both that he had been controlling and that her reactions were in some respects valid and appropriate response to his pressures. Through gaslighting interventions, which included a denial of his directive actions, he attempted to induce her to relinquish her own judgments about this interaction and to accept his judgment about what was taking place within herself and in her relationship with the analyst. His unconscious attempts to induce the patient to accept his judgment and also to deny the interaction succeeded, and after the fourth session she seldom consciously complained about his directive interventions.

Limited space prevents my documenting here the clinical evidence for the hypothesis that the patient throughout most of the analysis introjected not only the analyst's denial of this type of interaction but also other important interactions. During the rest of the analysis there was a gradual establishment and structuralization of a pattern of communication in which the analyst and the patient unconsciously colluded in denying some of the realities of their interactions.

In the different ways I earlier mentioned, the analyst unconsciously communicated to the patient his urgent wish that she not talk about the actualities of his controlling actions toward her. These unconscious communications were supported by his gaslighting manipulations, which unconsciously communicated the threat of further intimidation if she did not comply with the analyst's implicit and unconscious prescriptions for what she was supposed to talk about, how she was to talk, and when she was to talk in the analytic sessions. A common, unconscious communication of the analyst, "Don't talk about my controlling actions because I'm troubled by what you say," was transmitted to the patient through his denials. The patient unconsciously perceived these communications and responded to them by also denying the interaction.

The analyst unconsciously offered modes of communication (Types B and C) that the patient could use defensively to avoid thinking and talking about the analyst's directive interventions and their impact. These modes of communication could be used as screens to support what they both denied. To an increasing degree they shared one denial reaction in which important interactions such as the ones discussed in this chapter were not talked about or analyzed. Gradually and unconsciously a mode of interaction was established, and then maintained throughout the analysis, that had pathologically symbiotic qualities wherein the patient complied with the analyst's need to direct and control important aspects of her experience and expression. The aspect of that symbiotic interaction that is the focus of this chapter is the largely unconscious and interactional process by which they came to deny their interaction. This shared denial defended both against the awareness of the unconscious gratifications they attained in their symbiotic merger.

The Analyst's Denials

Probably the most frequently used way in which the analyst denied the meaning of his actions toward the patient and the validity and appropriateness of her responses to his controlling actions was his repeated failure to acknowledge or confirm to the patient the valid aspects of her conscious and unconscious communications regarding his directive interventions. Another way the analyst denied his directive and controlling interventions was by his defensive use of transference interpretations as a means of displacing the patient's emotional reactions from himself onto the patient's parents. Often when the patient expressed anger at the analyst for what he had done to her, the unconscious communication in the analyst's interpretations was something similar to the following: "You are really angry at your father, not at me." I do not mean to imply that the patient's angry reactions did not contain transference components. All communications contain both transference and nontransference aspects. In our thinking about the issue we should avoid falling into the polarized ways of thinking shown by the patient and the analyst, wherein they tended to view the reactions as either transference or nontransference. My point about the analyst's use of the transference concept is not that he was entirely incorrect in that judgment but that he frequently made transference interpretations to defend himself against the awareness of the actualities of his controlling actions on the patient and unconsciously to induce her also to deny these realities. Everything the patient says or does in the analytic situation is influenced by the analyst, and a comprehensive description and/or explanation of the patient's communication must take into account the interpersonal context. This perspective is similar to the bipersonal field concept (Baranger and Baranger 1966, Langs 1976a) by which it is postulated that every intervention between the two parties to the analytic situation, and every experience within either, is a product of the field and, as such, receives contributions from both its members.

Dewald, like many other analysts and therapists, appears to view the patient's mind as a closed system. In the analytic session, in his discussion of those sessions, and in his theoretical writings on the psychoanalytic process, he shows little awareness of the existence of unconscious communication or the unconscious meanings of his interactions with patients. In the classical psychoanalytic literature, the "intrapsychic" spatial metaphor is often reified and used to denote a closed system disconnected from transactions with the environment. The interactional concept advanced here and in Chapters 11 and 13 rejects the mistaken view of the analyst as one who observes and interprets events taking place within the psyche conceptualized as a system isolated from conscious and unconscious interpersonal influences.

The Patient's Denial

As the analysis proceeded, the patient's response to the analyst's pressures and directives showed a gradual change. She adopted the analyst's view that what she experienced in the analytic hours stemmed almost exclusively from the realms of fantasy and transference. What the patient denied about the analyst's directiveness and its emotional effects on her did not disappear; rather, what was denied "returned" in the form of derivatives. These derivatives were the products of the patient's ego's revisions of unconscious introjects, fantasies, and perceptions of the analyst evoked by his controlling interventions.

Changes in the patient's defensive functioning could also be observed in the patient's differing response to the analyst's directive questions. In the early sessions she tended to respond to his questions by describing her interactions with the analyst and others. As the analysis proceeded, she less often referred to actual interpersonal experiences and more often regressed and described conscious sexual and aggressive fantasies. Data from the process notes support the hypothesis that she developed a learned response to his questions in which the questions became signals for her to regress and to produce the kind of conscious sexual and aggressive fantasies the analyst expected her to have.

The Idealizing Transference and Vertical Splits

The patient's denial of these and other interactions with the analyst did not, of course, derive exclusively from her introjection of the analyst's defensive attitudes. The denial she introjected was assimilated and integrated with her preexisting defensive organization. Even before the analysis she tended to use denial in her relationships with men and to perceive and relate to them as wholly bad or wholly good. Indeed, the clinical data in Dewald's book indicate the presence of what Kohut (1971) calls a *vertical split*, in which one set of the patient's self-representations and object representations of men and the affects and interactions related to those representations was defensively kept separate, through disavowal, from a contradictory set. Dewald's process notes contain convincing evidence that he unconsciously supported the denial defenses underlying the vertical split and the related phenomena of the patient's idealizing transference.

Another important effect of the shared denial was the unconscious mutual enactment of the idealizing transference. A prominent and prolonged feature of this enactment was the patient's compliance with the analyst's directiveness.

In his epilogue to Dewald's book, the analyst James Anthony discusses how the patient in his follow-up interview with her showed a marked tendency toward splitting her representations of her therapists. Anthony noted her idealization of Dewald and her denigration of her former therapist, Mr. Harris. In my view, the patient came to the analysis with the need to express and work through an idealizing transference. She hoped to find a father figure who, unlike her own father, was both strong and incorruptible. The analyst's unconscious assumption of a directive role with the patient and his denials of his directiveness and its disturbing effects on the patient fostered her idealization of the analyst and the related vertical split. Her idealization served as a defense against her perceptions of the analyst's mistakes and shortcomings and, at the same time, gave her a means of denying her conflicts over aggression toward the analyst. Another and nondefensive source of her idealization was the revival in the analytic situation of an archaic object relation in a way first described by Kohut (1971). (For a further discussion of the different forms and meanings of idealization, see Dorpat 1979 and Gedo 1975.)

Consequences of the Denied Interaction

The shared denial of the aforementioned interactions had far-reaching effects and consequences on the analytic process and the patient. Our investigation of the denied interaction in the first four sessions provided data on the denial's short-term effects. In order to test hypotheses regarding the long-term effects, one would have to present extensive documentation from the whole analysis. Because this would be impractical, my goal here is the more limited one of describing briefly and generally the conclusions I reached after studying the entire book.

The major unrecognized and unanalyzed resistances in the analysis were of the interactional kind, and in many instances these resistances involved the shared denial discussed earlier. Langs (1981) establishes the foundations for a clinical theory of interactional resistances and discusses the relationships between defensive operations and resistances. The defensive avoidance by both the analyst and the patient of conflicts and fixations connected with issues of power, control, and autonomy was inextricably linked with their shared denial. This resulted in the failure to recognize or to analyze transferences (especially, I think, the idealizing transference) associated with the separation-individuation phase of development.

The structure and content of what Dewald called the patient's "transference neurosis" was strongly influenced by an unrecognized and predominantly defensive eroticized transference (see Blum 1973 for a discussion of the eroticized transference). As I noted in the examination of Session 4, the analyst tended to facilitate the patient's defensive sexualization of anxiety, a prime component of her eroticized transference.

Concluding Remarks

This investigation and the studies reviewed in Chapter 11 demonstrate that both the form and the content of denials are unconsciously and strongly influenced by the deniers' need to adapt to what others want of them. The unconscious wish to preserve a threatened relationship with significant others is a powerful dynamic in the formation and maintenance of denial responses.

A systematic study of the implications of this investigation for the psychoanalytic theory of technique is beyond the scope of this chapter. Classical psychoanalytic theories contain conceptual errors and omissions that readily lend themselves to the kinds of erroneous interventions made by Dewald and others. The interactional perspective has been relatively neglected in the classical literature on psychoanalytic process and technique (Gill 1982). Perhaps one cause of Dewald's denials of his interactions with the patient stemmed from his own analytic training.

The conclusions of this study are consistent with the results of the previous studies of the interactional aspects of defensive functioning reviewed in the previous chapter. There are two findings from this investigation that go beyond what has previously been reported. One is the central importance of shared denial, a term used to describe situations in which two or more individuals unconsciously collude in denying particular interactions between them. Though the literature reviewed in Chapter 11 has emphasized that individuals do influence the defensive functioning of others, it did not note either the prevalence or the significance of shared denial in human interactions.

Another contribution of the present study has been the explication of *how* one individual may influence the defensive functioning of another person. Although consciously intended messages sometimes play some role in this, the findings of the present study indicate that an individual's unconscious communications often have powerful and direct influences on the unconscious processes and defensive activities of another individual. Few individuals recognize to what degree human beings unconsciously both perceive and respond to others' unconscious communications.

Psychoanalysis has from its beginnings highlighted the role of unconscious and endogenous forces in shaping thought and behavior, but it has paid little attention to how others can influence an individual's unconscious psychic functioning. What is a most remarkable finding of the present study, and worthy of much more intensive and systematic research is the fact that individuals unconsciously influence the unconscious processes of other persons. Psychoanalysis has recognized how much goes on *within* persons that is beyond conscious awareness, but it has only begun to discover what transpires *between* individuals that is also unconscious. The classical psychoanalytic approach has tended to overlook unconscious communication and how the derivative manifestations of unconscious interactional processes of projection, introjection, and perception may be decoded from the patient's verbal communications, dreams, and symptoms.

13

Interactional Denial and Symptom Formation

In this chapter I shall present the findings and conclusions of a study of some of the interactional factors in the pathogenesis of a particular symptom complex experienced by an analytic patient described in Dewald's (1972) book. This report will be limited to an examination of Sessions 176, 177, and 178 and to a discussion of the formation and meaning of the following four elements of the symptom complex: (1) dyscontrol, (2) rage and helplessness, (3) genital sensations, and (4) ideas about cutting her wrists.

The patient developed similar symptoms at numerous times in the early and middle phases of the analysis, and an examination of these occasions indicates the presence of a consistent interactional pattern of events preceding each occurrence of the symptoms. In Chapter 12, for example, I hypothesized that the analyst's directive interventions and his projective identifications in Session 2 played a critical role in the patient's dyscontrol and the emergence of the conversion symptoms of genital sensations. A study of the symptom complex occurrences and the transactions preceding the symptom complex in Sessions 176, 177, and 178 will provide further tests of the interactional hypothesis proposed in Chapter 12. The major hypothesis presented and tested in this chapter is that the analyst-analysand shared denial played a crucial and causal role in the pathogenesis of the patient's dyscontrol and consequent symptom formation.

The major hypothesis and other hypotheses were validated by a repeated examination of the analyst's and the patient's communications both before and during many episodes of the symptom complex in the sessions presented in this chapter and in many other sessions.

There have been few psychoanalytic studies of the therapist's contributions to symptom formation. The literature contains occasional brief discussions about therapists who unconsciously encourage or evoke acting-out behaviors in their patients. A review of the literature did not locate any systematic studies of the analyst's contributions to symptom formation occurring during analytic hours. The prevailing tendency is to attribute such symptoms to the transference neurosis and to ignore or to discount possible contributions from the analyst.

Langs (1982b) holds that disturbing interventions by the therapist and the unconscious perception-introjects so generated are important sources for the patient's symptoms. He notes that symptoms may be founded and sustained on the introjection of implications of the therapist's interventions, and he defines *interactional symptoms* as "emotional disturbance[s] in either participant to the therapeutic dyad with significant sources from both participants" (1982b, p. 529). Langs describes *interactional syndromes* as clusters of interactional symptoms.

Langs (1982b) distinguishes between the *transference neurosis* or *syndrome* and the *interactional syndrome,* and he suggests that the term *interactional syndrome* be used when there are significant contributions from the unconscious perceptions and introjects of the analyst's pathology. In contrast, the transference neurosis or syndrome derives mainly from the patient's unconscious conflicts and fantasies regarding the analyst. Langs (1976b, p. 585) claims that many symptoms that appear during the course of an analysis that have previously been viewed as components of the transference neurosis are seen, with more careful scrutiny, to be in fact derived from the analytic interaction and to contain both transference and nontransference elements.

The causal significance of interpersonal and social factors in symptom formation has been studied by family therapists and others, but except for child psychoanalysts few investigators have focused on the crucial role of *unconscious* interactional factors.

Session 176

In Session 176 the analyst was especially active, and 15 out of his 20 interventions were questions of the type described in Chapter 12 of this book. During the first interchange the patient spoke about thoughts of killing herself, and she mentioned feeling that the analyst had been mad and disgusted with her the day before. Then the analyst responded, "You felt that I was mad and disgusted with you on Monday. What was the detail of that?" In reply to the analyst's question, she cried and answered, "I felt that you were giving up on me and that you were saying, 'Ugh, to hell with her.' It was nothing that you or I said, it was just a feeling I had." She went on to tell about feeling desperate and alone.

In the previous session there had been several interventions, such as both the first and the last intervention of the analyst, suggesting that the analyst had indeed been mad and disgusted with her. Therefore, her feeling could have had some basis in reality. After the analyst's directive questioning, the patient denied that her feeling was related to their communicative interaction, by saying, "It was nothing that you or I said, it was just a feeling I had."

Introjected Denial

The patient's denial (i.e., "It was nothing you or I said . . .") stemmed from her introjection of the analyst's attitude that her affective reactions were unrelated to the analyst-analysand communicative interactions. This type of denial was not typical of her attitude at the beginning of the analysis in which she made causal connections between what she felt about the analyst and what was going on in the analytic hours. The patient's denial was similar to the analyst's, as shown by a systematic review of the process notes and the discussions of the individual sessions that indicates that Dewald rarely acknowledged any relationship between the patient's communications and what was taking place at either conscious or unconscious levels in their interactions. His interpretations and explanations of her communications typically ascribed them to wholly endogenous and transferential sources isolated from the ongoing analyst-analysand transactions. A review of the sessions before Session 176 provides abundant evidence for the hypothesis first presented in Chapter 12 that the patient gradually introjected the analyst's attitude, thereby sharing with him a denial that her experiences had anything to do with what took place in their interactions.

Returning now to the analyst's first intervention in this session, which ends with the question, "What was the detail of that?" the analyst's directive questions gradually became signals or cues that the patient used to regress and to disavow the realities of her interactions with the analyst. First the analyst, and later also the patient, treated and spoke about her affects and her fantasies as if they were derived wholly from sources within herself, such as her past realtionships, and as if they had nothing to do with their here-and-now interactions. A communicative pattern was established in which the patient and the analyst unconsciously colluded in denying important meanings of their communications.

In the early part of this session she cried much of the time as she told about her fears of being alone and her thoughts of killing herself. During the middle section of the session, her predominant affect was one of anger at her parents, and she described her fears of being abandoned if she were to express her anger. The analyst commented, "I think you want to tell me how much you hate me too. What comes to your mind about that?" In response to his question, the patient began to express anger at the analyst, together with fears that her aggression would make the analyst fall apart or be weak and incapable of handling her feelings, as she believed her father to be.

The Analyst's Projective Identification

After about two-thirds of the session had passed, she reported a dream:

> I had a dream that I was swimming and I was having my period. There was a lot of blood in my hair and I felt something in my hand. First I thought it was a shark but then it turned out there was a penis in that water and that was why I felt that I can't dive in.

Without waiting for the patient's associations to the dream, Dewald made the following interpretation:

> I think the fantasy was that you can take your father away from your mother and that way you can have his penis for yourself. And so you have the same fantasy about me with the idea of taking me away from my wife and having my penis for yourself.

Dewald's aggressive interpretation of her wish to take him away from his wife in order to have his penis for herself came after the patient had frequently made comments about her fears that he was weak like her father and that he could not handle the situation with her. Perhaps he made this startling and arbitrary interpretation because he had unconsciously felt provoked and demeaned by the patient's belittling remarks.

Dewald's provocative and disturbing interpretation was a projective identification in which he unconsciously attempted to project his own conflicts onto the patient. He did not wait to hear the patient's associations to the dream, and his interpretive remarks appear to have arisen mainly from his countertransference reactions. The analyst was off the mark in the timing as well as the content of his interpretation. The shocklike quality of this intervention was similar to that of the interventions that preceded and evoked dyscontrol in other instances of the symptom complex. Other examples of psychically disruptive interventions described in Chapter 12 included abruptly changing the topic of dialogue and contradicting the patient's perceptions.

The following interchange follows the analyst's interpretation and shows the emergence of the symptom complex:

Patient: If I could just separate you and my father. I keep telling myself, "It's not that way with Dr. Dewald." But then I always think about

my father and I lose it. If I can convince myself that my father
would never give in to me, then I know I'll be all right. – – – – Now I
have an impulse to cut my wrists. I've got such a feeling in my vagina
and clitoris right now and it's as if I have a penis in it and I feel as if
I'll have an orgasm. – – – – Now I'm so mad at you.

Analyst: Let's look at the details of both sets of feelings. Both the sexual
feelings and also the feeling of being mad.

Patient: It's a feeling in my vagina and then I think of you as a God- damned
bastard!

According to the process notes, the patient continued to talk about different
elements of the symptom complex for the remainder of this session, and her
nonverbal communications were those of crying and "fury."

Denial and Dyscontrol

Let us now examine the patient's denial expressed just after Dewald's
interpretation and immediately before she began having symptoms such as
the genital sensations and the fantasy of cutting her wrists. She said, "If I
could just separate you and my father. I keep telling myself, 'It's not that way
with Dr. Dewald.'" Her statement arose, I assume, out of a wish to hold
onto an image of Dr. Dewald as the idealized object who was different from
her father. The explicit denial ("not that way with Dr. Dewald") defended
her against the unconscious perception that in reality it indeed *was that way*
with Dr. Dewald. His untimely interpretations repeated traumas she had
sustained at the hands of her father and her uncle. Her denial, I hypothesize,
was an unconscious last-ditch attempt to prevent herself from consciously
perceiving the meaning of the analyst's destructive intervention and from
recognizing the nature of her painful subjective responses to the intervention.
This denial triggered her dyscontrol and deprived her of the means for using
her conscious and secondary-process psychic resources for understanding
and coping with the minitraumatic effects of the analyst's intervention.
Without the denial, she may have been able to acknowledge the analyst's
erroneous intervention, avoided the dyscontrol and symptom complex, and
dealt with the experience in a more conscious and rational manner.

The Symptom Complex

The patient's symptoms can be viewed as the by-products and displacements
of the patient's denied interactions with the analyst. Embedded in the
symptoms are evidences of the patient's unconscious introjection of the
analyst's projective identification. The introjected hostility is defensively

turned against herself in the fantasy of cutting her wrists. A systematic review of the symptom complex in the entire book reveals a fairly constant manifest pattern consisting of four interrelated elements: (1) affective and cognitive dyscontrol; (2) intense affects of rage, helplessness, and anxiety; (3) genital (both clitoral and vaginal) sensations; and (4) ideas and fantasies of cutting her wrists.

Affective and Cognitive Dyscontrol

In this and other sessions the patient manifested affective and cognitive dyscontrol both before and during the times she experienced and spoke about other elements of the symptom complex. Evidence for the occurrence of dyscontrol came both from the patient's subjective reports of her state of mind and from an objective assessment of her psychic functioning. There was a partial and temporary breakdown of the patient's higher-level secondary-process functioning.

In Chapter 9 we discussed the dyscontrol hypothesis of symptom formation in which we posited that denial implies dyscontrol—the loss of direct, conscious control over what is denied. The cognitive arrest in denial reactions brings about dyscontrol and the impairment of higher-level psychic functions. This compromises their regulatory action and control over lower-level functions, with the consequence that the contents and products of the lower-level functions emerge as symptoms. Later in this chapter I shall discuss how the shared denial and dyscontrol contributed to symptom formation in the patient.

Rage and Helplessness

The patient's rage and helplessness were derived from her unconscious perceptions and introjections of the analyst's unconscious communications. These interactions undoubtedly replicated and evoked unconscious memories of severe childhood traumata. One was the sadomasochistic relationship with her father, and the other was a specific and major traumatic sexual seduction by her uncle. The emergence into consciousness and the partial working through of the sexual seduction occurred later in the analysis. The proximal cause of her rage and helplessness was the patient's pathological introjection of what the analyst was projecting onto her.

Her rage was partially prompted by a defensive need to overcome her helplessness. Probably the patient unconsciously at times preferred the tension and activity that accompanies rage to the inactivity and passivity of feeling and being helpless.

Helplessness and the Idealizing Transference

The patient's sense of helplessness also stemmed from her inability to make the analyst listen to and respond to her need for him to be a strong and incorruptible father figure. This inability arose partially out of her difficulties in clearly communicating her need and, more significantly, from the analyst's empathic failures to respond analytically to this transference wish. Her wish for an idealized self object was frequently misinterpreted by the analyst as arising from oedipal wishes. At different times she spoke of wanting the analyst to be strong, not to give in to her, and to help her feel safe.

Genital Sensations As a Conversion Symptom

I have designated the patient's genital sensations as conversion symptoms for two reasons. First, they did not arise in the usual or normal contexts. A study of the context in which these sensations occurred provides no evidence that the patient was either consciously or unconsciously concerned with desires for sexual intercourse with a libidinal or whole object. Next, and quite to the contrary, they appeared in settings and contexts in which she felt overwhelmed with intense conflict, rage, and evidences of dyscontrol and helplessness.

The patient's conversion symptom was a variety-of-release phenomenon in which the breakdown in higher-level psychic functioning caused the disinhibition of lower-level psychic functions and the emergence of symptoms, the products of uninhibited primary-process functioning. Dyscontrol in the patient was a temporary impairment of secondary-process functioning with a diminished ability for thinking and communicating with verbal symbols. At such times her verbal communications shifted from a predominantly Type A to a predominantly Type B mode. In other words, language was used for action discharge rather than for symbolic communication. Both the genital sensations and the wrist-cutting impulses were the fragmentation products of a pathological regressive process set in motion by the patient's dyscontrol over her thinking and communication.

Engel (1968) and others have written about conversion symptoms as being a primitive mode of preverbal communication. This patient's need to communicate persisted in the face of her regression and the temporary impairment of her higher-level psychic functions. Her unconscious interactions with the analyst and her conflicts became symbolized in the sensorimotor mode of thinking and communication. Conversion symptom formation contains a regression to the stage of development of consciousness when ideas and affects are represented by bodily sensations, a phenomenon that occurs normally before about age two.

Past experiences that were replicated and represented in the genital sensations probably included masturbatory experiences and the traumatic sexual seduction by her uncle. The conversion symptom constituted a reliving in timeless sensory experience of the overwhelming stimulation that she sustained in that traumatic seduction, revived but not remembered in her interactions with the analyst.

Contrary to Dewald's view of these erotic experiences, the patient's genital sensations did not represent a return of repressed oedipal longings for a whole object, a person. Rather, they were products of a pathological regressive process in which the genital sensations were used defensively to protect against further fragmentation of the self.

Defensive Erotization

The patient's defensive erotization in her conversion symptom and elsewhere defended predominantly against conflicts over hostility, the threats of object loss, and fragmentation of the self; and it represented the turning of childhood traumatic seduction into active repetition for mastery. While discussing her symptoms in Session 2, the patient said that she experienced the genital sensations whenever she became "mad" and "anxious." Her linkage of the genital sensations with feeling mad and anxious is confirmed by the repeated reports of the symptom complex in the process notes of many sessions. The patient's comparison of the genital sensations with masturbatory experiences in Session 2 suggests that the sensations were brought about by wishes for the kind of self-comfort and relief previously provided by masturbation. According to Coen's (1981) review of sexualization as a mode of defense, many kinds of sexual activity (heterosexual, perverse, autoerotic, sexual fantasies, and the like) may serve as a defense against unconscious conflicts and unpleasurable affects.

The function of pathological sexual activity in restituting or maintaining fragile self-representations has been investigated by Kohut (1971, 1977), by Stolorow and Lachmann (1980), and others. Psychosexual experiences in development contribute crucially to the articulation and consolidation of self- and object representations. According to Stolorow and Lachmann, in defensive sexualization, it is the early infantile function of the erotic experience that is retained and regressively relied on—"its function is maintaining the structural cohesion and stability of crumbling, fragmenting, disintegrating self and object representations" (p. 149). Kohut (1971, 1977) relates the defensive use of the sexual mode to a need for intense feeling stimulation to reassure the self that it is alive and whole, for defense against depressive affect, and as a mode for the expression of incorporative wishes to fill in missing narcissistic structures.

Interactional Factors in Dyscontrol and
Symptom Formation

In previous examinations of two of the patient's explicit denials in Session 176 —(1) "It was nothing you or I said," and (2) "It's not that way with Dr. Dewald"—I hypothesized that these derivatives stemmed from the patient's introjection of the analyst's denial of certain interactions. Before continuing my discussion of how this shared denial brought about the patient's dyscontrol and symptoms, I want to emphasize that neither the analyst nor the patient was *consciously* aware of these interactions or of their causal effects on the patient's dyscontrol and symptom formation.

The shared denial prevented both the analyst and the analysand from comprehending these interactions, from talking about them, and from doing anything about them. It is precisely because these interactions were unconscious that they had such recurrent and powerful cognitive and affective effects on both parties. Not the least of these effects were the episodes of dyscontrol and symptom formation.

The patient's denial was an important proximal cause of her dyscontrol and consequent symptoms. Her denial of these interactions and her responses to them imply she had unconsciously suspended use of her higher-level psychic abilities for conscious understanding and control over what was denied. Consequently, she did not perceive the controlling quality of the analyst's interventions, and she did not understand how her angry, helpless feelings were related to the analyst's interventions. In other words, for defensive purposes, the patient did not allow herself to understand the directiveness of the analyst's interventions and her responses to them. However, as we have shown with observations made in this chapter and in Chapter 12, the patient continued to perceive unconsciously and to react with conflicts, introjections, and other responses to the analyst's communications.

Because what was denied was not processed by secondary-process mechanisms and verbal thought, it then became processed unconsciously by the primary process and perhaps also (as I suggested in Chapter 6) by the mechanisms subserving the repetition compulsion. The analyst's unconscious communications evoked unconscious perceptions, introjects, fantasies, and conflicts, and these unconscious contents were disguised by the ego's adaptive and defensive functions to emerge later as derivatives in her verbal communications and symptoms. The denied interactions with the analyst "returned" unconsciously encoded in the patient's communications, and here I include her symptoms as a primitive form of communication. We can then, in principle, decode and analyze her symptoms as we have previously decoded and analyzed her verbal communications for disguised evidences of the patient's denied interactions with the analyst.

Denial, Contradictory Communications, and Dyscontrol

How did the denied interactions contribute to the patient's dyscontrol and symptom formation? What part did the analyst's communications and denials play in causing the symptom complex? To answer these questions we first need to look at the role of denial and screen behavior in contradictory communications. In Chapter 12 I discussed the contradictory messages contained in the analyst's directive questioning in which the conscious message "*Do* tell your thoughts and feelings about me" was contradicted by the unconscious and encoded message "Do *not* tell your thoughts and feelings about me." This unconscious prohibitory communication was supported by other interventions, such as the analyst's gaslighting interventions wherein he manipulated the patient to give up her perceptions of and protests against his directive actions and to substitute for her perceptions his view that what she experienced arose entirely from endogenous (e.g., transferential) sources.

The explicit or conscious communication in contradictory communications is a screen behavior created to bolster and maintain the subject's denial of the unconscious communication. It follows that a contradictory communication contains an affirmation expressed in the conscious message, a negation in the unconscious message that contradicts the affirmation, and an implicit denial.

As shown in Chapter 12, this type of implicit denial was repeated many times by Dewald in his interventions, and a study of Sessions 176, 177, and 178 will provide further examples. In these sessions the analyst encouraged, even pressured, the patient to ventilate her angry feelings and fantasies about him. At the same time, the analyst unconsciously communicated in different ways the message "Do *not* tell about your anger to me!"

I shall now turn from the sending to the receiving side of contradictory communications. Because of the interactional denial the patient *consciously* heard and responded to only the analyst's manifest or conscious communications. His unconscious communications (e.g., *not* to talk about her anger toward him) were then registered, unconsciously perceived, and responded to by the patient. Her unconscious perceptions and her disturbed responses to these perceptions were unconsciously processed by her primary process and later "returned" as verbal derivatives or as symptoms.

Contradictory communications evoke contradictory perceptions and contradictory responses in the receiver, who introjects the sender's implicit denial. The receiver's unconscious perceptions of the sender's communication is contradictory to the receiver's conscious reception of the sender's communication. Accordingly, the receiver's unconscious responses will contradict his or her consciously intended responses. Individuals subjected to contradictory communications may internalize (at least temporarily) the contradictory communications and the implicit denial. The incongruity between the contradictory perceptions and between the contradictory responses to those perceptions is itself a source of conflicts and confusion. The receiver's internalization and adoption of the implicit denial produces a cognitive dyscontrol over the psychic functions required for understanding the contradictory communications. Consequently, the receiver of contradictory communications is often not able to employ secondary-process thinking and verbal thought adaptively for rational thinking, reality testing, and the delay of primary-process discharge.

For example, recall the patient's explicit denial in Session 176—"It's not that way with Dr. Dewald"—expressed just before her having symptoms. The patient's conscious perception of the analyst as *not* like her father was contradicted by, and in conflict with, her unconscious perception that he *was* like her father. The analyst's contradictory communications caused unconscious conflicts between the patient's wishes to believe her own perceptions of what he was communicating and her wishes to believe his explicit communications about what was occurring in their relations.

To this point, we have studied the presence of contradictory communications contained in the analyst's questions. Other kinds of interventions may also contain contradictory communications. Interpretations that contain projective identification, such as the interpretations examined in Session 176, are disruptive to the recipient's psychic functioning because they contain contradictory communications. The metacommunication (i.e., "this is an interpretation") conveyed when an analyst interprets contradicts the unconscious communications contained in the projective identification. Part of this contradiction is that interpretations are explanatory statements ostensibly designed to enlighten the patient. Interpretations should be given in a neutral mode wherein the analyst does not attempt to control or to influence the patient except by providing insight. By definition, projective identification contains mainly unconscious attempts to control and influence the recipient by means other than insight and understanding.

What the therapist communicates unconsciously in projective identification is then opposed to what he or she should be doing in interpreting. The disturbing effects of projective identification are made doubly so when such controlling communications are delivered in an interpretive mode of speaking, because of their contradictory, cognitively disrupting, and confusing effects. On the basis of clinical evidence, Bateson (1972) postulates that communications with double messages place the receiver in a "double bind" and that the double bind plays a causal role in the etiology of schizophrenia.

Session 177

In Sessions 177 and 178 the patient had several recurrences of the same symptom complex, and as indicated earlier, the interactional pattern of events in those sessions was similar to that observed in Sessions 2 and 176. In Session 177, eight out of 11 interventions and in Session 178 eight of ten interventions were questions of the directive type.

In each session, using questions and other interventions, Dewald brought sustained pressure on the patient to reveal her destructive fantasies about the analyst. He interpreted behaviors such as vagueness and silence as defenses against aggression. In a compliant response to these pressures and directives, the patient described her conscious fantasies of attacking or destroying the analyst. She spoke about her fears of her anger's destroying the analyst and his not being able to take it. Dewald then made the following defense interpretation: "So we can see that your thought that I'd be weak and destroyed and unable to tolerate your anger really represents a defense against your own sense of helplessness and your own feeling of being weak."

Again in this interpretation, as he did in Session 176, the analyst responded to the patient's complaint that he was weak and unable to tolerate her anger by a deprecatory remark. His communication ignored the valid aspects of her statements about him, and the unconscious communication in his defense interpretation could be restated as "It is you, not I, who is the weak and helpless one."

The patient's dyscontrol began soon after the analyst's defense interpretation. She became enraged and exclaimed, "When you say that it makes me want to kill you! You reduce me to just being a baby! . . . I hate you for making me *feel* so weak and helpless! – –* I'm *not* and I know I can destroy you!"

The analyst then queried, "What's the fantasy?" Note that the analyst's communication (i.e., "What's the fantasy?") functioned as a defensive diversion from the actualities of the immediate and affectively charged interaction with the patient, and it served to deny what was taking place in the analyst-analysand relationship. By his focus on conscious fantasy he again unconsciously communicated his denial of certain interventions, his wish for the patient to share in this denial, and his wish that the patient should not think about or say what he had done to make her feel angry and helpless.

She began to cry and to tell about her fantasies of destroying her father, her mother, and the analyst. She exclaimed, ". . . and the more helpless I feel, the madder I feel. I want to stand here and just give you hell!"

Conscious or Unconscious Fantasy?

The analyst often pressed the patient by questions and other interventions to express her fantasies, and the patient usually complied by presenting vivid

_____
*Each dash (–) represents a 30-second period of silence.

erotic and aggressive fantasies. As Anthony notes in the book's epilogue, the patient was unusually adept at creating affectively charged fantasies.

Dewald repeatedly made two mistakes in his conceptualization and interpretations of the meaning and function of her conscious fantasies. One was to treat these fantasies as wholly transferential. Her conscious fantasies had both transference and nontransference elements and should be viewed as derivatives of both. Her conscious imagery, such as that from Session 4 described in Chapter 12 in which she visualized the analyst sitting on her and squashing her, expressed in a metaphorical way important unconscious perceptions of how the analyst was treating her.

The conceptual error to the detriment of the analyst's technique and the analytic process was his confusion of *conscious* fantasies with *unconscious* fantasies. In his interventions in the analysis and his discussions of the analytic hours, he treats her conscious fantasies as if they were unconscious fantasies. The emergence into consciousness of unconscious fantasies through interpretation or other means and their working through play a crucial role in the devleopment of insight and the resolution of symptoms and transferences. This process and the products of this process should not be confused with the patient's expressions of conscious fantasies.

As Langs (1982a) notes, therapists sometimes become seduced into believing that apparently loaded instinctual drive material directly expresses unconscious content and that patients are then directly expressing their basic unconscious wishes without defense. Dewald's view is therefore incorrect, because even the most blatant communications have both manifest and latent, direct and encoded, implications.

The Symptom Complex

As I noted earlier, the patient showed signs of dyscontrol and rage after the analyst interpreted her thoughts of his being weak as a projection of her own weakness. Then Dewald asked, "What's the fantasy?" The patient cried and described her fantasies of destroying her father, her mother, and the analyst. Again, the analyst asked, "What's the detail?" She replied,

> I feel as if I'd die and that scares me. I can't imagine ever being mad here and then just walking out and being able to function and being able to return. It's like the end of the world and everyone dies. I know that these are all just excuses for me not to be mad.

After talking more about how helpless and how angry she felt, she said,

> You're just like my father and you're telling me, "Be a big girl." [Elaborates.] He'd always get disgusted if I'd ever act like a baby.

It makes me so mad! Now the idea of wanting to cut my wrists
comes to my mind. – – – – But then I get that sexual feeling every
time!

Derivatives of Unconscious Introjects and Percepts

Observe in the above quotation the patient's apology for *not* being mad (i.e.,
"I know that these are all just excuses for me not to be mad"). If we consider
her apology as a derivative, then we could speculate that it derives from her
unconscious perceptions of the analyst's pressures to become angry. Perhaps
also the patient's apology arose out of her introjection of what I earlier
postulated to be the analyst's deprecatory unconscious communication (i.e.,
"It is you, not I, who is the weak and helpless one") contained in his defense
interpretation.

These hypotheses are supported by another derivative ("You're just like
my father and you're telling me 'Be a big girl'"). This derivative probably
also stems from both the patient's unconscious introjection and her perception of the analyst's demeaning attitude toward her unconsciously conveyed
in his defense interpretation.

Interactional Aspects of the Wrist-Cutting Fantasy

An important dynamic in the genesis of the patient's wrist-cutting fantasies
was her introjection of the unconsciously hostile contents contained in the
analyst's projective identifications. Cutting her wrists meant cutting the
hateful introjected object. At the same time, the wrist-cutting fantasy symbolized her need to maintain her relationship with the analyst. The wrist-
cutting fantasy stemmed from unconscious wishes to appease the analyst and
restore her relationship with him. Cutting her wrists meant preserving her tie
to the analyst and protecting him from her hatred for him. Many clinical
studies of suicidal subjects have demonstrated that suicide threats and
attempts stem from powerful needs for restoring and/or repairing a relationship when its loss has been threatened. As Simpson (1976) explains, the
expression of wrist-cutting impulses and the act of wrist cutting have multiple
conscious and unconscious aims, including gaining attention, the need to be
loved and cared for, reducing tension, and the need for punishment.

The unconscious life-restoring and life-preserving wishes contained in
her thoughts of cutting herself are similar to the life-affirming aims expressed
in her genital sensations. Wrist-cutting wishes and overt actions occur most
commonly during states of depersonalization and/or depression. The life-

affirming wishes that are denied in depersonalization and depression "return" in the wrist-cutting fantasy. Wrist cutting is unconsciously viewed as a means of reintegration, repersonalization, and dramatic return to reality and life from the dead state of unreality. Recall the patient's statement, "It's like the end of the world and everyone dies," just before she admitted wanting to cut her wrists. Rosenthal and associates (1972) characterize these unconscious meanings of the wrist-cutting act as "I bleed; therefore I am alive," and "I do have insides, I can see them."

Session 178

At the beginning of this session the patient talked of a frightening dream that panicked and awakened her. In the dream she was running with a huge butcher knife, and without meaning to, she slit a baby's head with the knife. During most of the hour the analyst asked her for associations to different elements in the dream. She responded by describing fantasies of both seducing and destroying her father. During much of the hour she was anxious and crying. Midway through the hour she recalled a pleasant childhood memory of playing on a couch with her father. She became anxious as she told of having intense and alternating feelings of love and hate. At this point she began to show evidence of dyscontrol, as shown by her statement "I feel as if everything is all swimming around me and there are all kinds of voices and firecrackers and it's all so wild." With escalating emotional turmoil she made a plea for the analyst's help:

> I'm all emotion inside and I want to let it out by talking
> and to get your attention and to have you understand
> that I'm so nervous. [Then she was silent for one
> minute.] Suddenly I'm frightened and I want to cut my
> wrists.

Referring to her one minute of silence, the analyst responded with the confrontation, "I think there was a connecting thought or fantasy left out there between the feeling of being excited and having me understand and being frightened and wanting to cut your wrists."

Just after the patient had exhibited much turmoil and had asked for his help, the analyst chided her for her minute's silence and claimed that she had left something out. Here again, I think, we can view his unempathic confrontation as a projective identification in which he attempted to deal with his own conflicts and impatience by projecting them onto the patient.

The patient responded to the analyst's confrontation, "I felt that you really don't care and that you don't want to listen and understand me. You're not going to give me any attention and love and I hate you." She cursed him and accused him of trying to ruin her world. In a setting of mounting rage and anxiety, she again reported having different parts of the symptom complex:

> I'm so mad at you! I have a sexual feeling in my vagina.
> I feel like I'm going to die! I want to take your God-
> damned penis and snap it off. That's the only kind of
> woman I can be! – – – – I feel completely helpless. I want
> you and your attention so badly but I know I'll never
> get it and I don't know what to do. – – – – I want to
> yell and scream and go wild and I want to see you fall
> apart and say, "God, what have I done?"

Dewald asked, "And what else comes to mind about that?"

The patient replied, "Then you'd pick me up and love me and tell me that you're so sorry. Then I get a sexual feeling and I feel like cutting my wrists." After further rageful ventilation of her feeling that the analyst had reduced her to being like a child, she made her final hostile outburst of the hour: "I hate *you* and it's not my father. It's *you*. I hate your *guts*. I feel like walking out of here. But I'm scared to death. And you just sit there and give me absolutely nothing."

As in Sessions 2, 176, and 177, the patient's reports of having sexual sensations and wishes to cut her wrists occurred in the context of dyscontrol, rage, and helplessness. And again, the symptom complex was triggered by an intervention containing a projective identification.

The Shared Denial

The patient's derivative "I hate *you* and it's not my father" may be considered to be a confrontation that indirectly refers to the analyst's persistent denials that the patient's anger had anything to do with the analyst's communications. Dewald denies the meaning of her confrontation, and in his discussion of Session 178, he writes,

> She illustrates the intensity of this transference experience when
> she says, "I hate *you* and it's not my father. It's *you*." For the
> moment the therapeutic alliance has been suspended, the self-
> observing ego functions are decreased, and she is again experi-
> encing the relationship to me as if it were really the childhood
> situation with the father.

The patient denied that her hatred for the analyst had anything to do with her relationship with her father, and the analyst in his discussion of the sessions and in his interactions with the patient denied that he had contributed to the patient's hatred. He viewed her hatred as entirely a transference experience. Actually, both Dewald and the patient were right, and in another way both were wrong. Her hatred stemmed from her interactions with both the analyst and her father. All human experience is shaped by both the past and the present, by transference and nontransference. Transference is not a separate entity or a discrete kind of object relation; rather, it is an aspect of all object relations and all experience.

Although the patient directly vented her hatred for the analyst in this session, she continued to deny different meanings of her angry relations with the analyst—meanings connected with the here-and-now interactions as well as those arising from the past. A study of the patient's angry outbursts against the analyst shows that after the third session she rarely directly said what there was about the analyst or his communications that had provoked her anger.

As the analysis progressed, the patient, like the analyst, seldom attempted to connect, to relate, to correlate, to make sense of her emotions in terms of her ongoing communicative interactions with the analyst. Her communications about her ideas, feelings, and fantasies were discussed, interpreted, and treated by both the analyst and the analysand as if they were experiences disconnected and isolated from the background of analyst-analysand interactions from which they had emerged.

These findings support the hypothesis that the analyst and the analysand gradually developed a shared myth, an unconscious, tacit agreement in which she could become angry at him as long as she, like the analyst, would ascribe her anger to transferential sources and that her angry ideas and perceptions would be labeled as fantasies. In this way first the analyst and then the patient, in a merging and defensive compliance with the analyst, denied that her angry responses had anything to do with the analyst's unconscious communications and controlling actions.

Interactional Aspects of Rage and Helplessness

The patient's intense sense of helplessness experienced both immediately before and during the times she had the genital sensations and the wishes to cut her wrists stemmed in part from the bind she was placed in by the analyst's contradictory communications. For example, to be openly angry with him went against his unconscious prohibitions. At the same time she felt she should be angry with him in order to comply with his pressures on her to express her angry emotions and fantasies.

Many of the analyst's interventions in the sessions just reviewed were directed at the patient's defenses against aggression and anxieties over aggression. He conceived of her aggression toward him as arising from the frustration of her oedipal wishes, and he often interpreted her aggression as transferred from her relations with her father. The analyst's attribution of her aggression to oedipal origins was reductionistic and simplistic because there is abundant evidence in the process notes that her aggressive impulses had additional sources and meanings, in both the past and in the here-and-now interactions with the analyst.

Much of her rageful behavior fits the description and dynamics Kohut (1972) discusses in his study of narcissistic rage. The patient's rage was triggered and inflamed by the analyst's directive questions and projective identifications. This emphasis on the proximal stimuli for her rage reactions should not be construed as discounting the developmental roots of her propensity for rage in her past relationships, fixations, and traumas.

The patient's rage reactions contributed to her dyscontrol, which also intensified her rage. Narcissistic rage emerges when there is some threat to the subject's sense of self. Any event or situation that threatens the individual's sense of identity or self-cohesion may be a powerful factor in rage reactions. The patient's cognitive dyscontrol triggered rageful emotions because the dyscontrol temporarily impaired her capacities for rational thinking, for maintaining her sense of self-cohesion and her boundaries between reality and fantasy and between past and present. Even the momentary loss of control over these vital psychic functions may evoke rage. Examples of this phenomenon are the overwhelming anxiety and rage reactions frequently observed in patients having cognitive dyscontrol as a result of brain damage (Goldstein 1975). (See Chapter 16 for a discussion of affective reactions to brain damage.)

Kohut (1971, 1977) wrote that separation from or loss of control over another person perceived as a self object may lead to threatened fragmentation, loss of self-cohesion, and narcissistic rage. There is clinical evidence in the sessions reported that this was an element in the genesis of the patient's rage reactions. In Session 178, for example, she became enraged when after she had told the analyst about her nervousness and her need for understanding, he told her that she had left out a "connecting thought or fantasy." She wished for a merger with an idealized self object, and when instead the analyst was confrontive and critical, she became enraged. Disruptions of self-object transferences may lead to intense feelings of rage and helplessness.

Actual or threatened loss of the self object for the subject means the loss of an extended part of the self. The self-object is experienced in much the same way as the subject experiences the self or the body. Threatened loss or separation from the self object evokes feelings of helplessness and rage similar to what occurs when one loses a body part or a body function.

Conclusions

As we have observed in this chapter and in Chapter 12, the patient—in defensive compliance with the analyst's unconscious communications— gradually adopted his denial of his controlling interventions. These studies have reported on why she denied, what she denied, and how she denied. This chapter has demonstrated that their shared denial played a critical role in the patient's dyscontrol and in the formation of a particular symptom complex experienced during the analytic hours.

One can view the conscious and unconscious effects of the analyst's controlling interventions from both an affective and a cognitive point of view. These interventions provoked disturbing affects and conflicts that revived the patient's preexisting conflicts. An important factor was the patient's introjection of the analyst's projective identifications. The analyst's contradictory communications evoked cognitive dyscontrol. In these communications the conscious or manifest communication was used to screen the contradictory, unconscious communication. The patient's introjection of the contradictory messages impaired her higher-level (secondary-process) functions, and this dyscontrol in turn led to the emergence of her symptoms.

This chapter's focus on the nontransference aspects of the patient's perceptions and reactions should not be construed to mean any downgrading of transference issues. One reason that the denied interactions caused symptoms was that these interactions repeated past traumatic relationships among the patient, her father, and her uncle. The analyst's controlling mode of relating and communicating to the analysand and her compliance with the analyst replicated similar aspects of the patient's relationship with her father. The mutual, unconscious acting out of this pathologically symbiotic kind of object relation and the shared denial of this kind of interaction prevented both the analyst and the analysand from attaining insight into the differences as well as the similarities between her earlier father-child relations and her current relations with the analyst.

The denied, unconscious nature of these interactions accounts for their pathogenic power in producing dyscontrol and symptom formation. Individuals can usually cope with consciously experienced intense affects and disturbing perceptions. Because the patient lost conscious cognitive and affective control over what was denied, she developed the symptom complex. What was denied returned in the form of symptoms, a type of communication based on primary-process mechanisms. Symptoms emerge when conflicts and perceptions unfold outside consciousness and are subjected to uncontrolled primary-process mechanisms (Langs 1982a).

This study's findings and conclusions have important implications for explaining the interpersonal and social factors involved in symptom formation and perhaps also for other kinds of psychiatric disturbances. Everyone has at times evoked upsetting emotions or anger, helplessness, and frustration in others. Such temporary and conscious unpleasurable affective experiences usually have little significance in symptom formation. In this study, the necessary condition responsible for symptom formation was the shared denial. The findings from this study suggest the testable hypothesis that interactional symptoms arise in interpersonal situations in which one individual, through contradictory and perhaps also other kinds of communications, manipulates another individual in such a way that the other individual is not able to use effectively his or her higher-level psychic functions for coping with stress and conflict.

It is premature to generalize and extend the conclusions reached in this study to other therapeutic situations. Nevertheless, I suspect that shared denial contributes to symptom formation far more often in analytic and psychotherapeutic situations than most mental health professionals realize. According to Langs (1982a, 1982b), many psychoanalysts and therapists deny important therapist-patient interactions, and beginning with Freud, many classical analysts have used the transference concept defensively to screen out of their awareness the unconscious impact on patients of their interventions.

Many therapists, like Dewald, view the patient's communications almost entirely in terms of internal conflicts, defenses, and transferences disconnected and isolated from the events and transactions of the therapy hours. They appear to conceptualize the patient's mind as a closed system separated from its environment. As a result, such individuals perceive their analytic role as confined to that of the detached observer and objective interpreter of events in that closed system. This widely held therapeutic stance and the theories used to support it can effectively be used to deny the powerful effects of the therapist's unconscious communications on the patient's psychic functions and communications.

The implications of this investigation for the theories of the analytic process and technique could be the subject of other studies. Such studies may lead to modifications of psychoanalytic theories of the psychoanalytic process and technique to include a systematic account of how the unconscious communications of the analyst may contribute to the patient's defensive operations and symptom formation. This and similar studies should demonstrate that the communicative method advanced by Langs (1978, 1980, 1981, 1982a, 1982b) and employed in this chapter and Chapter 12 could greatly assist therapists in listening to their patients and themselves. In this way, instances of interactional denial and interactional symptoms could more quickly be detected and rectified, if not entirely prevented.

14

The Working Through of Denial
in the Therapeutic Process

In this chapter a case study is used to illustrate and explain the conditions in the patient and the patient-analyst relationship needed to work through denial. What occurred in the patient both before and after she lifted and worked through her denials is explained by the cognitive arrest theory. Working through denial reractions transforms primitive forms of mentation into more adaptive and reality-syntonic modes of cognition and communication.

Case Study

The patient was a 32-year-old married nurse who was seen in once-a-week psychotherapy. One of her complaints was that she had been acting like her own mother in being "cold" and "bitchy" toward her two stepchildren. She also feared that leaving her own three-month-old son with a baby-sitter while she went to work would harm him and that he would be "emotionally abandoned" by her as she had been by her mother. Before the birth of her son she had been drinking excessively. She described her father as a "softy," a nice man who was "always helping people."

I had previously seen the patient for several brief periods of psycho-therapy extending back 13 years. Each time she came in during some kind of interpersonal crisis and abruptly terminated after she had resolved the crisis and had begun to feel better. On one occasion she had been troubled about her relationship with her first husband, who had been physically abusive to her. She used the therapy at that time to protect herself and obtain a divorce.

Though she was seen on a once-a-week basis, I limited nearly all my interventions to interpretations that focused on here-and-now transferences or to interventions designed to create and to maintain a psychoanalytic frame.

Projective Identification

During the first five months the sessions had a similar structure, in that during each hour the patient tried to induce me to act out with her the role of an idealized and omnipotent caretaker. She used a variety of maneuvers and manipulations to get me to tell her what to do, what to think, and what to feel. She asked questions, played the part of being helpless, and urged me to give her advice and moral directives. Her major mode of communication was what Langs (1978) has called the Type B mode, and much of what she communicated to me could be viewed as projective identification.

In one session her projective identification became especially intense, and she put unremitting pressures on me to give her advice and directives. She said she was going to stop her psychotherapy and that she was going to obtain help from an alcoholism counselor who she knew would tell her what to do. I succumbed to her pressures and, in a tone of irritation, lectured to her about the differences between psychoanalytic psychotherapy and alcoholism counseling. She agreed to continue with the psychotherapy. My response to the patient's projective identification stemmed from what Grindberg (1962) calls *projective counteridentification.* In other words, I had acted out rather than contained and analyzed the role cast on me by the patient, and my lecturing remarks were themselves also a type of projective identification. In a way, she had succeeded in having the analyst rather than herself be the one to concerned about "emotional abandonment." By her manipulations and her threats of leaving therapy she had evoked in me her unconscious conflicts about being abandoned.

At the beginning of the next session she turned toward me and said gently, "You know you really did manipulate me last time by the way you talked to me about psychotherapy."

I replied, "Yes, I did."

"Of course," she added, "I have put a lot of pressure on you, and I know I've tried to manipulate you at times to answer my questions." Here she was indirectly referring to the many interpretations I had made about how she had tried to maneuver and manipulate me into acting out the roles and contents she had projected onto me. Her benevolent confrontation that I had also manipulated her was, I think, motivated by her loving and therapeutic need to assist me. Searles (1975) and Langs (1981) describe the mainly unconscious therapeutic communications of patients and how they unconsciously perceive and attempt to remedy their therapists' emotional disturbances. In a short time the analytic frame was restored, and I was able to maintain a more interpretive and neutral stance toward her conflicts regarding emotional abandonment and her projective identifications.

Constructive and Pathological Symbiotic Relations

One day the patient again behaved in a helpless fashion, and she asked me what she should do about her infant son. She wanted me to tell her if she should give up working and stay home in order to care for him. I responded with the interpretation that she was pretending both to herself and to me that she could not decide for herself. "You are turning over to me your own abilities for thinking and deciding," I added.

Her response was to tell about how eager her father had been to help her and to give her advice. She felt that the only time she received much attention in her parental family was when she presented a "problem" to them. The patient was relieved and gratified that she could use her own mind in her relations with me and that she did not have to turn over the "good" parts of herself to me. My interpretation and her response to it marked a change from a predominantly pathological symbiotic relationship to a more normal and constructive symbiosis. She no longer pressed me for answers to her questions and began to perceive our relationship more as a cooperative alliance. The relationship was mainly a symbiotic one because she perceived and treated me at most times as a need-fulfilling self object rather than as a whole object.

In the ensuing several months she experienced in every session one or two brief periods when she felt "bad." In writing about her experience I have used her word *bad* to give the reader some idea of her inchoate and inarticulate state of mind. She literally did not know and could not say what she felt bad about. Though the nature and meaning of these bad feelings were not clear to the patient or to myself, it was obvious that she was handling them differently from the way she had previously. Whereas before she had attempted to manipulate me into doing something about her feeling bad, now she was attempting to talk about her dysphoric emotions and to reflect on them.

The Dissolution of Denial

A remarkable and lasting change in her defensive denial occurred in one session in which she lifted her defenses and ventilated her intense feelings of self-hatred. She began the session telling that she had never felt so bad about herself as she had in the past few days. Crying profusely, she exclaimed that she wanted to kill the bad part of herself. In an increasingly anguished way she scolded and berated herself for both real and imagined wrongdoings. She said she wanted to run away from me and find some place to hide. Because she seemed poised to bolt and run from her chair, I felt it was necessary to intervene. I interpreted her projection, saying that I thought she feared I would hate her as much as she was hating herself. She revealed that she had figured out that many of her problems had come about because of this bad part of herself. In the past, she explained, she had used alcohol or had run away whenever she had started to feel the way she now did. I wondered aloud whether one reason she wanted to run away from me was that it was so painful for her to tell me what she was feeling. Running away, I surmised, was a kind of emotional abandonment of herself. By running away she was doing to herself what she felt her mother had done to her. For her this was a most painful and difficult session, and throughout most of the hour she struggled between intense wishes to stay and equally intense wishes to run away.

She went on speaking about the bad part of herself and she angrily described herself as a "terrible mother," "a negligent wife," and a "not-so-good nurse." Crying again, she told of how she had broken all of the Ten Commandments, including the one about not killing—referring to the time when she had had an abortion. Toward the end of this tumultuous hour she regained her composure and thanked me for not reassuring her or minimizing her emotions, as her parents had. She closed the hour by stating, "I have never put into words or told anybody about these bad feelings about myself." A later section will explain the implications and consequences of her ability to put into words for the first time these disturbing emotions.

Working Through and Reconstruction

In the succeeding several months this patient made rapid progress as she worked through the implications and meanings of her telling me about the bad part of herself. We traced her self-hatred back to the emotional abandonment by her mother and to a traumatic separation from her mother when she was one year old. At that time, her mother had developed eclampsia and was hospitalized for over a month before delivering a baby girl. During this time the patient was cared for in her grandparents' home. She was able to understand that she had felt responsible for the separation from her mother and that the so-called bad part of herself was an amalgam of guilt and rage over the loss of her mother. Considerable analytic work was done on her impulsive tendencies to run away from me and from others. Avoiding and removing herself from close relationships stemmed from a defensive, unconscious identification with her mother's physical and emotional abandonments.

For the first time in her life she was able to comprehend the differing contributions made by reality and fantasy to her dysphoric emotions. She realized that blaming herself for her mother's hospitalization and emotional abandonments was based on fantasy and not fact. In a futile attempt to preserve her representation of a good, need-fulfilling mother, she had unconsciously introjected and applied to herself the badness of her mother.

Anniversary Reaction

Both the patient and the analyst recognized that the patient's highly charged abreaction about the bad part of herself came at the time of her son's first birthday. In a sense, this was an anniversary reaction in that unconsciously she wanted to come to terms with and resolve the traumas engendered by her mother's leaving her at one year of age and, at the same time, protect her baby son from a similar misfortune. During the following months she made steady progress in the treatment and began to feel and to look much healthier and happier than before. She decided to leave her nursing job temporarily in order to stay home and care for her son. She was able to resolve some long-standing conflicts with her husband, and her relationships with others, including most notably her son, were strikingly more mutually gratifying.

The portion of her treatment summarized above can be divided into three periods according to the different ways in which the patient attempted to communicate and to deal with her dysphoric affects. In the first period, she attempted to repeat, by projective identification, the pathological symbiotic relation she had with her father, and she perceived and related to the analyst as one who would offer her magical means of emotional relief and direction. The second period began after a successful interpretation regarding her projective identification. She began to use the therapist's interpretation that she was defensively turning over to him her thinking abilities as permission to think for herself. During this time she continued to relate to the analyst as a self-object, but she began to form an alliance in which she could cooperate with the analyst in talking about and understanding her emotions. The third period—the working-through period—began when she lifted the denial and worked through the traumatic experiences underlying her self-hatred.

What Was Denied

In the first part of her treatment she first denied and then projected onto the analyst her painful feelings about emotional abandonment. As we have seen, she managed to evoke in the therapist the fear of abandonment that she unconsciously had defended against by denial and projective identification. Her excessive drinking and promiscuity were used to deny the bad part of herself. The most important denied contents concerning the disavowal of the meanings related to her painful affects. Only in the working-through period of treatment did she gradually construct, with the therapist's assistance, these personal meanings. These previously denied meanings included the significance of her mother's physical abandonment when she was one year old and her mother's later emotional abandonments, her defensive and hostile identification with the abandoning mother, her anger at her mother for the abandonment, the causal relationships between her acting out behaviors (e.g., excessive drinking, running away from others) and her dysphoric affects, and finally the unconscious reasons for blaming herself for her mother's abandonments.

It would not be accurate to say that she had repressed these meanings. These personal meanings were not created before the therapy and then repressed. They did not exist in the unconscious; they were articulated and created only after some dissolution of her denial. Actually, the first time she recognized and established as part of her representational world the meanings associated with her bad feelings was when she talked about her painful emotions in her psychotherapy hours.

Making the unconscious conscious was not merely or only a process of translating what was unconscious into consciousness. The full personal meanings of what she had previously denied were appreciated and recognized as they never had been before. This new consciousness was more than the synthesis and integration of what had previously been dissociated from conscious awareness. Working through denial is a formative and creative endeavor in which previously unconscious memories and fantasies are used to construct revised representations and meanings of the self and its object world.

Unlike denial, repression is failing to recall psychic contents (e.g., memories) that have received verbal representation. In working through repression the patient remembers something that he or she formerly could not recall: some psychic content becomes conscious that had been conscious before it was repressed. In contrast, what has been denied has never been transformed from its primary-process elements through the symbolization process into verbal representations. When the denial defense is resolved, a new consciousness of what was denied is created. (Further discussion about the relationship between defense and memory pathology may be found in Chapter 15.)

Loewald (1980) conceptualizes working through as a process in which the resistance of the unconscious—the repetition compulsion—is overcome. Working through is the strenuous task of helping lift unconscious processes onto a new level of integration, the level of secondary process. In addition to the resistance associated with repression, another resistance—the repetition compulsion—was recognized by Freud (1926). In reptition compulsion, the unconscious resists the transformation of primary into secondary process. He described this resistance as the "attraction exerted by the unconscious prototypes upon the repressed instinctive processes" (p. 159). According to Loewald (1980), the products of working through are not a copy, a rerecording, but a new version of something old. The working through of the above patient's denials was a creative and reconstructive activity in which she verbalized for the first time in her life what she had previously denied.

How the Patient Denied

In the weeks after she revealed to herself and the therapist the bad part of herself, the patient made some insightful comments on different facets of her denying. She explained that she had kept her negative feelings "secret" from herself. She had tried to "hide" them, and she had "denied" that part of herself. Never before had she "acknowledged" this painful aspect of her experience and her personality. By "running away" from painful situations she had avoided facing a part of herself. These quotations indicate how she had previously denied the personal significance of her painful affects. In working through her denial she attained considerable insight, as the above quotations attest, into her specific modes of denial.

One can deny in thought, fantasy, and overt motoric action. The patient's acting out behaviors (e.g., excessive drinking, running away, promiscuity) had been used to escape and reject her dysphoric feelings. Gradually the patient was able to understand the relationship between her self-destructive acting out and her previously unconscious wishes to destroy and "get rid of" the bad part of herself. Understanding and verbalizing the emotions, images, and memories associated with these painful emotions proved to be of decisive value in controlling her acting-out propensities. Her creating new and realistic meanings of her painful emotions gave her new methods to tame and control her impulses. Freud (1900) emphasized that the development of the secondary process causes a delay or detour between impulse and overt action. Being able to reflect on and speak about her painful affects gave this patient a delay between her wishes and their enactment.

Cognitive Arrest in Denial

Chapter 1 explained that what is denied is not put into words and that denial includes a specific cognitive arrest that prevents the subject from attaining a realistic view of whatever he or she is denying. Working through what has been denied means verbalizing and avowing what the denial has previously kept unconscious. What is denied is *disavowed*, whereas working through some denied content includes an *avowal* as part of the self of what has previously been rejected. The words *denied content* in the above sentence do *not* mean verbal or secondary-process content. As used here, content refers to the primary-process, presymbolic elements. Because of the cognitive arrest in denial reactions, these embryonic, presymbolic elements have not been transformed into symbolic, verbal forms. A critical aspect of working through a denial defense is the transformation of primitive, embryonic forms of thinking about painful experiences into more adaptive, reality-syntonic modes of cognition and communication.

The cognitive arrest hypothesis regarding denial may be used to explain what occurred in the above patient both before and after the hour when she lifted the denial defense against her dysphoric affects. Verbalizing these emotions for the first time in her life aided her in understanding herself and the history of her relationships with significant others. Previously, these dysphoric emotions were the experiential and conscious aspects of an unconscious negative introject in which certain self-representations were merged and undifferentiated from object-representations of her bad, abandoning mother. Working through these affects of primitive guilt and rage helped her differentiate between her mother and herself and allowed her to distinguish better between fantasy and reality. In other words, the dissolution of her defense against feeling bad was accompanied by the formation of new and/or improved boundaries between herself and the objects of her needs, between the present and the past, and between reality and fantasy.

Patient–Analyst Interactions

The therapist's major contribution to working through the denial is in establishing and maintaining the conditions in the therapeutic situation that allow and foster the patients' own mainly unconscious efforts to deal constructively with their denials and the painful affects warded off by denial. The prime condition for facilitating this patient's resolution of her denial defense was in maintaining a neutral attitude and a secure psychoanalytic frame that provided a safe holding environment for the patient. This included avoiding antianalytic deviations such as giving advice, directives, and educational interventions. A review of 22 supervised analytic cases shows that the major cause of analytic failure is frame errors, such as using antianalytic methods, made by the analytic candidates (Dorpat 1984).

The analyst's other major contribution in the patient's working through of her denial defense was the transference interpretations concerning her projection of the good parts of herself (her rights and abilities for thinking and making decisions) onto the analyst. As a result of the work done by both the analyst and the analysand on her need for a magical and omnipotent self object to relieve her from facing the bad feelings in herself, she was able to obtain some understanding of her pathologically symbiotic relationship with her father. Her use of the interpretations regarding this projective identification helped her reestablish her confidence in her own capabilities for thinking and making decisions.

Many of the major elements of her denial reaction had been interpreted and discussed before the hour when she lifted the defense. These interpretations paved the way and prepared the patient for ultimately dissolving her denials. I would like to emphasize that these elements were treated by means of interpretive interventions that focused on the patient-analyst interactions. As they became involved in the analytic interactions, issues of abandonment and running away were repeatedly interpreted. Also interpreted were the patient's projections onto the analyst of her self-punishing and self-rejecting attitudes. Most important, interpretations that focused on the patient's denial of her own mental functions and their projection onto the analyst aided her avowing and using her autonomous abilities for self-reflection and decision making. The position advanced here is in agreement with the views of Gill (1982), who emphasizes the therapeutic significance and priority of here-and-now transference interpretations.

Weiss (1982) argues persuasively that patients are likely to lift their defenses and to experience a warded-off content when they unconsciously decide that it is safe for them to do so. He shows that the operations of the unconscious mind are regulated by the ego's assessments of danger and safety. Patients are able to lift their defenses and talk about previously warded-off contents when their relationship with the therapist offers them a feeling of safety. The therapist's maintenance of a neutral attitude and a secure psychoanalytic frame are the foremost conditions needed for providing a safe holding environment for the patient.

Identifications with the Analyst Introject

Working through denial reactions requires insight into the what, how, and why of denial alongside the structure-building internalizing of patient-analyst interactions. There is a growing tendency by many analysts to view internalization and the development of insight as two interrelated processes that explain therapeutic progress (Meissner 1981). This patient's internalization of her interactions with the analyst was essential to her working through of her denial defense and to her psychic development. After the decisive session in which she lifted the denial, the patient often spoke about the "tools" she had acquired or learned in her treatment. By tools she referred to her emerging capacities for tolerating and containing her emotions and, above all, to her growing abilities for putting her feelings into words, first in the sessions with the analyst and, later, alone in her thinking. The tools she spoke about are similar to the analyst's professional functions (e.g., acceptance, empathic listening, and interpretation).

An earlier paper describes two stages in the internalization of patient-analyst relations (Dorpat 1979). These stages include, first, the formation of an analytic introjection through the introjection of patient-analyst relations and, second, the establishment of new or improved ego and superego functions by selective identifications with the analytic introject. By first introjecting her relations with the analyst, the patient gradually formed a stable analytic introject. Later, she developed her tools for self-reflection and self-understanding, by making selective identifications with the analyst introject.

Denial and Projective Identification

Denial is an important aspect of projective identification, and the patient in this study used projective identification in the early period of her treatment to avoid thinking about her painful emotions. What the patient denied was then projected onto the therapist. In an interpretation described earlier, both the patient's denial and her projective identification were interpreted. The interpretation focused on her denial in fantasy (i.e., pretending she could not think or decide for herself) and her projection of thinking and deciding functions onto the therapist. One of the factors that distinguishes pathological projection from normal projection is denial. As a normal psychic mechanism, projection plays a role in such activities as empathy and interpersonal perception. But in pathological projection, what is defensively attributed to someone else is also denied as some content or function of the self.

Unconscious destructive fantasies also were central to this patient's denials. The intense aggression in her earlier attitude toward herself when she felt bad was indicated by comments she made after the hour when she lifted the denial. Speaking of her former attitude, she spoke at different times of how she had earlier tried to "kill," "reject," "destroy," and "get rid of" the "bad" part of herself. These quotations provide a hint of the content of the underlying unconscious fantasies that had energized her denials.

Libidinal Motives in Projective Identification

The patient's response to several of my interpretations of her projective identifications was that she was "giving the good parts" of herself to me. She spoke of how she had hoped to please me as she had previously pleased her father by turning over to him those "good" parts of herself. Her associations to these interpretations provided the information needed for reconstructing her pathological symbiotic relationship with her father. The father had been orphaned at age two, and he had projected onto the patient his own fears of abandonment. He had treated her as if she were a young child whom he had to advise, direct, and help by thinking for her. In so doing he had compromised her autonomy and confidence in her own abilities. In order to please him and maintain a relationship with him, she had played the part of a helpless girl who needed him to solve her problems.

Many studies have emphasized the presence of conscious or unconscious hostile wishes to the object in patients' projective identifications. Though I do not dispute that this is a common dynamic, I do disagree with the idea that hostile wishes to the object are a universal or defining feature of projective identification. In this patient and in two analytic patients who manifested similar kinds of projective identification, hostile impulses played a minimal role in their projective identifications. The unconscious wishes underlying their projections were loving wishes to give, to please, and to sacrifice some part of themselves for the analyst. These patients had unconsciously directed their hostility against themselves and had denied their own psychic abilities. Then, in what they considered to be a loving act, they had attributed to the analyst these functions and the moral authority to regulate them. In so doing, they are replicating with the analyst earlier pathological symbiotic relationships in which the motives for attributing idealized powers and abilities onto the analyst were viewed as acts of love and surrender. At times these generous impulses were fused with passive-receptive sexual desires. Over time, in these three cases, it became abundantly clear to both the patients and the analyst that their self-sacrificing gifts had been unconsciously designed to bolster the fragile self-esteem of their earlier symbiotic partners, including both parents and spouses.

The point of the foregoing discussion is to underscore the neglected importance of predominantly unconscious loving motives to some forms of projective identification. Unfortunately, in the three patients noted above, these libidinal impulses were used to repeat and maintain pathological symbiotic relationships, and they required the unconscious, self-destructive sacrifice and denial of the patients' autonomous ego and superego functions.

Projective Identification and Transference

Classical psychoanalytic writings on transference emphasize the *displacement* of affects and attitudes toward parents onto the analyst, whereas Kleinian analysts and others stress the importance of *projection* of aspects of the self onto the analyst. Displacement and projection are not mutually exclusive; they may occur together. For example, the patient displaced onto the therapist from her relations with her father the wishful expectation that he would advise and direct her. At the same time, she was also projecting onto the therapist idealized powers of thinking and decision making. When projective identification is a prominent mode of defense and relatedness, both displacement and projection in transference reactions often occur simultaneously.

The patient's displacement onto the analyst of her pathological symbiotic relations with her father should not be called father transference, because the relations that were transferred were predominantly of a self-object rather than a whole object type. The term *father transference* accurately describes transferences in which the analyst is perceived and treated as a whole object. As Kohut (1971) explains, in self-object transferences, the therapist is valued for the function(s) that he or she symbolizes, and not for his or her separate and personal characteristics.

Projective Identification and Countertransference

The case study section above shows two different responses by the therapist to the patient's projective identification. In the first instance, the therapist reacted to the patient's threats to terminate the therapy by scolding her and lecturing. In so doing he enacted his countertransference and participated with the patient in a mutual projective identification. The second vignette explained the analyst's interpretation that the patient was turning over to the analyst her abilities for thinking and deciding. The therapist's lecturing approach may have helped prevent the patient's running away from treatment, but it did not have any therapeutic effects. In contrast, the therapist's interpretive responses did lead to therapeutic and constructive change in the patient. She was able to internalize the analyst's implicit communication that she could think and decide for herself. Using these abilities, she was later able to work through her denials and conflicts over abandonment.

Ogden (1982) describes three phases in projective identification, with the first two phases attempting to evoke in the recipient the subject's disavowed feelings. The nature and quality of the third phase is decisive for the patient's working through of some unconscious conflict. This phase includes the psychological processing of the projection by the recipient and finally the reinternalization of the modified projection by the subject. In the second vignette in which the therapist responded with an interpretation, there was a therapeutic reinternalization by the patient that provided one of the conditions for her later working through of her denial reaction.

Before the patient could reach the working-through period, the analyst had to process and "metabolize" what was projected onto him. We commonly think of working through as a process that occurs solely within the patient.

But the evidence from this and many other cases strongly suggests that there is an interactional component of working through. The patient could begin to work through and master conflicts and traumas concerning abandonment only after the analyst had first processed and, in a sense, worked through the conflicts associated with abandonment that the patient had evoked in him by her repeated threats to quit treatment.

The therapist's countertransference is an amalgam of the therapist's preexisting tendencies and conflicts and his or her affective responses to the role that the patient attempts to force on him or her. Pressures placed on the therapist are often subtle and persistent, and the projector's manipulation can rekindle the therapist's unconscious conflicts. Being the recipient of the patient's projective identifications can be extremely frustrating and stressful. Therapists often feel helpless and controlled and unable either to relieve their own discomfort or to find some therapeutic and interpretive response to the patient. One way to conceptualize these frustrations is to view them as constituting a group of dilemmas concerning how the therapist should respond to the patient's projective identifications.

The therapist should not act out with the patient the role that is attributed to him or her. Unfortunately, it is not possible completely to avoid doing this, because, as Sandler (1976) observes, the analyst's emotional response to the patient—his or her countertransference—is created partly from his or her responses to the patient's pressures on him or her and from sources within himself or herself.

Frequently, therapists are unwittingly drawn into states of mutual projective identification. With patients who use more subtle forms of projective identification, therapists may not be aware of what "hit" them, who "hit" them, and how they were "hit." Particularly in the therapy of more disturbed patients, temporary episodes of mutual projective identification do occur, even with competent therapists. Although it is not possible always to avoid mutual projective identification, it is both necessary and possible for therapists to detect the presence of mutual projective identification and to disengage themselves from it. The communicative method outlined and used in Chapters 12 and 13 is a valuable tool for detecting and investigating the complex unconscious interactions in mutual projective identifications.

Unless conditions are suitable for interpretation, the therapist's silence in response to the patient's projective identification is usually the preferred technique. But sometimes even silence itself may appear to the patient to verify the patient's projection of the dead, unresponsive, and isolated parts of himself or herself. Silence does communicate something, and as Watzlawick and colleagues (1967) explain, it is not possible for one to *not* communicate.

Even when the therapist does succeed in communicating in a manner that does not completely agree with the patient's projection, he or she may face the frustrating prospect of being ignored or discounted. As discussed in

Chapters 7 and 11, the patient who uses projective identification will frequently deny the meaning of any communication that disagrees with his or her projection. The patient may negatively hallucinate communications that do not fit his or her preconceptions and expectations of the object.

Patients whose predominant mode of communication is through projective identification also tend to receive communications in the same mode. Or, as Langs (1982b) explains, individuals who are Type B senders are also Type B receivers. They "hear" in the Type B mode. Because their communications are mainly designed to manipulate and control others, they unconsciously assume that others communicate with them in the same way. Oftentimes they do not understand the analyst's interpretations as interpretations, and they frequently misunderstand interpretations as directives or other modes of interpersonal manipulation.

My purpose in emphasizing the inevitability of these dilemmas is to undercut some of the more common ways in which therapists seek to avoid recognizing their emotional difficulties in containing and responding to their patients' projective identifications. Acknowledging these dilemmas and the conflicts they engender is necessary in order to create constructive solutions to the dilemmas and to devise therapeutic interventions.

For some therapists a common way of avoiding these dilemmas and stresses is by engaging in mutual projective identification with the patient. Often, therapists are unaware of their participation in a Type B field. They have unconsciously identified with the role cast on them by the patient and acted out this role in their interactions with the patient. Some therapists are aware of participating in mutual projective identification, but they rationalize their interventions as necessary deviations required by the contingencies of the therapy situation or by the patient's psychopathology.

Summary

A case study was used to illustrate and explain conditions in the patient and the patient-analyst relationship that are necessary for working through defensive denial. The cognitive arrest theory was used to describe what occurred in the patient both before and after she lifted the defensive denial. A decisive change in her defensive organization occurred after the patient was able to lift her defenses and to speak about her feelings of self-hatred. In succeeding hours she worked through what she had denied, how she denied, and why she had denied the different meanings of her many lifelong emotions of self-hatred that had first been evoked by the abandonment of her mother when she was one year old and later by her mother's emotional abandonment.

The process of becoming conscious of these meanings was a formative process in which unconscious contents, memories, and fantasies were used to construct new personal meanings and representations of herself and others. In contrast with repressed content, what has been denied has never been transformed from its primary-process elements through the symbolization process into verbal representations.

A crucial aspect of working through denial reactions is the transformation of primitive, embryonic forms of thinking about painful experiences into more adaptive, reality-syntonic modes of cognition and communication. Conditions in the therapeutic situation that foster working through include maintaining a psychoanalytic frame and interpretations that give priority to interpretations of transferences in the here-and-now. Two basic processes in working through include the development of insight and the internalization of patient-analyst interactions.

Transference and countertransference aspects of projective identification were discussed, and guidelines for overcoming the inevitable frustrations and stresses engendered by patients' projective identification were outlined.

15

Defense and Memory Pathology

Though the psychoanalytic literature from Freud on contains many discussions about the relationship between repression and memory, little has been written about the kinds of memory pathology caused by denial reactions. The cognitive arrest theory explains the enactive memories, screen memories, and gaps in memory brought about by denial. The major hypothesis advanced in this chapter is that denial prevents the formation of representational memories of whatever is denied. This hypothesis is supported by experimental studies (summarized in the last section of this chapter) that show that long-term memory depends on attention. Permanent storage of information requires an act of focal attention.

Veridical representational memories of denied past experiences cannot be recalled or recovered in analysis or elsewhere because they were never formed. Denial is an interruption of the normal process of thought and percept formation, with the consequence that what is denied does not attain conscious levels; and the denier, therefore, does not form an *accurate* verbal representation of what he or she has denied. The term *accurate* is emphasized because the denying individual does form screen memories, wish-fulling distortions, and displacements of the denied event.

When the repression defense is lifted in analysis, the patient is able to recall something that he or she had been conscious of at some previous time. In contrast, when denial is lifted, the patient creates new ideas and memories of the previously denied event. What I shall later write about denial and memory pathology is similiar to what others have written about the consequences of primal repression. The concept of repetition compulsion functioning (described in Chapter 6 as a consequence of primal repression) is similar to the concept of *enactive* memory.

In what follows I shall summarize the clinical findings regarding pathological memorial activities associated with denial reactions that have led me to formulate the hypothesis of denial's blocking the formation of representational memory and that provide evidential support for it.

Denial and Memory Pathology

The patient described in the previous chapter did not in her treatment recall accurate and specific memories of her mother's physical abandonment when she was one year old. Generally, her psychotherapy did not bring about the recall of memories that once were conscious. Rather, the memory activity linked with the working through of her denial was a reconstructive process in which she created new memories and meanings regarding her mother's physical and emotional abandonments, her responses of rage and guilt, and her need both to repeat and to deny these traumas. With her, the principal kind of memory pathology was enactive memory. Before her psychotherapy, she did not have accurate representational memories of her mother's abandonments and her affective reactions to them.

The main types of pathological memorial activity associated with denial are enactive memory, screen memories, and deficits or gaps in memory. Clinical observations made during the psychoanalytic psychotherapy or the psychoanalysis of patients who suffered traumas in childhood, such as the suicide of a parent, indicate that their denials of the trauma prevented them from forming accurate memories of the event and the circumstances surrounding the event (Dorpat 1972). Several studies demonstrate that the trauma of parental death is often defended against by the surviving child's denials of important meanings of the parental death (Altschul 1968, Bowlby 1980, Dorpat 1972, Furst 1967).

At times such traumatized patients become confused and disorganized when their unconscious responses to traumas are revived in the analytic situation. There are huge gaps in their recollections covered over by patently distorted screen memories. In the treatment of traumatized patients it became obvious to me and oftentimes to the patients that they could not remember important relationships and events connected with the trauma. Even when I took into account their current defensive need to repress and to distort their memories, it still seemed as if a major part of their difficulty in recalling the past was a consequence of the ways that their memories were established during their disturbed and traumatized state.

Rubinfine (1973) explains why patients recall past traumatic events in a disorganized and confused manner. He argues persuasively that the state of consciousness in which a percept is recalled is similar to the state of consciousness in which the percept was originally registered. Registration of percepts during a disorganized altered state of consciousness prevents the percepts from becoming objects of focal attention. Such unconscious perceptions are restricted to drive-organized schemas and are processed by the primary process, much in the same way as the day residue is processed in dreams.

Enactive Memory and Representational Memory

A primitive kind of memorial activity observed in patients who have denied past events is the acting out of past traumatic events and relationships. Loewald (1976) distinguishes between *representational* and *enactive* memory. A defining property of the enactive form of remembering is that it is unconscious—that is, the individual is not aware that he or she is repeating something from the past. In representational remembering, the individual recalls something from the past that is consciously distinguished from the present. Enactive memory shares the timelessness and lack of differentiation of the primary process and the unconscious. Affective states and moods may also often be understood as forms of nonrepresentational remembering. The distinction between enactive and representational memory resolves itself into that between unconscious and preconscious memory. Unconscious memory follows the laws of the primary process, whereas preconscious memory (i.e., representational memory) is regulated by the secondary process (Loewald 1976).

Freud (1914) distinguished between consciously remembering and repeating the past, and he claimed that repeating the past is an unconscious form of remembering. Repeating, in the sense of reenacting past experiences in the present, is remembering by action and affect rather than by thought.

An example of enactive memory is seen in the patient described in Chapters 8 and 9 who, as a young child, had been ignored by his mother and who unconsciously repeated that interaction by ignoring his analyst and others. Through interpretations linking reconstructions of the past with present transference reactions, his unconscious memories (i.e., enactive memories) were lifted from total unconscious states to a higher level of consciousness. In this way psychoanalysis aided him in constructing new ideas, representations, and memories regarding himself and his object relationships.

Screen Memories and Repression

In working analytically with patients who had suffered childhood trauma I at first incorrectly assumed that once their repression resistances had been lifted, they would be able to produce clear and accurate memories of the past traumatic events. This proved to be a false hope because even when these patients had progressed to the point that they wanted to remember the trauma, they either were not able to do so or they produced screen memories. Working through their repression resistances against thinking about and remembering the trauma did not, in the main, bring about therapeutic change or the recovery of memories providing valid insights into the trauma or themselves.

An example of an emotionally powerful and enduring kind of defensive screen activity observed by several clinicians in survivors of trauma is *survivor guilt* (Niederland 1961). For example, many patients who were survivors of parental suicide defended themselves against overwhelming unconscious feelings of rage and helplessness evoked by the trauma, by maintaining an irrational emotion of guilt over the suicide (Dorpat 1972, Warren 1972). Until they obtained therapy or analysis, their screen memories asssociated with guilt feelings were used to prevent the emergence of memories linked with rage and helplessness regarding their parents' suicide.

Screen memories, screen percepts, and screen affects formed at or near the time of a traumatic event may later be repressed, and in psychoanalytic therapy these unconscious screen memories and affects may be recalled after there is some lifting of the repression. The clinician should be cautious about considering or interpreting such screen memories as accurate reproductions of the traumatic event. As Freud (1899) and others have shown, screen memories serve a defensive function in analysis, just as they originally served a defensive screening function at the time of the trauma.

When the memory and meaning of a past event have been obscured by denial, the memories that are either immediately available to consciousness or recovered after repression has been lifted are nearly always screen memories, distorted half-truths defensively constructed either at the time of the past event or later to avoid painful recognition of the personal meanings and truths regarding the event.

Defense and Memory Gaps

Memory gaps—the inability to remember past experiences—often stem from denial and repression acting together. Repression is nonrecallability, and I am using the term *repression* to describe situations in which persons, for unconscious defensive reasons, are not able to recall representational memories. To the extent that elements of some past eperience were denied at the time of the experience, veridical representations were never formed. Though aspects of any disturbing event may be denied, denial reactions and the consequent failure to form accurate representational memories are probably most prominent following acute or chronic trauma. By *chronic trauma* I mean cumulative types of trauma and stress stemming from disruptive and pathological parent-child relations.

Denial, together with the disorganizing emotional turmoil at the time of trauma, prevents individuals from forming accurate representational memories and reality-syntonic meanings regarding the traumatic experience. Clinical findings from the treatment of such individuals strongly suggest that such denials of traumatic experiences are usually maintained unaltered for many years unless psychoanalytic treatment assists the patients in working through the denial (Altschul 1968, Dorpat 1972). Some degree of denial is an invariable reaction to trauma, though the duration and the particular form of denial depend on many variables pertaining to the individual's defensive structure and the nature of the trauma (Greenacre 1967, Horowitz 1976). The mastery of traumatic events and relationships in the analytic situation includes the patient's working through emotional responses to the trauma and the defenses that have prevented the patient from remembering, understanding, and overcoming the trauma.

Reconstruction and Denial

An important empirical generalization about the working through of denied past events and relationships is that patients in psychoanalytic treatment are able to articulate new meanings, ideas, and memories regarding the previously denied occurrences. In working with these patients, one gains the definite and repeated impression that these ideas had never previously been put into words and that the original experience had taken place at a level of psychic integration that was not amenable to preconscious or conscious integration. The reconstruction of denied past experiences in the therapeutic situation is a creative and structure-forming psychic activity in which the patient establishes new conceptualizations about his or her past experiences and himself or herself. The therapeutic resolution of denied past relationships revived and repeated in the transference as enactive memories is the *construction*, not the recovery, of representational memories. The analytic reconstruction of denied past events and relationships requires, first, the analyst's interpretive construction of new meanings regarding the patient's unrememberable past and, second, the patient's formation of representational memories. This reconstructive task is optimally carried out by transference interpretations that link current reactions to the analyst with denied past experiences. The relationships between denial and the reconstruction of past trauma in analytic treatment were also discussed in Chapters 9 and 14.

In contrast, working through repressed reactions requires the recall of percepts and ideas that had been conscious at one time. Though the recovery and working through of repressed representational memories plays some varying part in the therapeutic process, a much more extensive effort is usually required for working through denied events and relationships.

Defense As Preventing Permanent Forgetting

Another memory defect associated with defense is the inability to forget permanently whatever has been defended against (G. Klein 1966). Denied and repressed memories remain active and unconsciously influence in remarkable and diverse ways the individual's thinking and character. Pathological unconscious ideas persist with such freshness and affective strength because they have been blocked from the normal wearing-away processes by which past events are normally and permanently forgotten. Defense prevents immediate access to unconscious content, but it also preserves it for later use.

Repression is not forgetting. George Klein (1966) distinguishes between repression (defined as *nonrecallability*) and normal forgetting. Forgetting implies either temporary or permanent unavailability. Permanent forgetting of some experiences is normal and expectable, because such experiences have been dissipated through the gradual absorption and assimilation of the past with the ongoing record of experience. Because repressed memories are not recalled, they are not corrected and assimilated, and so they are retained unconsciously in a motivating and inhibitory capacity.

The implications of these concepts of memory pathology for theories of psychoanalytic technique and process are clear. A short-range strategy of psychoanalytic treatment is to assist the patient's remembering, reconstructing, and avowing the meaning of events and relationships that he or she has repressed and denied. A longer-range product of such constructive and reconstructive endeavors is the ability to *forget permanently* those experiences that were formerly unrememberable and unforgettable.

Focal Attention and Long-Term Memory

Contemporary theories of cognitive psychologists about long-term memory are congruent with the hypothesis that denial prevents the formation of representational memories. Experimental research verifies what William James (1890, pp. 403–404) writes about attention. He notes that individuals may attend to and remember only one of two contemporaneous sensations. The immediate effects of attention, he claims, are to make us perceive, conceptualize, distinguish, and remember better than we could otherwise. Attention means withdrawing from some things in order to deal more effectively with and to remember other things.

Cognitive psychologists agree that memory formation is dependent on focal attention. We can consciously remember only what we have previously attended to (Mandler 1975, Neisser 1967, Norman 1969, Triesman and Reilly 1969). Neisser (1967, p. 23) and others present convincing evidence for the hypothesis that the effects of preattentive cognitive processes are limited to the immediate present; more permanent storage of information requires an act of focal attention. Experimental evidence indicates that individuals have only a short-term memory for material not attended to. Norman (1969) writes, "Events to which we do not consciously attend cannot receive the proper analysis and organization which is necessary for both complete understanding and retrieval" (p. 179).

Cognitive psychologists view problem solving and recall as constructive psychic acts based on information from earlier acts (Neisser 1967). Memory storage retains information about mental acts rather than copies of information. Thus, what is used and recovered in forming conscious remembrances of an event will be based partly on the traces of mental acts performed and stored at the time of the event. The conclusions derived from experimental studies on long-term memory are remarkably similar to the clinical hypothesis advanced by Rubinfine (1973). As noted earlier, he believes that the state of consciousness in which a percept is recalled is similar to the state of consciousness in which the percept was originally registered.

Summary

The clinical and experimental evidence reviewed in this chapter supports the hypothesis that denial prevents the formation of representational memories of whatever is denied. Denial is an arrest of the normal process of thought and percept formation, with the result that whatever is denied does not attain explicit conscious awareness. This explicit awareness is necessary for long-term memory formation. The failure to form accurate representational memories in denial reactions is related to the pathological memorial activity (e.g., enactive memory, screen memory, and memory gaps) associated with denied past events.

Experimental studies demonstrate that the permanent storage of information (i.e., long-term memory) requires conscious acts of focal attention. Because the denier avoids giving focal attention to whatever he or she denies, he or she does not form long-term representational memories of it. The reconstruction in the analytic situation of past experiences defended against by denial is a formative psychic activity in which the patient establishes new concepts and memories of past experiences. In contrast with work with repression, the therapeutic resolution of denied past events concerns the formation and not the recall of representational memories. The memories defended against are both unrememberable and unforgettable. Defense prevents permanent forgetting because denied and repressed memories are blocked from the normal wearing-away process by which the records of past experiences are assimilated and permanently and normally forgotten.

16

Denial and Brain Function

Important clinical observations, investigations, and neurologists' theories of denial reactions seldom appear in the psychiatric and psychoanalytic literature. This overview of studies of denial reactions in patients with brain damage is presented with the expectation that psychoanalytic theories of denial will profit from integrating the knowledge gained from sister disciplines, the neurosciences. The first section of this chapter concerns studies of the anosognosia syndrome in brain-damaged persons. The second section covers the denial responses of patients who have had the so-called split-brain operation (commissurotomy of the corpus collosum). The final section on the relationships among disconnection syndromes, perceptual defenses, and denial reviews clinical studies that demonstrate that the interruption of neural pathways to the speech centers is conducive to denial reactions.

Studies of Anosognosia

The neurological literature contains many reports of patients with brain disease who denied disabilities or parts of the body. The concept of denial, but not the term *denial*, was described in the neurological literature, according to Weinstein and Kahn (1955), as early as 1885. At that time, Von Monakow told of patients who reacted to blindness by denying their disability. The term *anosognosia* was introduced by Babinski (1914) to denote denial or unawareness of left hemiplegia. Subsequently, other reports of patients with brain disease noted that different kinds of disabilities may be denied: right and left hemiplegia, blindness, alexia, deafness, auditory agnosia, hemiballismus, and headaches.

The literal meaning of the word *anosognosia*—lack of knowledge of disease—is not wholly accurate because, as Weinstein and Kahn (1955) demonstrate, anosognosia patients do have an unconscious perception of the disabilities they deny. Their patients did evidence some rudimentary and distorted awareness of their disabled extremities by referring to them as "a dummy" and "a rusty piece of machinery." Also, the very fact of the selectiveness of their denial of disability indicated some awareness of their deficit, as the patients never ignored or expressed delusions about a member of the body that was not disabled.

At first, the term anosognosia was used to describe verbal negation of the paralyzed limb. Later, other clinical manifestations were included under the rubric of anosognosia. According to Weinstein and colleagues (1964), they include the patient's

> verbal negation of the paralyzed limb, denial of their existence, and delusions, illusions and hallucinations concerning the affected side involving the phantom of an extra limb, and neglect of, and inattention to, one side of the body. (p. 376)

For the purposes of this chapter, the words *denial* and *anosognosia* will be considered synonymous. This usage is in accord with that of Weinstein and Kahn (1955), who interpreted all of the clinical manifestations of anosognosia as constituting either an explicit or an implicit denial of illness. They defined explicit verbal denial as the direct negation, in words, of the disability. In their study, forms of implicit denial included withdrawal, inattention, pain asymbolia, altered sexual behavior, hallucinations, and change in mood.

Cutting (1978) and Weinstein and Kahn (1955) discuss the varied hypotheses of anosognosia that have been advanced, ranging from psychodynamic interpretations to detailed neurophysiological explanations. In my opinion, neither the psychodynamic nor the neurophysiological hypotheses alone can completely explain anosognosia. As the following discussion will demonstrate, a comprehensive explanatory theory must take into account both psychodynamic and neurophysiological factors.

Much of the discussion in the older neurological literature focused on the questions of whether anosognosia is a unitary kind of dysfunction that is produced by a focal lesion or whether it is an aspect of a more generalized disturbance in brain function and behavior. Studies by Cutting (1978), Nathanson, Bergman, and Gordon (1952), and Weinstein and his associates (1955, 1964) proved that the various forms of anosognosia are not discrete entities that can be localized in different parts of the brain. Weinstein and Kahn (1955) argue convincingly that the location of the lesion, in the parietal or frontal lobe, is what determines the physical disability that may be denied, and not the mechanism of denial.

Psychodynamic Factors in Anosognosia

The observations of Guthrie and Grossman (1952), Nathanson and his associates (1952), and Weinstein and his associates (1955, 1964) demonstrate that anosognosia behaviors are subjectively meaningful and can be interpreted psychodynamically. In this respect anosognosia behaviors are no different from psychiatric symptoms in patients who do not have brain damage. The various forms of denial found in patients with brain disease are manifestations of a defensive psychological attitude temporarily adopted by the patient with gross structural defects of the central nervous system, as a means of protecting against the recognition of life-threatening illness and/or disability. Guthrie and Grossman (1952) and Weinstein and Kahn (1955) show convincingly that the premorbid personality is an important factor in the genesis of denial reactions among brain-damaged patients. They found that patients with anosognosia had used the same type of denial defense in other situations before the onset of the brain disease.

Because denial of illness is also frequently found in seriously ill medical patients who do not have brain disease, some doubt has been expressed as to whether somatic factors play any role in the denial reactions of patients with brain disease. Aitken-Swan and Easson (1959) report that 19 percent of a sample of 231 cancer patients denied the presence of a malignancy. In a study of 100 cancer patients, Gilbertson and Wangenstein (1962) found that 20 percent denied their illness. Croog, Shapiro, and Levine (1971) report that 20 percent of a sample of 345 men who were interviewed three weeks after a myocardial infarction said they had not had a heart attack. The above percentages of denying patients in samples of cancer and heart patients may be compared with the percentage of deniers—28 percent—found in the study of 100 consecutive hemiplegic patients by Nathanson and his associates (1952).

A comparison of the clinical case descriptions of the denying cancer and heart disease patients with the clinical descriptions of the anosognosia patients reveals a striking qualitative difference in the kinds of denial reactions. Generally, denial reactions in brain-damaged patients, especially in patients with right hemisphere damage, have more gross distortions of reality and delusional qualities than do the denial behaviors reported in cancer and heart patients. For example, one patient reported by Weinstein and Kahn (1955) identified her paralyzed left arm as her seven-year-old daughter. Another patient, who had sustained a left hemiplegia as a result of shooting herself in the head, denied her disability and stated that a friend of hers had been shot in the head. One woman with left hemiplegia had the delusion of having two left arms. Weinstein and Kahn (1955) tell of several patients who claimed that their paralyzed extremities actually belonged to someone else.

Somatic Factors in Anosognosia

In my view, there is convincing evidence that somatic factors in patients with brain damage do help form denial reactions. Evidence for this hypothesis comes from a study of 100 consecutive hemiplegia patients carried out by Nathanson, Bergman, and Gordon (1952). All 28 of the patients who denied their hemiplegia had an "organic mental syndrome," as demonstrated by some degree of disorientation and other symptoms and signs of defects in higher mental functions. In contrast, a majority of the hemiplegia patients who did not deny their illness also did not have the organic mental syndrome. Other studies of anosognosia patients indicate that anosognosia is associated with disturbances in higher mental functions (Cutting 1978, Ullman 1962, Weinstein and Kahn 1955). All of the phenomena observed in anosognosia syndrome—the denial of illness, disorientation, confabulation, delusional reduplication,* and nonaphasic language disturbances—are part of an over-all pattern of behavior that appears at certain levels of defective brain function (Weinstein and Kahn 1955).

Anosognosia occurs only under certain physical conditions; it does not take place in all patients with brain damage. In their discussion of somatic factors in their series of anosognosia patients, Weinstein and Kahn (1955) point out:

> The conditions of brain pathology were those which by virtue of rapidity of development, diffuseness, bilaterality or midline situa-tion or through the effects of increased intracranial pressure or subarachnoid bleeding produced diffuse delta wave activity in the EEG record. (p. 87)

Another finding implicating somatic causal factors is that the presence and degree of denial in studies of anosognosia patients are positively corre-lated with the degree of brain function impairment (Weinstein and Kahn 1955). When the patients in the Weinstein and Kahn (1955) investigation attained an improved level of brain function, their denial symptoms tended to disappear.

As noted earlier, in brain-damaged persons the symptom—disorientation —is frequently found in conjunction with the denial of illness. Weinstein and Kahn (1955) found that disorientation for place and time, like the anosognosic delusion itself, could not be attributed to defects in memory, calculation, or sensory perception. Disorientation, like explicit denial, is a symbolic form of adaptation that the patient uses to avoid overwhelming anxiety, the "catas-trophic reaction" of brain-damaged persons first described by Goldstein (1948).

*Delusional reduplication refers to the patient's reduplication for place, person, time, or parts of the body.

When the content of the patients' disorientation expressions in the Weinstein and Kahn (1955) study was analyzed, it was found that their distortions were both meaningful and unconsciously intentional. The substituted time or place often expressed their denial of illness or symbolized their feelings about their disability. Hospitalized patients with disorientation for place usually located the hospital at a place close to their home or place of business. One patient, for example, incorrectly maintained that her home was across the street from the hospital. The psychic content of their disorientation expressions could be understood as symbolic wish fulfillments. Thus, one patient who denied her paraparesis and her tracheotomy referred to the hospital as the "Fresh Air Roller Skating Academy."

Hemisphere Differences in Denial Responses

Before proceeding with a discussion of the cerebral hemispheres, anosognosia, and aphasia, I shall briefly review some basic neuroanatomy. The neural pathways carrying information from one side of the body cross over and connect chiefly with the opposite side of the brain. The left hemisphere controls motor functions on the right side of the body and, in right-handed persons, contains the speech area. Damage to the left hemisphere in right-handed persons thus tends to produce aphasia and sensorimotor disabilities on the right side of the body.

It is believed that the anosognosia syndrome occurs much more frequently with right-hemisphere lesions than with left-hemisphere lesions. Aphasia occurs far more often in patients who have sustained injuries to the left hemisphere. Weinstein and his colleagues (1963, 1964) provide convincing evidence for the hypothesis that the predominance of anosognosia for right-hemisphere lesions over left-hemisphere lesions is explained on the basis of the aphasic patient's loss of metaphorical speech. They conclude that damage to the left-hemisphere speech area deprives the patient of the use of metaphorical speech needed for the formation of denial reactions.

Weinstein and his associates (1963, 1964) evaluated the relationship between anosognosia and aphasia in patients who had lesions of the left hemisphere and who showed anosognosia or aphasia. In the 28 patients studied, the severity of the anosognosia was inversely proportionate to the degree of aphasia. Patients with marked anosognosia had little or no aphasia, and the aphasic patients in general did not manifest denial. Nearly all of the aphasic patients admitted both the aphasia and their sensorimotor deficit.

The skeptical reader could argue against the hypothesis of Weinstein and his colleagues (1963, 1964) on the basis that aphasic patients may actually deny their disability, but because of their aphasia, they cannot communicate their denial. This objection to Weinstein's hypothesis disappears in light of the observations made by him and his associates that the aphasic patients in their study did not, in the main, exhibit *nonverbal* expressions of denial such as indifference, inattention, or neglect of the disabled body members. In contrast, the nonaphasic patients expressed both verbal and nonverbal kinds of denial.

Weinstein and his associates (1964) report that manifestations of anosognosia associated with right-hemisphere lesions tend to be more bizarre than those with left-hemisphere involvement. Patients with left-hemisphere lesions rarely represent their disabilities in delusional or other metaphorical language. Weinstein and his colleagues (1963, 1964) call the various manifestations of the anosognosic syndrome *metaphorical* because the patient's feelings about the self were expressed in terms of the somatic, spatial, and temporal aspects of the environment. For example, one patient called his paretic left side his "dead mother." It was hypothesized that the aphasia patients did not use or misuse metaphor, as did the anosognosia patients, because the damage to their speech centers had deprived them of the capacity to use metaphor. Their hypothesis was supported by the results of a test concerning the interpretation of idioms, which revealed that the aphasia patients had a statistically significantly greater deficit of metaphorical speech than did the anosognosia patients.

Aphasia is negatively correlated with denial reactions because damage to the left-hemisphere speech centers impairs the subject's abilities for understanding and speaking in metaphors. The capacity for metaphorical speech appears to be a necessary condition for denial reactions. The tools, as it were, of denial reactions are symbols; when the subject is deprived of the use of symbols, he or she is no longer able to use the denial defense.

The fact that damage to the speech areas tends to deprive the individual of the denial defense probably accounts for the greater emotional disturbance found in patients with left-hemisphere lesions, as compared with patients with right-hemisphere lesions. Denial reactions occur more frequently following right-hemisphere lesions, and depressive and anxiety reactions are observed much more often following left-hemisphere lesions. Gainotti (1969) reported on 150 cases of unilateral cerebral lesions in which he compared the incidence of the indifference reaction with the incidence of the catastrophic reaction. With left-hemisphere lesions, the incidence of catastrophic reactions was 62 percent, whereas with right-hemisphere lesions it was only 10 percent. In contrast, the incidence of *la belle indifference* was 33 percent with right lesions and 11 percent with left lesions. In their comparison of right and left temporal lobe epileptics, Bear and Fedio (1977) found that right-temporal epileptics exhibited denial, whereas left-temporal epileptics exaggerated their emotional difficulties. In addition to the reports on anosognosia and temporal lobe epileptic patients, there are other clinical investigations such as studies with the Wada carotid artery amobarbitol test and reports on the effects of unilateral electroconvulsive shock treatment that show that there are major differences between the two hemispheres in the quality of affective reactions to injuries of the hemispheres (Galin 1974).

In summary, the unconscious defensive need to deny disability plays an important role in the functional symptoms of brain-damaged patients. Both psychodynamic and neurophysiological hypotheses are needed for a comprehensive explanation of the anosognosia syndrome. Physical damage to the brain plays a role in the genesis of the brain-damaged person's denial reactions. The meaning and defensive function of the denial reactions can be explained psychodynamically. Denial reactions occur most frequently following right-hemisphere lesions, and depressive and anxiety reactions are observed much more often following left-hemisphere lesions. Aphasia and anosognosia tend to be mutually exclusive symptoms, because damage to the speech area impairs the patient's capacities for understanding and speaking in the metaphors required for the formation of denial responses.

Split-Brain Studies

Recent studies on the function of the two cerebral hemispheres, especially investigations of split-brain patients, promise to shed light on the neurophysiological correlates and mechanisms of denial. The two hemispheres communicate through the corpus collosum which joins the hemispheres anatomically. Sectioning of the corpus collosum prevents sensory information that enters one hemisphere from the opposite side of the body from being transferred to the other hemisphere. A group of severe epileptics were treated by the split-brain operation involving commissurotomy, cutting down the midline the interconnections between the two hemispheres (Sperry 1982). Ingenious and subtle tests showed that the operation had clearly separated the specialized functions of the two hemispheres.

The split-brain surgery dramatically delineated the two major modes of consciousness that normally are integrated in each person. Each hemisphere appears to have its own conscious sphere for sensation, perception, and other mental activities, and in split-brain patients the entire cognitive activity of one hemisphere is detached from the corresponding experience of the other. Writing on the effects of the operation, Sperry (1964) said, "Everything we have seen so far indicated that the surgery has left each of these people with two separate minds, that is, with two separate spheres of consciousness" (p. 29).

In tests examining the capacity of the split-brain patients to speak with reference to information specifically lateralized to one or the other hemisphere, very different responses were obtained from the right and left hemisphere. Although spoken descriptions of stimulus material obtained from the left hemisphere showed little or no impairment, the right hemisphere in the same tests was incapable of speech. For example, when a patient held a pencil (hidden from his sight) in his right hand, he could verbally describe it correctly. But when the pencil (again hidden from sight) was placed in his left hand, he could not accurately describe it. Recall that information from the left hand informs the right hemisphere, which possesses only a limited capacity for speech. With the corpus collosum severed, the left (verbal) hemisphere is no longer connected with the right hemisphere and does not "know" what is in the left hand. The right hemisphere, though it cannot "speak," can "understand" language and act intelligently on the basis of what it has understood.

Split-brain patients who received specific information only in the right hemisphere responded with denial reactions. Gazzaniga (1967) reported that for a considerable time after the split-brain operation, when an object was placed in the left hand of the patients, they generally "denied" its presence. When a pencil was placed in the left hand of the split-brain patients, it might go unnoticed, or more frequently, the patient would recognize it but call it a "can opener" or a "cigarette lighter." Gazzaniga and Sperry (1967) believed that such confabulations and rationalizations came presumably from the left hemisphere and were based on whatever indirect cues happened to be available to that hemisphere. The confabulations and similar behaviors of these patients remind us of the screen behaviors in denial reactions discussed in Chapter 1.

In certain mental processes the right hemisphere is on a par with or superior to the left. The right hemisphere can generate an emotional reaction. In one of the experiments, a photograph of a nude woman was presented to the right hemisphere of a split-brain patient (Gazzaniga 1967). At first the patient said that she saw nothing, but then a smile spread over her face and she began to chuckle. When asked what she was laughing at, she said, "I don't know . . . nothing . . . oh—that funny machine." Although the right hemisphere could not "say" what she had seen, the sight nevertheless elicited an emotional response. The patient's reactions to the photograph strike the psychoanalyst as similar to the hysteric patient's denial of sexual feelings and thoughts.

In the above and similar tests, a clear split was observed between two independent consciousnesses which in normal individuals are usually integrated and in communication. This division in the split-brain patients is similar to Freud's concept of the defensive splitting of the ego in which there are also two separated and unintegrated kinds of consciousness. This process seems to underlie the defense of denial in which the verbal mechanism is deprived of access to emotional information in other parts of the system (Fingarette 1969).

The Relationship Between Hemispheric Modes and the Primary and Secondary Processes

In a general way, the responses of the two separate hemispheres are analogous to the differences and conflicts between the conscious and unconscious processes described by Freud. The secondary-process workings of the conscious mind are similar to the kinds of mental operations mediated by the left hemisphere, and the right hemisphere functions are like those of the primary process and the unconscious system. The right hemisphere, for example, processes and interprets nonverbal information.

Galin (1974) was the first to draw a parallel between hemispheric modes and those processes designated as primary and secondary processes. The psychoanalyst McLaughlin (1978) built on and expanded the viewpoint of Galin. Both suggested that the primary-process modes, as ordinarily conceptualized in psychoanalysis, seem formally similar to the cognitive modes, assigned to the recessive hemisphere. Likewise, secondary-process modes are similar to the workings of the dominant hemisphere. McLaughlin's (1978) clinical observations support the concept of a congruence between hemispheric functions and their interworkings and those attributed to primary and secondary processes and their interrelationships.

McKinnon (1979) studied the semantic forms in the primary and secondary process and compared them with the semantic forms of the right and left hemispheres, and he found that they were homomorphic. The descriptive features of the semantic forms of the primary and secondary processes are structural and logical homologues of, respectively, the right hemisphere and the left hemisphere. The left hemisphere mode tends to be verbal, sequential, detailed, and analytic, whereas the right-hemisphere mode is characteristically nonverbal, synthetic, coherent, and spatial.

Let us examine the denial reactions of the split-brain patients and compare them with the denials of psychiatric patients. When information was presented to only the right hemisphere of split-brain patients, they were not able to integrate this information into explicit (verbal) awareness. Their confabulations and other distortions of reality have the same form as the denials of psychiatric patients. The simultaneous activity in the split-brain patients of two levels or kinds of consciousness that were not integrated with each other is another similarity between the denial behaviors of the split-brain patients and the denials of psychiatric patients.

The failure of the split-brain patients to integrate, to represent, and to verbalize correctly the information received into the right hemisphere occurred because the split-brain operation had severed the neural pathways from the right brain to the speech centers in the left brain. These patients were trying to appraise what was happening to them, even though they lacked the information necessary for making an accurate appraisal. It seems most probable that anxiety over their inability to make an accurate appraisal prompted them to deny their disability through a confabulated response.

The Functional Commissurotomy Hypothesis of Defense

On the basis of findings from the split-brain operation and from other clinical and experimental evidence of left and right cerebral hemispheric specialization, Galin (1974), Hoppe (1977), and Ornstein (1972) hypothesize that in individuals with intact brains, mental events in the right hemisphere can become disconnected from the left hemisphere by inhibition of neural transmission across the cerebral hemispheres. In their views, this blocking of information or "functional commissurotomy" provides the neurological underpinnings of psychic defense.

McKinnon (1979) offers cogent criticisms of the functional commissurotomy hypothesis. He claims that this hypothesis tends to be a "narrow localizationalist" conception of higher cerebral functioning because it implies that complex psychological functions such as defense correlate with distinct and local parts of the cortex.

Hoppe (1977) proposes that denial is due to the blocking of the interhemispheric stream, by which thing-presentations cannot be connected with the word-presentations of the left hemisphere. His study of 12 commissurotomy patients revealed a paucity of dreams, fantasies, and symbols. Their fantasies were unimaginative and tied to reality; their symbolization was concrete, discursive, and rigid. He notes the similarity of their impoverishment of feelings and fantasies with those of psychosomatic patients. Hoppe hypothesizes that in severe psychosomatic disorders there is a defensive functional commissurotomy that prevents certain emotions and gestalt perceptions in the right hemisphere from being verbalized by the left hemisphere. Instead, these emotions are hypercathected in the right hemisphere, leading to the resomatization of affect and the formation of psychosomatic symptoms.

Grotstein (1980) speculates about the existence of an inborn splitting defense. He cites the work of Gazzaniga and LeDoux (1978), who found that the corpus collosum and the deep cerebral commissures that unite the two cerebral hemispheres do not begin to myelinate (and therefore to function) until about three or four months of age and do not complete myelination until adolescence. Grotstein believes that this inborn splitting may be a mechanism for achieving anesthesia of painful experience by keeping the two hemispheres and the different modes of consciousness from communicating with each other before the individual is sufficiently mature to integrate the two modes of consciousness.

Although the hypotheses of Galin (1974), Grotstein (1980), Hoppe (1977), and Orenstein (1972) that denial and other defensive processes are mediated by some sort of functional commissurotomy may be true in some instances, it does not seem likely that a functional commissurotomy is a necessary condition for denial reactions. Damage to the corpus collosum is only one of several kinds of brain lesions that can facilitate denial reactions. The following section of this chapter argues that a critical anatomic factor in many, if not all, of the denial reactions of brain-damaged persons is some disruption of neural connections to the speech centers in the brain.

Perceptual Defects, Disconnection Syndromes, and Denial

What was written above about the effects of interrupting the transmission of information from the right brain to the left brain in split-brain patients generally applies also to other situations in which there is an interruption of input to the speech area. Next, I shall briefly review studies that indicate that the interruption of information to the speech centers facilitates denial behaviors. The interruption can occur at any place from the sensory end organs and peripheral sensory channels to pathways proximal to the speech area.

The psychoanalyst Linn (1953) emphasizes the reciprocal relationship between denial and disturbances of perception and provides clinical evidence that interferences with perception facilitate denial. Given a person's predisposition to denial, lesions of the somatic perceptual apparatuses weaken the person's hold on reality and thus contribute to denial reactions. For example, the neurological literature contains many reports of patients who deny their blindness or deafness. Persons who deny blindness often report visual experiences that are obviously confabulations, and they act as if they could see quite well.

Brown (1972) also believes that the interruption of sensory input to higher centers predisposes to denial. He notes that complete blindness is usually required for the blindness to be denied, and he concludes that the "denial of blindness results from visuosensory loss, where the lack of new information permits the conviction that vision has remained unchanged" (p. 240). According to Brown, another condition for the denial of blindness is confusion or a disturbance of consciousness. With regard to the denial of hemiplegia, Brown (1972) and others before him have emphasized the causal importance of the interruption of sensory information, particularly kinesthetic information, from the affected limb. If awareness in patients with hemiplegia is otherwise normal (e.g., if there is no organic brain syndrome), the existence of the limb in visual awareness will guarantee the maintenance of the percept, *disabled limb*, in the patient's body schema. Brown holds that if there is an overall reduction in awareness, such as occurs with an organic brain syndrome, there will be a failure of the disabled limb percept to overcome the effects of kinesthetic loss. This situation will facilitate the denial of the disability, because the patient may interpret the absence of information from the afflicted limb to mean the absence of impairment.

Disconnection Syndromes and Denial

The hypothesis that denial reactions are facilitated by the interruption of neural channels to the speech centers is supported by the studies of Geschwind (1965) on agnosia* and the disconnection syndromes. Disconnection syndromes may occur as a result of disruption between activities within the same hemisphere or as the result of disruption between the two hemispheres (e.g., the split-brain condition). Disconnection syndromes result from cutting sensory-speech connections. Geschwind (1965) provides convincing evidence that agnosic disorders result from disconnections from the speech area, and he views such disorders as "naming disturbances." An example of visual agnosia was the patient who misidentified a picture of a key as a violin.

The disorder "associative visual agnosia" was originally described by Lissauer (1889), who characterizes it as an inability to name, describe, or give the use of objects visually perceived in the presence of an intact ability to draw the object or to identify it through the sensory channels. The agnosic disturbance is a circumscribed one: unlike the aphasic's tendency to misname everything, the visual agnosic's inability is confined to a very limited area such as the naming of colors. Visual agnosia has been interpreted as a kind of "psychic blindness" in which there is a retention of visual sensory capacities with the loss of the signs and symbols through which visual conceptual recognition takes place. Geschwind (1965) describes one patient with a color-naming defect who could match colored papers and correctly sort slips of two slightly different shades of green into different piles, but was unable to articulate or even to select the correct names for the colors themselves.

Confabulation is the most common form of denial observed in agnosic patients and in other patients with the disconnection syndrome. According to Brown (1972), confabulation in patients with brain damage is a sign of an interruption in the perceptual process. As noted in Chapter 10, it is possible to distinguish a first stage of perception, during which sensory information is processed and registered, from a second stage, in which there is a conceptual identification of the perceived object. The cognitive defect in agnosic patients

---

*Agnosia is defined by *Dorland's Medical Dictionary* as "loss of the power to recognize the import of sensory stimuli. The varieties correspond with the several senses and are distinguished as auditory, visual, olfactory, gustatory, and tactile."

that predisposes to denial responses resides in the second or conceptual stage of perception.

Geschwind (1965) and Weinstein and his associates (1964) agree on three conditions that predispose to confabulation responses in patients with brain damage: (1) Confabulation is an attempt to fill in the gap of performance of some type, and it does not occur in the absence of a defect. (2) Confabulation is less marked in the presence of aphasia. (3) The presence of some overall impairment of awareness, such as occurs in the acute or the chronic brain syndrome, is conducive to confabulation. A fourth condition advanced by Geschwind (1965) is that confabulation is more likely to occur in the presence of lesions of the association areas than it is in cases of damage to primary sensory pathways up to and including the primary sensory cortex.

Discussion

The clinical and experimental evidence just reviewed demonstrates the presence of a cognitive defect in the denial reactions of brain-damaged persons. These findings support my hypothesis advanced in Chapter 1 that a critical factor in denial reactions is an arrest of secondary-process thinking about something mentally painful to the denying subject. In order to avoid unpleasurable affects, the denying subject aborts his or her thinking about some painful object at a primary-process level. The different forms of screen behavior, such as confabulation observed both in psychiatric patients without brain damage and in brain-damaged patients, are needed by these individuals to fill the gaps created by their cognitive defect.

The cognitive arrest theory presented in Chapter 1 holds that the cognitive defect in denying patients with intact brain function is brought about by the patient's unconscious fantasy attacks on some painful object. These attacks cause a temporary arrest of the patient's thinking at a primitive level and prevent the patient from forming realistic representations of whatever is disturbing. In anosognosia patients, the causes of the cognitive defect are more complex, as both somatic and psychodynamic factors appear to be operative. As evidenced by their symptoms (e.g., disorientation) of an organic brain syndrome, they have a physically caused impairment of the symbolic function. At the same time, their defensive aim of negating the facts and meanings of their disability contributes to their failure to think or to speak realistically about their disability.

In contrast, the cognitive defect in patients suffering from one of the disconnection syndromes (e.g., agnosic patients and split-brain patients) is a circumscribed defect and is not a generalized defect in the symbolic function. The confabulations and failures of split-brain patients to think or speak realistically about certain experiences come about because the commissurotomy has blocked the transmission of information about those experiences from the minor hemisphere to the speech area in the dominant hemisphere.

Many brain-damaged persons are not able to create an accurate conceptual knowledge of whatever they are denying. In the anosognosia patients this occurs partially because of a generalized defect in their symbolic function. In the disconnection syndromes the failure to develop a conceptual knowledge of what they are denying comes about because of specific disconnections from the speech area. Similarly, in psychiatric patients who do not have brain damage, there is a failure to develop a veridical and reality-appropriate conception of whatever they are denying. Their defect stems from their unconscious and defensive need to avoid conceptualizing something emotionally painful.

The presence of denial per se is not dependent on a structural brain lesion, because denial often does occur in the absence of any structural brain lesion. Weinstein and Kahn (1955) state, "Some motivation to deny illness and incapacity exists in everyone and the level of brain function determines the particular perceptual-symbolic organization, or language in which it is expressed" (p. 123). They argue that the effect of the brain lesion is to provide a milieu of function in which any incapacity or defect *may* be denied. Pathological changes in brain function affect the pattern rather than the elements or contents of the symbolic expressions of denial. A psychodynamic perspective is required for the understanding of the contents and unconscious meanings of specific denial behaviors in brain-damaged patients, just as it is in the denials of persons with intact brain functions.

The defensive aim of avoiding the recognition of reality is only one of several possible motives in denial behaviors. At the same time that the denying patients are defending themselves, they are also attempting to make sense to themselves and others of their situation. The gap in the patients' performance caused by their cognitive defect generates a need to provide some meaningful and coherent account of themselves and their present situation. This need is illustrated in the confabulations of the split-brain patients. When their speech areas were deprived of whatever information was needed for them to construct a realistic appraisal of what was taking place, they used whatever cues were available to them to confabulate an account.

Denial reactions of brain-damaged persons provide a kind of natural experiment for testing the hypothesis advanced in Chapter 1 of the nature of screen behaviors in the denials of psychiatric patients. There I hypothesized that the subjects unconsciously design screen behaviors to fill in the gaps created by their disavowal of reality. This disavowal deprives them of using verbal representations to describe veridically their unpleasurable situation. Now let us suppose that we could design an experiment in which we could temporarily deprive subjects of their capacities to use language for thinking and speaking realistically about something. We could, in principle, do this by interfering with their capacities for receiving, integrating, and interpreting information about the something or other in question.

This, as we have just seen in the studies reviewed, is precisely what happens in the denial reactions of brain-damaged persons. Because the interruption of information to speech centers deprives them of the means for accurately symbolizing certain events, they then resort to various kinds of screen behavior to fill in the gaps created by their cognitive defect.

Much information from the studies of psychologists and neuroscientists shows that the highest level of consciousness is connected with the function of verbal thought and that it is also linked with capacities for abstract or secondary-process thought. The outstanding discovery of the investigation of split-brain patients is the uniqueness and exclusiveness of the dominant hemisphere in respect to the highest level of consciousness (Popper and Eccles 1977). According to Eccles, the commissurotomy investigations are important because they have shown that the hemisphere containing the speech centers has the amazing property of being in liaison with the subject's self-conscious mind in respect to both giving and receiving. Self-consciousness is derived only from neural activity in the dominant hemisphere (Popper and Eccles 1977). The speech area in the dominant hemisphere is essential to the higher mental processes involving symbolization and abstraction capacities. The denial reactions of patients with brain damage have a property in common with denial in patients who do not have brain damage. Both groups have an impairment of cognition caused by the subject's failures to integrate adequately and to symbolize certain kinds of information.

The abstract capacity (or symbolic function), according to Goldstein (1975), is the expression of the brain's most complex function and the one that suffers first when the brain is damaged. Brown (1972), Cutting (1978), Weinstein and colleagues (1955, 1964), and others maintain that the fundamental defect in brain-damaged persons that underlies and explains the functional symptoms (e.g., denial, disorientation, and defects in attention) pertains to language and the symbolic function. Comparing defects in the abstract attitude in schizophrenics with brain-damaged patients, Goldstein (1975) notes that schizophrenics show a selective nonuse of abstraction ability, which concerns only a definite part of the world, whereas patients with brain damage tend to have a generalized defect in the abstract attitude.

Summary

This chapter presented an overview of denial reactions in patients with brain damage, with the aim of integrating knowledge obtained from neurological studies with psychoanalytic theories of denial. Anosognosia is a unique and most interesting kind of symptom because the available evidence indicates that both psychodynamic and neurophysiological hypotheses are required for a comprehensive explanation of the anosognosia syndrome. Anosognosia symptoms are unconsciously intentional and meaningful denial behaviors. They can be interpreted psychodynamically as a manifestation of defensive attitude adopted by the patient to avoid recognizing a life-threatening illness and/or disability. Anosognosia is associated with other disturbances of the higher mental functions (e.g., disorientation) found in brain-damaged patients.

The higher frequency of anosognosia that occurs in right-hemisphere lesions, in comparison with left-hemisphere lesions, is explained on the basis of the aphasic patient's loss of metaphorical speech. Damage to the speech area tends to deprive the patient of the metaphorical speech needed for the formation of denial reactions.

Studies were reviewed indicating that the interruption of information to the speech area facilitates denial reactions. The interruption can occur anywhere from the peripheral sensory channels to the pathways proximal to the speech area. Lesions of the somatic perceptual apparatuses tend to weaken the person's hold on reality and thus contribute to denial responses. Investigations of brain-damaged patients and patients having had the split-brain operation support the cognitive arrest theory of denial.

The cognitive defect in the split-brain patients stems from the interruption of information from the minor hemisphere to the speech area of the dominant hemisphere. In patients with agnosia, the cognitive defect results from the disconnection of pathways from the cortical projection area to the speech area. The different forms of screen behavior (e.g., confabulation) observed in both psychiatric patients without brain damage and brain-damaged patients are motivated by the defensive aim of filling in the gaps created by their cognitive defect.

REFERENCES

Abend, S. M. (1975). An analogue of negation. *Psychoanalytic Quarterly* 44:631–637.

Aitken-Swan, J., and Easson, E. (1959). Reaction of cancer patients on being told of their diagnosis. *British Medical Journal* 1:799–814.

Allport, F. H. (1955). *Theories of Perception and the Concept of Structure*. New York: John Wiley.

Altschul, S. (1968). Denial and ego arrest. *Journal of the American Psychoanalytic Association* 16:301–318.

Arieti, S. (1955). *Interpretation of Schizophrenia*. New York: Brunner.

—— (1978). The structural and psychodynamic role of cognition in the human psyche. In *On Schizophrenia, Phobias, Depression, Psychotherapy, and the Farther Shores of Psychiatry*. New York: Brunner/Mazel.

Arlow, J. (1966). Depersonalization and derealization. In *Psychoanalysis: A General Psychology*, ed. R. M. Loewenstein, L. M. Newman, M. Schur, and A. J. Solnit. New York: International Universities Press.

Anthony, E. J. (1961). A study of "screen sensations." *Psychoanalytic Study of the Child* 16:211–245.

Atkins, N. B. (1970). Panel report: Action, acting out, and the symptomatic act. *Journal of the American Psychoanalytic Association* 18:631–643.

Babinski, J. (1914). Contribution a l'étude des troubles mentaux dans l'hemiplegie organique cerebrale (anosognosie). *Review of Neurology* 68:380–387.

Bak, R. C. (1968). The phallic woman: The ubiquitous fantasy in perversion. *Psychoanalytic Study of the Child* 23:15–35.

Baranger, W., and Baranger, M. (1966). Insight in the analytic situation. In *Psychoanalysis in the Americas*, ed. R. E. Litman. New York: International Universities Press.

Basch, M. F. (1974). Interference with perceptual transformation in the service of defense. *Annual of Psychoanalysis* 2:87–97. New York: International Universities Press.

——— (1976). Developmental psychology and explanatory theory in psychoanalysis. *Annual of Psychoanalysis* 4:229–263.

——— (1981). Psychoanalytic interpretation and cognitive transformation. *International Journal of Psycho-Analysis* 62:151–176.

Bateson, G. (1972). *Steps to an Ecology of Mind.* New York: Ballantine.

Bear, D., and Fedio, P. (1977). Quantitative analysis of interictal behavior in temporal lobe epilepsy. *Archives of Neurology* 34:454–465.

Beisser, A. R. (1979). Denial and affirmation in illness and death. *American Journal of Psychiatry* 136:1026–1030.

Békésy, G. (1967). *Sensory Inhibition.* Princeton, N.J.: Princeton University Press.

Benjamin, J. D. (1965). Developmental biology and psychoanalysis. In *Psychoanalysis and Current Biological Thought*, ed. N. S. Greenfield and W. C. Lewis. Madison: University of Wisconsin Press.

Beres, D. (1956). Ego deviation and the concept of schizophrenia: Defense functions of the ego. *Psychoanalytic Study of the Child* 11:164–236.

Bernheim, H. (1884). *De la Suggestion dans l'État Hypnotique et dans l'État de Veille.* Paris: Octave Doine Editeur.

Bion, W. R. (1959a). Attacks on linking. *International Journal of Psycho-Analysis* 40:308–315.

——— (1959b). *Experiences in Groups.* New York: Basic Books.

——— (1967). *Second Thoughts: Selected Papers on Psycho-Analysis.* New York: Jason Aronson.

Blum, H. P. (1973). The concept of erotized transference. *Journal of the American Psychoanalytic Association* 21:61–76.

Boszormenyi-Nagy, I. (1967). Relational modes and meaning. In *Family Therapy and Disturbed Families*, ed. G. H. Zuk and I. Boszormenyi-Nagy. Palo Alto, Calif.: Science and Behavior Books.

Bourguignon, A., and Manus, A. (1980). *Hallucination, negative, deni de la realite, et scotomization. Annales Medico-Psychologiques* 138:129–153.

Bowlby, J. (1961). Processes of Mourning. *International Journal of Psycho-Analysis* 42:317–340.

——— (1980). *Attachment and Loss. Volume 3: Loss, Sadness and Depression.* New York: Basic Books.

Brazelton, T. B. (1980). Neonatal assessment. In *The Course of Life, I*, ed. S. I. Greenspan and G. H. Pollock. Bethesda, Md.: N.I.M.H.

Brenner, C. (1972). Affects and psychic conflict. *Psychoanalytic Quarterly* 44:5–28.

——— (1981). Defense and defense mechanisms. *Psychoanalytic Quarterly*, 50: 557–569.

Breuer, J., and Freud, S. (1893–1895). Studies on hysteria. *Standard Edition* 2.

Breznitz, S. (1983). The seven kinds of denial. In *The Denial of Stress*, ed. S. Breznitz. New York: International Universities Press.

Broadbent, D. E. (1958). *Perception and Communication.* London: Pergamon Press.

Brodey, W. M. (1965). On the dynamics of narcissism: I. Externalization and early ego development. *Psychoanalytic Study of the Child* 20:165–193.

Brown, J. W. (1972). *Aphasia, Apraxia, and Agnosia.* Springfield, Ill.: Chas. C Thomas.

Brown, W. P. (1961). Conceptions of perceptual defense. *British Journal of Psychology.* Monograph Supplement No. 35.

Bruner, J. S. (1964). The course of cognitive growth. *American Psychology* 19:1–5.

———, and Postman, L. (1949). Perception, cognition, and behavior. *Journal of Personality* 18:14–31.

Buber, M. (1970). *I and Thou.* New York: Scribner's.

Buchsbaum, M. (1976). Self-regulation of stimulus intensity: Augmenting/reducing the average evoked response. In *Consciousness and Self-Regulation*, vol. 1, ed. G. E. Schwartz and D. Shapiro. New York: Plenum Press.

Cain, A. C. (1972). Children's disturbed reactions to parental suicide: Distortions of guilt, communication, and identification. In *Survivors of Suicide*, ed. A. C. Cain. Springfield, Ill.: Chas. C Thomas.

Calef, V., and Weinshel, E. M. (1981). Some clinical consequences of introjection: Gaslighting. *Psychoanalytic Quarterly* 50:44–66.

Coen, S. J. (1981). Sexualization as a predominant mode of defense. *Journal of the American Psychoanalytic Association* 29:893–920.

Cohen, J. (1980a). Structural consequences of psychic trauma. A new look at *Beyond the Pleasure Principle*. *International Journal of Psycho-Analysis* 61: 421–438.

——— (1980b). Towards a general theory of repression. Paper presented at the Annual Meeting of the American Psychoanalytic Association, San Francisco, May 1980.

Croog, S., Shapiro, D., and Levin, S. (1971). Denial among male heart patients. *Psychosomatic Medicine* 33:385–398.

Cutting, J. (1978). Study of anosognosia. *Journal of Neurology, Neurosurgery, and Psychiatry* 41:548–555.

Dahl, H. (1965). Observations on a "national experiment": Helen Keller. *Journal of the American Psychoanalytic Association* 13:533–550.

de Monchaux, C. (1962). Thinking and negative hallucination. *International Journal of Psycho-Analysis* 43:311–314.

Dewald, P. A. (1972). *The Psychoanalytic Process.* New York: Basic Books.

Dixon, N. F. (1971). *Subliminal Perception: The Nature of a Controversy.* London: McGraw-Hill.

Dorpat, T. L. (1968). Regulatory mechanisms of the perceptual apparatus on involuntary physiological actions. *Journal of the American Psychoanalytic Association* 16:319–334.

——— (1971). Phantom sensations of internal organs. *Comprehensive Psychiatry* 12:27–35.

——— (1972). Psychological effects of parental suicide on survivors. In *Survivors of Suicide*, ed. A. C. Cain. Springfield, Ill.: Chas. C Thomas.

——— (1973). Suicide, loss, and mourning. *Life-Threatening Behavior* 3:213–224.

——— (1974). Drug automatism, barbiturate poisoning and suicide behavior. *Archives of General Psychiatry* 31:216–220.

——— (1975). Dyscontrol and suicidal behaviors. In *Self-Destructive Behavior*, ed. A. R. Roberts. Springfield, Ill.: Chas. C Thomas.

——— (1976). Structural conflict and object relations conflict. *Journal of the American Psychoanalytic Association* 24:855–874.

——— (1977). Depressive affect. *Psychoanalytic Study of the Child* 32:3–28.

——— (1978). Psychological aspects of accidents. *Annual of Psychoanalysis* 6:273–

283, ed. Chicago Institute for Psychoanalysis. New York: International Universities Press.

―― (1979). Introjection and the idealizing transference. *International Journal of Psychoanalytic Psychotherapy* 7:23–53.

―― (1981). Basic concepts and terms in object relations theories. In *Object and Self: A Developmental Approach*, ed. S. Tuttman, C. Kaye, and M. Zimmerman. New York: International Universities Press.

―― (1984). Technical errors in supervised analysis. In *Listening and Interpreting: The Challenge of the Work of Robert Langs*, ed. J. Raney. New York: Jason Aronson.

Eissler, K. (1953). Notes upon the emotionality of a schizophrenic patient and its relation to problems of technique. *Psychoanalytic Study of the Child* 8:199–251.

―― (1962). On the metapsychology of the preconscious: A tentative contribution to psychoanalytic morphology. *Psychoanalytic Study of the Child* 17:9–41.

Emde, R. N., and Robinson, J. (1979). The first two months. In *Basic Handbook of Child Psychiatry*, ed. J. Noshpitz. New York: Basic Books.

Engel, G. L. (1968). The psychoanalytic approach to psychosomatic medicine. In *Modern Psychoanalysis*, ed. J. Marmor. New York: Basic Books.

Erdelyi, M. (1974). A new look at the new look: Perceptual defense and vigilance. *Psychological Review* 81:1–25.

Erikson, E. H. (1950). *Childhood and Society*, rev. ed. New York: Norton.

Esman, A. H. (1983). The "stimulus barrier"—A review and reconsideration. *Psychoanalytic Study of the Child* 38:193–207.

Feldman, S. S. (1959). *Mannerisms of Speech and Gestures in Everyday Life*. New York: International Universities Press.

Fenichel, O. (1941). *Problems of Psychoanalytic Technique*. New York: Psychoanalytic Quarterly.

―― (1945). *The Psychoanalytic Theory of Neurosis*. New York: Norton.

―― (1954). *The Collected Papers of Otto Fenichel*. Second series. New York: Norton.

Fine, B. B., Joseph, E. D., and Waldhorn, H. F., eds. (1969). *The Mechanism of Denial*. Monograph III. New York: International Universities Press.

Fingarette, H. (1969). *Self-Deception*. New York: Routledge & Kegan Paul.

Fisher, C. (1954). Dreams and perception: The role of preconscious and primary modes of perception in dream formation. *Journal of the American Psychoanalytic Association* 2:389–445.

―― (1956). Dreams, images, and perception: A study of unconscious-preconscious relationships. *Journal of the American Psychoanalytic Association* 4:5–48.

―― (1957). A study of the preliminary stages of the construction of dreams and images. *Journal of the American Psychoanalytic Association* 5:5–60.

Flavell, J. (1956). Abstract thinking and social behavior in schizophrenia. *Journal of Abnormal Social Psychology* 52:208–211.

――, and Draguns, J. (1957). A microgenetic approach to perception and thought. *Psychological Bulletin* 54:197–216.

Fleming, J., and Altschul, S. (1963). Activation of mourning and growth by psychoanalysis. *International Journal of Psycho-Analysis* 44:419–431.

Fraiberg, S. (1969). Libidinal object constancy and mental representation. *Psychoanalytic Study of the Child* 24:3–47.

Framo, J. L. (1970). Symptoms from a family transactional viewpoint. In *Family Therapy in Transition*, ed. N. W. Ackerman. Boston: Little, Brown.

Frank, A. (1969). The unrememberable and the unforgettable: Passive primal repression. *Psychoanalytic Study of the Child* 24:48–77.

——, and Muslin, H. (1967). The development of Freud's concept of primal repression. *Psycholanalytic Study of the Child* 22:55–76.

Frankel, L. (1963). Self-preservation and the development of accident proneness in children and adolescents. *Psychoanalytic Study of the Child* 18:469–473.

Freud, A. (1936). *The Ego and the Mechanisms of Defense*. New York: International Universities Press.

Freud, A. (1965). *Normality and Pathology in Childhood*. New York: International Universities Press.

Freud, S. (1895). Project for a scientific psychology. *Standard Edition* 1:281 343.

—— (1899). Screen memories. *Standard Edition* 3:301–323.

—— (1900). The interpretation of dreams. *Standard Edition* 5:1–627.

—— (1901). The psychopathology of everyday life. *Standard Edition* 6:1 290.

—— (1905a). Fragment of an analysis of a case of hysteria. *Standard Edition* 3:122.

—— (1905b). Jokes and their relation to the unconscious. *Standard Edition* 8:1–236.

—— (1905c). Three essays on the theory of sexuality. *Standard Edition* 7:125–248.

—— (1907). Delusions and dreams in Jensen's *Gradiva*. *Standard Edition* 9:1–96.

—— (1909). Notes upon a case of obsessional neurosis. *Standard Edition* 10:151–318.

—— (1910). The psycho-analytic view of psychogenic disturbance of vision. *Standard Edition* 11:209–218.

—— (1911a). Formulations regarding the two principles in mental functioning. *Standard Edition* 12:213–226.

—— (1911b). Psycho-analytic notes on an autobiographical account of a case of paranoia (dementia paranoides). *Standard Edition* 12:3–82.

—— (1912). A note on the unconscious in psychoanalysis. *Standard Edition* 12.

—— (1914). Remembering, repeating, and working through. *Standard Edition* 12:145–156.

—— (1915a). Instincts and their vicissitudes. *Standard Edition* 14:109–141.

—— (1915b). Repression. *Standard Edition* 14:146–158.

—— (1915c). The unconscious. *Standard Edition* 14:161–215.

—— (1917). A metapsychological supplement to the theory of dreams. *Standard Edition* 14:219–235.

—— (1918). From the history of an infantile neurosis. *Standard Edition* 17:3–123.

—— (1920). Beyond the pleasure principle. *Standard Edition* 18:1–64.

—— (1923). The ego and the id. *Standard Edition* 19:3–68.

—— (1923). The infantile genital organization: An interpolation into the theory of sexuality. *Standard Edition* 19:141–148.

—— (1924a). The economic problem of masochism. *Standard Edition* 19:157–170.

—— (1924b). The loss of reality in neuroses and psychoses. *Standard Edition* 19:183–190.

—— (1924c). Neurosis and psychosis. *Standard Edition* 19:148–156.

—— (1925a). Negation. *Standard Edition* 19:234–239.

—— (1925b). Some psychical consequences of the anatomical distinction between the sexes. *Standard Edition* 19:243–258.

—— (1926). Inhibitions, symptoms and anxiety. *Standard Edition* 20:77–174.

—— (1927a). Fetishism. *Standard Edition* 21:152–159.

—— (1927b). The future of an illusion. *Standard Edition* 21:3–9.

—— (1933). New introductory lectures on psychoanalysis. *Standard Edition* 22:1–82.

—— (1936). A disturbance of memory on the Acropolis. *Standard Edition* 22: 239–248.

—— (1937). Construction in analysis. *Standard Edition* 23:256–270.

—— (1938). Splitting of the ego in the process of defense. *Standard Edition* 23:273–278.

—— (1940). An outline of psycho-analysis. *Standard Edition* 23:144–207.

Frosch, J. (1970). Psychoanalytic considerations of the psychotic character. *Journal of the American Psychoanalytic Association* 18:24–50.

Furman, E. (1974). *A Child's Parent Dies*. New Haven, Conn.: Yale University Press.

Furst, S. S. (1967). *Psychic Trauma*. New York: Basic Books.

Gainotti, G. (1969). Reactions "catastrophiques" et manifestations d'indifference au cours des atteintes cerebrales. *Neuropsychologia* 7:195–204.

Galenson, E., and Roiphe, H. (1980). The preoedipal development of the boy. *Journal of the American Psychoanalytic Association* 28:805–828.

Galin, D. (1974). Implications for psychiatry of left and right cerebral specialization. *Archives of General Psychiatry* 31:572–583.

Garma, A. (1946). The genesis of reality testing. *Psychoanalytic Quarterly* 15:161–174.

Gazzaniga, M. (1967). The split brain in man. *Scientific American* 217:24–29.

——, and LeDoux, J. (1978). *The Integrated Mind*. New York: Plenum Press.

——, and Sperry, R. (1967). Language after section of the cerebral commissures. *Brain* 90:131–148.

Gedo, J. (1975). Forms of idealization in the analytic transference. *Journal of the American Psychoanalytic Association* 23:485–505.

—— (1979). *Beyond Interpretation*. New York: International Universities Press.

——, and Goldberg, A. (1973). *Models of the Mind*. Chicago: University of Chicago Press.

Geschwind, N. (1965). Disconnexion syndromes in animals and man. *Brain* 88: 237–294, 585–644.

Gilbertson, V., and Wangenstein, O. (1962). *The Physician and the Total Care of the Cancer Patient*. New York: American Cancer Society.

Gill, M. M. (1963). *Topography and Systems in Psychoanalytic Theory*. Psychological Issues Monograph 10. New York: International Universities Press.

—— (1977). Psychic energy reconsidered: Discussion. *Journal of the American Psychoanalytic Association* 25:581–598.

—— (1982). *Analysis of Transference, Vol. 1: Theory and Technique*. New York: International Universities Press.

Glover, E. (1937). Symposium on the theory of the therapeutic results of psycho-analysis. *International Journal of Psycho-Analysis* 18:125–189.

—— (1939). *Psycho-Analysis*. London and New York: Staples Press.

—— (1947). *Basic Mental Concepts*. London: Imago.

Goldberger, L. (1983). The concept and mechanisms of denial: A selective overview. *The Denial of Stress*, ed. S. Breznitz. New York: International Universities Press.

Goldstein, K. (1939). *The Organism*. New York: American Book.

—— (1948). *Language and Language Disturbance*. New York: Grune & Stratton.

—— (1975). Functional disturbances of brain damage. In *American Handbook of Psychiatry, Vol. IV*, ed. S. Arieti. New York: Basic Books.

Gorer, G. (1965). *Death, Grief, and Mourning*. New York: Doubleday.

Granit, R. (1955). *Receptors and Sensory Reception*. New Haven, Conn.: Yale University Press.

Green, A. (1977). Negative hallucination: A note as an addendum to a treatise on hallucinations. *Evolution Psychiatrique* 42:645–656.

Greenacre, P. (1958). Toward an understanding of the physical nucleus of some defence reactions. *International Journal of Psycho-Analysis* 39:69–76.

—— (1967). The influence of infantile trauma on genetic patterns. In *Psychic Trauma*, ed. S. S. Furst. New York: Basic Books.

Greene, W. A. (1958). Role of vicarious object in the adaptation to object loss: I. Use of a vicarious object as a means of adjustment to separation from a significant person. *Psychosomatic Medicine* 20:349–350.

—— (1959). Role of vicarious object in the adaptation to object loss: II. Vicissitudes in the role of the vicarious object. *Psychosomatic Medicine* 21:438–447.

Greenson, R. (1958). Screen defenses, screen hunger, screen reality. *Journal of the American Psychoanalytic Association* 6:242–262.

Grindberg, O. (1962). On a specific aspect of countertransference due to the patient's projective identification. *International Journal of Psycho-Analysis* 43:436–440.

Grotstein, J. (1980). *Splitting and Projective Identification*. New York: Jason Aronson.

Guthrie, T., and Grossman, E. (1952). A study of the syndromes of denial. *Archives of Neurology and Psychiatry* 68:362–371.

Haan, N. (1977). *Coping and Defending: Processes of Self-Environment Organization*. New York: Academic Press.

Habermas, J. (1971). *Knowledge and Human Interests*. Boston: Beacon Press.

Hackett, T. P., Cassem, N. H., and Wishnie, H. A. (1968). The coronary care unit: An appraisal of its psychological hazards. *New England Journal of Medicine* 279:1365–1370.

—— (1969). Detection and treatment of anxiety and treatment of anxiety in the coronary care unit. *American Heart Journal* 78:727–730.

Hartmann, H. (1939). *Ego Psychology and the Problem of Adaptation*. New York: International Universities Press.

—— (1950). Comments on the psychoanalytic theory of the ego. *Psychoanalytic Study of the Child* 5:74–96.

—— (1953). Contribution to the metapsychology of schizophrenia. *Psychoanalytic Study of the Child* 8:177–198.

—— (1964). *Essays on Ego Psychology*. New York: International Universities Press.

Hendin, H. (1964). *Suicide and Scandinavia*. New York: Grune & Stratton.

Hilgard, E. R. (1949). Human motives and the concept of the self. *American Psychologist* 4:374–382.

Hoffer, W. (1952). The mutual influences in the development of ego and id. *Psychoanalytic Study of the Child* 7:31–36.

Holt, R. R. (1976). Drive or wish? A reconsideration of the psychoanalytic theory of motivation. In *Psychology Versus Metapsychology*, ed. M. Gill and P. S. Holzman. *Psychological Issues*, vol. 9. New York: International Universities Press.

Hoppe, K. (1977). Split brains and psychoanalysis. *Psychoanalytic Quarterly* 46: 466–498.

Horn, G. (1976). Physiological studies of attention and arousal. In *Mechanisms in Transmission of Signals for Conscious Behavior*, ed. T. Desiraju. Amsterdam: Elsevier.

Horney, K. (1933). The denial of the vagina. *International Journal of Psycho-Analysis* 14:57–70.

Horowitz, M. (1976). *Stress Response Syndromes*. New York: Jason Aronson.

Hubel, D. H., Henson, C. O., Ruprecht, A., and Galambos, R. (1959). "Attention" units in the auditory cortex. *Science* 124:1279–1280.

Isaacs, S. (1952). The nature and function of phantasy. In *Developments in Psycho-Analysis*, ed. M. Klein, P. Heiman, and J. Riviere. London: Hogarth Press.

Isakower, O. (1938). A contribution to the patho-psychology of phenomena associated with falling asleep. *International Journal of Psycho-Analysis* 19:331–345.

Jackson, J. H. (1932). *Selected Writings of John Hughlings Jackson*. London: Hoddee & Stoughton.

Jacobson, E. (1957). Denial and repression. *Journal of the American Psychoanalytic Association* 5:61–92.

—— (1959). Depersonalization. *Journal of the American Psychoanalytic Association* 7:581–609.

James, W. (1890). *The Principles of Psychology, Vol. 1*. New York: Henry Holt.

Kanzer, M. (1957). Panel Report. Acting out and its relation to impulse disorders. *Journal of the American Psychoanalytic Association* 5:136–145.

Keith-Spiegel, P., and Spiegel, D. E. (1967). Affective states of patients immediately preceding suicide. *Journal of Psychiatric Residency* 5:89–93.

Kernberg, O. F. (1976). *Object Relations Theory and Clinical Psychoanalysis*. New York: Jason Aronson.

Klein, G. S. (1949). Adaptive properties of sensory functioning: Some postulates and hypotheses. *Bulletin of the Menninger Clinic* 13:16–24.

—— (1959). Consciousness in psychoanalytic theory: Some implications for current research in perception. *Journal of the American Psychoanalytic Association* 7:5–34.

—— (1966). Peremptory Ideation. In *Motives and Thought: Psychoanalytic Essays in Honor of David Rapaport*, ed. R. R. Holt. *Psychological Issues*. New York: International Universities Press.

—— (1976). *Psychoanalytic Theory—An Exploration of Essentials*. New York: International Universities Press.

Klein, M. (1935). A contribution to the psychogenesis of manic-depressive states. In

Contributions to Psycho-Analysis, 1921–1945. London: Hogarth Press.

——— (1946). Notes on some schizoid mechanisms. *International Journal of Psycho-Analysis* 27:99–110.

——— (1952). Some theoretical conclusions regarding the emotional life of the infant. In *Developments in Psychoanalysis*, ed. M. Klein, P. Heiman, and J. Riviere. London: Hogarth Press.

——— (1975). *Envy and Gratitude and Other Works*. London: Delacorte Press/ Seymour Lawrence.

———, Heinman, P., and Money-Kryle, R. (1955). *New Directions in Psycho-Analysis*. New York: Basic Books.

Knapp, P. H. (1967). Some riddles of riddance. *Archives of General Psychiatry* 16:586–602.

Kohut, H. (1971). *The Analysis of the Self*. New York: International Universities Press.

——— (1972). Thoughts on narcissism and narcissistic rage. *Psychoanalytic Study of the Child* 27:360–402.

——— (1977). *The Restoration of the Self*. New York: International Universities Press.

Kübler-Ross, E. (1969). *On Death and Dying*. London: Macmillan.

LaForgue, R. (1927). Scotomization in schizophrenia. *International Journal of Psychoanalysis* 8:473–478.

Laing, R. D. (1967). Family and individual structure. In *The Predicament of the Family*, ed. P. Lomax. New York: International Universities Press.

Lampl-De Groot, J. (1957). On defense and development. *Psychoanalytic Study of the Child* 12:121–126.

Langer, S. K. (1967). *Mind: An Essay on Human Feeling*, vol. 1. Baltimore and London: Johns Hopkins University Press.

Langs, R. (1975). The patient's unconscious percepts of the therapist's errors. In *Tactics and Techniques in Psychoanalytic Therapy, Vol. 2, Countertransference*, ed. P. Giovacchini. New York: Jason Aronson.

——— (1976a). *The Bipersonal Field*. New York: Jason Aronson.

——— (1976b). *The Therapeutic Interaction, Vol. II*. New York: Jason Aronson.

——— (1978). *The Listening Process*. New York: Jason Aronson.

——— (1979a). *The Supervisory Experience*. New York: Jason Aronson.

——— (1979b). *The Therapeutic Environment*. New York: Jason Aronson.

——— (1980). *Interactions: The Realm of Transference and Countertransference*. New York: Jason Aronson.

——— (1981). *Resistances and Interventions*. New York: Jason Aronson.

——— (1982a). *The Psychotherapeutic Conspiracy*. New York: Jason Aronson.

——— (1982b). *Psychotherapy: A Basic Text*. New York: Jason Aronson.

——— (1983). *Unconscious Communication in Everyday Life*. New York: Jason Aronson.

Lazarus, R. (1968). Emotion as coping process. In *The Nature of Emotion*, ed. M. Arnold. Baltimore: Penguin.

Lester, D. (1967). Fear of death of suicidal persons. *Psychological Reports* 20(3): 1077–1078.

Levitan, H. L. (1969). The depersonalizing process. *Psychoanalytic Quarterly* 37: 97–110.

Lewin, B. (1950). *The Psychoanalysis of Elation.* New York: Norton.

Lichtenberg, J., and Slap, H. (1973). Notes on the concept of splitting and the defense mechanism of the splitting of representation. *Journal of the American Psychoanalytic Association* 21:772–777.

Lindemann, E. (1944). Symptomatology and management of acute grief. *American Journal of Psychiatry* 101:141–148.

Linn, L. (1953). The role of perception in the mechanism of denial. *Journal of the American Psychoanalytic Association* 1:690–705.

Lipin, T. (1963). The repetition compulsion and "maturational" drive representations. *International Journal of Psycho-Analysis* 44:389–406.

Lissauer, H. (1889). Ein fall von seelenblindheit nebst einem beitrage zur̈r theorie dersalben. *Archiv Für Psychiatrie und Nervenkrankheiten* 21:222–270.

Litman, R. E. (1970). Suicide as acting out. In *The Psychology of Suicide*, eds. E. S. Shneidman, N. L. Farberow, and R. E. Litman. New Haven, Conn.: Yale University Press.

Livingston, R. B. (1959). Neurophysiology. In *Handbook of Physiology*. Washington, D.C.: American Physiology Society.

Loewald, H. W. (1970). Psychoanalytic theory and the psychoanalytic process. *Psychoanalytic Study of the Child* 25:45–68.

——— (1976). Perspectives on memory. In *Psychology Versus Metapsychology: Psychoanalytic Essays in Memory of George S. Klein*, ed. M. M. Gill and P. S. Holzmann. New York: International Universities Press.

——— (1978). Instinct theory, object relations, and psychic-structure formation. *Journal of the American Psychoanalytic Association* 26:453–506.

——— (1978). *Psychoanalysis and the History of the Individual.* New Haven, Conn.: Yale University Press.

——— (1980). *Papers on Psychoanalysis.* New Haven, Conn.: Yale University Press.

Luria, A. R. (1961). *The Role of Speech in the Regulation of Normal and Abnormal Behavior.* New York: Pergamon Press.

Lustman, S. L. (1957). Psychic energy and mechanisms of defense. *Psychoanalytic Study of the Child* 12:151–168.

Mahler, M. S. (1952). On child psychosis and schizophrenia: Autistic and symbiotic infantile psychoses. *Psychoanalytic Study of the Child* 7:286–294.

——— (1968). *On Human Symbiosis and the Vicissitudes of Individuation.* New York: International Universities Press.

———, and McDevitt, J. B. (1968). Observations on adaptation and defense *in statu nascendi. Psychoanalytic Quarterly* 37:1–21.

———, Pine, F., and Berman, A. (1975). *The Psychological Birth of the Human Infant: Symbiosis and Individuation.* New York: Basic Books.

Mandler, G. (1975). *Mind and Emotion.* New York: John Wiley.

Masterson, J. F. (1976). *Psychotherapy of the Borderline Adult.* New York: Brunner/Mazel.

McKinnon, J. A. (1979). Two semantic forms—Neuropsychological and psychoanalytic descriptions. *Psychoanalysis and Contemporary Thought* 2:25–76.

McLaughlin, J. (1978). Primary and secondary process in the context of cerebral hemispheric specialization. *Psychoanalytic Quarterly* 47:237–266.

Meerlo, J. A. M. (1962). *Suicide and Mass Suicide.* New York: Grune & Stratton.

Meissner, W. (1981). *Internalization in Psychoanalysis.* New York: International Universities Press.

Melzack, R., and Wall, P. O. (1965). Pain mechanisms: A new theory. *Science* 150:971–979.

Mischel, T. (1974). Understanding neurotic behavior: From mechanism to intentionality. In *Understanding Other Persons*, ed. T. Mischel. Totowa, N.J.: Rowman & Littlefield.

Modell, A. H. (1961). Denial and the sense of separateness. *Journal of the American Psychoanalytic Association* 9:533–547.

Moore, B. E. and Fine, B. D., eds. (1967). *A Glossary of Psychoanalytic Terms and Concepts.* New York: American Psychoanalytic Association.

Muir, R. C. (1982). The family, the group, transpersonal processes and the individual. *International Review of Psycho-Analysis* 9:317–326.

Nathanson, M., Bergman, P., and Gordon, G. (1952). Denial of illness. *A.M.A. Archives of Neurology and Psychiatry* 68:380–387.

Neisser, U. (1967). *Cognitive Psychology.* New York: Appleton-Century-Crofts.

——— (1976). *Cognition and Reality.* San Francisco: W. H. Freeman.

Niederland, W. (1961). The problem of the survivor. *Journal of the Hillside Hospital* 10:233–247, 1961.

Ninenger, E. V. (1965). Variations of archaic thinking in neurotics, borderline patients, and schizophrenics. *Psychoanalytic Quarterly* 34:633–636.

Norman, D. A. (1969). *Memory and Attention: An Introduction to Human Information Processing.* New York: John Wiley.

Ogden, T. H. (1982). *Projective Identification and Psychotherapeutic Technique.* New York: Jason Aronson.

——— (1983). The concept of internal object relations. *International Journal of Psycho-Analysis* 64:227–241.

O'Neill, E. (1956). *Long Day's Journey into Night.* New Haven, Conn.: Yale University Press.

Ornstein, R. E. (1972). *The Psychology of Consciousness.* San Francisco: W. H. Freeman.

Parkes, C. M. (1970). "Seeking" and "finding" a lost object. *Social Sciences Medicine* 4:187–201.

Pearson, G. H. J. (1953). A note on primal repression. *Bulletin of the Philadelphia Association of Psychoanalysis* 3:42.

Peterfreund, E. (1971). *Information, Systems, and Psychoanalysis.* Psychological Issues Monograph 25/26. New York: International Universities Press.

Peto, A. (1964). Variations of archaic thinking in neurotics, borderline patients, and schizophrenics. *Psychoanalytic Study of the Child* 19:73–92.

Petrie, A. (1967). *Individuality in Pain and Suffering.* Chicago: University of Chicago Press.

Piaget, J. (1929). *The Child's Conception of the World.* New York: Harcourt, Brace & World.

——— (1937). *The Construction of Reality in the Child.* New York: Basic Books, 1954.

———, and Inhelder, B. (1969). *The Psychology of the Child.* New York: Basic Books.

Polanyi, M. (1964). *Personal Knowledge.* New York: Harper & Row.

Pollock, G. H. (1978). Process and affect—Mourning and grief. *International Journal of Psycho-Analysis* 59:255–276.

Popper, K. R., and Eccles, J. C. (1977). *The Self and Its Brain.* New York: Springer International.

Pruyser, P. (1975). What splits in "splitting"? *Bulletin of the Menninger Clinic* 39:1–46.

Räkkölainer, V., and Alanen, Y. O. (1982). On the transactionality of defensive processes. *International Review of Psycho-Analysis* 9:263–272.

Rangell, L. (1959). The nature of conversion. *Journal of the American Psychoanalytic Association* 7:632–662.

Rapaport, D. (1951). Toward a theory of thinking. In *Organization and Pathology of Thought,* ed. D. Rapaport. New York: Columbia University Press.

—— (1960). *The Structure of Psychoanalytic Theory.* Psychological Issues, Monograph 61. New York: International Universities Press.

—— (1967). *The Collected Papers of David Rapaport,* ed. M. Gill. New York: Basic Books.

Robbins, M. D. (1976). Borderline personality organizations: The need for a new theory. *Journal of the American Psychoanalytic Association* 24:831–853.

Robertson, J. (1953). Some responses of young children to the loss of maternal care. *Nursing Times* 49:382–386.

Rochlin, G. (1967). How younger children view death and themselves. In *Explaining Death to Children,* ed. E. Groelman. New York: Beacon Press.

Rosen, V. H. (1955). The reconstruction of a traumatic childhood event in a case of derealization. *Journal of the American Psychoanalytic Association* 3:211–221.

Rosenblatt, A. D., and Thickstun, J. T. (1977a). Energy, information, and motivation: A revision of psychoanalytic theory. *Journal of the American Psychoanalytic Association* 25:537–558.

Rosenblatt, A. D., and Thickstun, J. T. (1977b). *Modern Psychoanalytic Concepts in a General Psychology, Parts 1 and 2.* Psychological Issues Monograph 42/43. New York: International Universities Press.

Rosenthal, R. J., Rinzler, C., Wallsh, R., and Klausner, E. (1972). Wrist-cutting syndrome: The meaning of a gesture. *American Journal of Psychiatry,* 11: 1363–1368.

Rothenberg, A. (1961). Psychological problems in terminal cancer patients. *Cancer* 14:1063–1073.

Rubinfine, D. L. (1962). Maternal stimulation, psychic structure and early object relations with special reference to aggression and denial. *Psychoanalytic Study of the Child* 17:265–282.

—— (1973). Notes toward a theory of consciousness. *International Journal of Psychoanalytic Psychotherapy* 2:391–410.

Rubinstein, B. B. (1976). Hope, fear, wish, expectation, and fantasy: A semantic-phenomenological and extraclinical theoretical study. *Psychoanalysis and Contemporary Science* 5:3–60.

Sandler, J. (1976). Countertransference and role-responsiveness. *International Review of Psycho-Analysis* 3:43–47.

———, and Joffe, W. G. (1967). Persistence in psychological function and development. *Bulletin of the Menninger Clinic* 31:227–257.

———, and Nagera, H. (1963). Aspects of the metapsychology of fantasy. *Psychoanalytic Study of the Child* 18:159–194.

———, and Sandler, A. M. (1978). On the development of object relationships and affects. *International Journal of Psycho-Analysis* 59:285–296.

Schachtel, E. (1959). *Metamorphosis*. New York: Basic Books.

Schafer, R. (1968a). *Aspects of Internalization*. New York: International Universities Press.

——— (1968b). The mechanisms of defense. *International Journal of Psycho-Analysis* 49:49–62.

——— (1975). Freudian and Kleinian theory and technique: Some features and problems in common. Lecture delivered to the Los Angeles Psychoanalytic Society and Institute, June 26, 1975.

——— (1976). *A New Language for Psychoanalysis*. New Haven, Conn.: Yale University Press.

Schilder, P. (1953). *Medical Psychology*. New York: International Universities Press.

Schnierla, T. C. (1959). An evolutionary and developmental theory of biphasic processes underlying approach and withdrawal. In *Nebraska Symposium on Motivation*, ed. M. R. Jones. Lincoln: University of Nebraska Press.

Schur, M. (1955). Comments on the metapsychology of somatization. *Psychoanalytic Study of the Child* 10:143–150.

——— (1966). *The Id and the Regulatory Principles of Mental Functioning*. New York: International Universities Press.

Searles, H. F. (1965). The effort to drive the other person crazy—An element in the aetiology and psychotherapy of schizophrenia. *Collected Papers on Schizophrenia and Related Subjects*. pp. 254–283. New York: International Universities Press.

——— (1975). The patient as therapist to his analyst. In *Tactics and Techniques in Psychoanalytic Therapy. Vol. II: Counter-transference*, ed. P. Giovacchini. New York: Jason Aronson.

——— (1979). The function of the patient's realistic perceptions of the analyst in delusional transference. In *Countertransference and Related Subjects*, ed. H. Searles. New York: International Universities Press.

Segal, H. (1964). *Introduction to the Works of Melanie Klein*. New York: Basic Books.

Shevrin, H., and Taussieng, P. W. (1965). Vicissitudes of the need for tactile stimulation in instinctual development. *Psychoanalytic Study of the Child* 209:310–339.

Schneidman, E. S., and Farberow, N. L. (1957). The logic of suicide. In *Clues to Suicide*, ed. E. S. Shneidman and N. L. Farberow. New York: McGraw Hill.

Siegman, A. J. (1967). Denial and screening of object images. *Journal of the American Psychoanalytic Association* 15:261–280.

Silverblatt, H. (1981). Denial of pregnancies extended to physicians. *Psychiatric News*, November 20.

Silverman, L. H. (1967). An experimental approach to the study of dynamic propositions in psychoanalysis: The relationship between the aggressive drive and ego regression—Initial studies. *Journal of the American Psychoanalytic Association* 15:376–403.

Silverman, L. H., Bronstein, A., and Mendelsohn, E. (1976). The further use of the subliminal psychodynamic activation method for experimental study of the clinical theory of psychoanalysis: On the specificity of relationships between manifest psychopathology and unconscious conflict: *Psychotherapy: Theory, Research, and Practice* 13:2–16.

Simpson, M. A. (1976). Self-mutilation and suicide. In *Suicidology: Contemporary Developments*, ed. E. S. Shneidman. New York: Grune & Stratton.

Solley, C. M., and Murphy, G. (1960). *Development of the Perceptual World*. New York: Basic Books.

Spence, D. P. (1967). Subliminal perception and perceptual defense: Two sides of a single problem. *Behavioral Science* 12:183–193.

Sperling, S. (1958). On denial and the essential nature of defense. *International Journal of Psycho-Analysis* 39:25–38.

Sperry, R. (1964). Problems outstanding in the evolution of brain function. James Arthur Lecture, American Museum of Natural History, New York.

——— (1982). Some effects of disconnecting the cerebral hemispheres. *Science* 217: 1223–1226.

Spiegel, D. E., and Neuringer, C. (1963). Role of dread in suicidal behavior. *Journal of Abnormal Social Psychology* 66:507–511.

Spitz, R. A. (1957). *No and Yes—On the Genesis of Human Communication*. New York: International Universities Press.

——— (1961). Some early prototypes of ego defenses. *Journal of the American Psychoanalytic Association* 9:626–651.

———, and Cobliner, W. G. (1965). *The First Year of Life*. New York: International Universities Press.

———, and Wolf, K. M. (1964). Anaclitic depression. *Psychoanalytic Study of the Child* 2:313–342.

Stamm, J. L. (1962). Altered ego states allied to depersonalization. *Journal of the American Psychoanalytic Association* 10:762–783.

Stein, M. H. (1965). States of consciousness in the analytic situation. In *Drives, Affects, Behavior, Vol. II*, ed. M. Schur. New York: International Universities Press.

Stewart, H. (1966). Negative hallucinations in hypnosis. *International Journal of Psycho-Analysis* 47:50–53.

Stewart, W. A. (1970). The split in the ego and the mechanisms of disavowal. *Psychoanalytic Quarterly* 39:1–16.

Stolorow, R. D., and Lachmann, F. M. (1980). *Psychoanalysis of Developmental Arrests: Theory and Treatment*. New York: International Universities Press.

Stunkard, A. (1959). Obesity and denial of hunger. *Psychosomatic Medicine* 21: 281–290.

Sullivan, H. (1956). *Clinical Studies in Psychiatry*. New York: Norton.

Trieseman, A. M., and Riley, J. G. R. (1969). Is selective attention selective perception or selective response? A further test. *Journal of Experimental Psychology* 79:27–34.

Ullman, M. (1962). *Behavioral Changes in Patients Following Stroke*. Springfield, Ill.: Chas. C Thomas.

Vogel, E. F., and Bell, N. W. (1960). The emotionally disturbed child as the family scapegoat. In *A Modern Introduction to the Family*, ed. N. W. Bell and E. F. Vogel. Glencoe, Ill.: Free Press.

Volkan, V. D. (1976). *Primitive Internalized Object Relations.* New York: International Universities Press.

Vygotsky, L. S. (1934). *Thought and Language.* Cambridge, Mass.: MIT Press, 1962.

Waelder, R. (1951). The structure of paranoid ideas. *International Journal of Psycho-Analysis* 32:167–177.

Wallerstein, R. S. (1967). Reconstruction and mastery in the transference psychosis. *Journal of the American Psychoanalytic Association* 15:556–569.

―――― (1976). Psychoanalysis as a science: Its present status and its future tasks. *Psychology Versus Metapsychology: Psychoanalytic Essays in Memory of George S. Klein*, ed. M. M. Gill and P. S. Holzman. New York: International Universities Press.

―――― (1981). The bipolar self: Discussion of alternative perspectives. *Journal of the American Psychoanalytic Association* 29:377–394.

Wangh, M. (1950). Othello: The tragedy of Iago. *Psychoanalytic Quarterly* 19:202–212.

―――― (1962). The evocation of a proxy: A psychological manoeuvre, its use as a defense, its purpose and genesis. *Psychoanalytic Study of the Child* 17:463–469.

Warren, M. (1972). Some psychological sequelae of parental suicide in surviving children. In *Survivors of Suicide*, ed. A. C. Cain. Springfield, Ill.: Chas. C Thomas.

Watzlawick, P., Beavin, J. H., and Jackson, D. D. (1967). *Pragmatics of Human Communication.* New York: Norton.

Waxenberg, S. E. (1966). The importance of the communication of feelings about cancer. *Annals of the New York Academy of Science* 25:1000–1005.

Weinshel, E. M. (1977). "I didn't mean it." Negation as a character trait. *Psychoanalytic Study of the Child* 32:387–419.

Weinstein, E. A. (1980). Affects and neuropsychology. *The Academy Forum* 24:12.

――――, Cole, M., and Mitchell, M. (1963). Anosognosia and aphasia. *Transactions of the American Neurological Association* 88:172–175.

――――, Cole, M., Mitchell, M., and Lyerly, G. (1964). Anosognosia and aphasia. *Archives of Neurology* 10:376–386.

――――, and Kahn, R. L. (1955). *Denial of Illness.* Springfield, Ill.: Chas. C Thomas.

Weisman, A. D. (1972). *On Dying and Denying: A Psychiatric Study of Terminality.* New York: Behavioral Publications.

Weiss, J. (1982). *Psychotherapy Research: Theory and Findings.* Mount Zion Hospital and Medical Center, Bulletin 5.

Werner, H. (1948). *Comparative Psychology of Mental Development.* Chicago: Follett.

―――― (1956). Microgenesis and aphasia. *Journal of Abnormal Social Psychology* 52:347–353.

―――― (1957). *Comparative Psychology of Mental Development.* New York: International Universities Press.

Whitman, R. M. (1963). Remembering and forgetting dreams in psychoanalysis. *Journal of the American Psychoanalytic Association* 11:752–774.

Williams, G. (1957). *The Sanctity of Life and the Criminal Law.* New York: Knopf.

Wynne, L. C. (1965). Some indications and contraindications for exploratory family therapy. In *Intensive Family Therapy*, ed. I. Boszormenyi-Nagy and J. L. Framo. New York: Hoeber.

Yalom, I. D. (1980). *Existential Psychotherapy.* New York: Basic Books.

Zinner, J., and Shapiro, R. (1972). Projective identification as a mode of perception and behavior in families of adolescents. *International Journal of Psycho-Analysis* 53:523–531.

Index